DATE DUE

GAYLORD			PRINTED IN U.S.A.

THE IRISH

THE IRISH

Emigration, Marriage, and Fertility

Robert E. Kennedy, Jr.

UNIVERSITY OF CALIFORNIA PRESS

Berkeley / Los Angeles / London

University of California Press
Berkeley and Los Angeles, California
University of California Press, Ltd.
London, England

Copyright © 1973, by
The Regents of the University of California

ISBN: 0-520-01987-3
Library of Congress Catalog Card Number: 70-187740
Printed in the United States of America
Designed by Jim Mennick

To my wife

❧ Contents

❧ Acknowledgments

I am greatly indebted to the staff of the Central Statistics Office, Dublin, for its generous cooperation and assistance. Two members of its staff deserve special mention: M. D. McCarthy, who, as Director of the Central Statistics Office when I arrived in Dublin in 1965, introduced me to the large amount of available statistical information; and Matthew Collinge, Head Librarian, who not only met my frequent requests for material with competence and cheerfulness, but who also brought many additional sources to my attention.

For valuable suggestions, criticisms, and concrete examples I am particularly grateful to K. H. Connell, Queen's University, Belfast; Conor K. Ward, University College, Dublin; Michael Wright, Dublin; James O'Shea, Dublin; and in the United States, Gordon F. Streib, Cornell University; and Alfred McClung Lee, City University of New York.

The present organization of the text and several points made in the major arguments are the results of the suggestions and criticisms of those who read earlier drafts of the manuscript. On demographic matters I owe much to William Petersen, Ohio State University; Kingsley Davis, University of California, Berkeley; Calvin Goldscheider, University of California, Berkeley; and to D. V. Glass, London School of Economics and Political Science. My interpretation of Irish history and customs was greatly aided by comments from L. P. Curtis, Jr., University of California, Berkeley; and from Kieran D. Flanagan, University College, Cork. The flaws which remain are entirely my own responsibility.

For assistance in preparing the final draft, I would like to thank Grant Barnes of the University of California Press for his patience; Harry Foreman, Director of the Population Study Center, University of Minnesota, for making available the facilities of the Center; and Terry Roiger, for her diligence in typing the manuscript itself. The book would not have been possible without the assistance of my wife. She acted not only as typist, editor, copyreader, and critic, but also as a source of additional insights into Irish life and customs.

My work in Ireland was supported in part by a United States Public Health Service Fellowship, 5-Fl-MH-28,935-02 BEH, from the National Institute of Mental Health.

R.E.K., Jr.

✤ List of Tables

Statistical Appendix Tables

EXPLANATORY NOTE

The commonly used names for the two Irelands, "Ireland" and "Northern Ireland," are used consistently throughout this work even for the period before the Anglo-Irish treaty of 1921. The alternative would have been for me to make up my own names for the two parts before partition, and for the reader to keep in mind a sequence of official names for Ireland after 1920 (Southern Ireland, 1920–22; Irish Free State, 1922–37; Ireland, 1937–49; and Republic of Ireland, 1949 to the present). The word Eire simply means Ireland in the Irish language. The use of the term "32 Counties" will distinguish references made to the whole of Ireland (composed of the 26 counties of Ireland and the 6 counties of Northern Ireland).

CHAPTER I

Basic Issues and Interpretations

WHILE all other European nations increased in population during the last century, the population of Ireland decreased at every census except one between 1841 and 1961; the number of persons living in Ireland in 1966 was less than half that of 1841. Of all Western European countries, Ireland has the greatest amount of postponed marriage and permanent celibacy, and yet it also has the highest marital fertility rate. Because of these anomalous patterns, many social scientists agree with the claim of some persons of Irish birth or ancestry that the word "Irish" is a synonym for "unique."[1] Flattering as this idea might be to the Irish, it is unsettling to social scientists to admit the existence of an apparent exception to so many well known and widely accepted theories concerning population growth, urbanization, emigration, age at marriage, and family size. The aim of this book is to distinguish some of the more interesting elements of Irish life which are indeed peculiar to Ireland from those which Ireland shares, to a greater or lesser degree, with other countries.

In many areas of life where the Irish appear unique today, they were not at all unusual a century ago. To explain how these changes took place is one of the major purposes of this book. There are some difficulties, however, in using the historical approach to construct a sociological "explanation." One is the possibility that the change under study was caused by a factor overlooked by the investigator. Another is in distinguishing which of an associated group of changes took place first and hence would be more likely to be the cause rather than the effect of the other changes. With the first difficulty, the best any investigator can do is make his interpretation with an open mind; there is no methodological substitute for imagination. In an attempt to gain insight into Irish behavior as the Irish themselves see it, my wife and I lived in Ireland for almost two years from 1965 through 1967. I accepted the fact that individuals — not aggregate rates — move, marry, and have babies, and that before meaningful interpretations can be made of the various measures based on aggregate data, one must first understand the actions of at least a few real persons. My personal experiences in Ireland were limited and not representative in any statistical sense, of course, but they did provide ideas which could be tested by turning to statistical data.

This brings us to the second difficulty in using historical materials for sociological explanation. There are several methodological techniques which could be used *if* the changes were quantitative in character and *if* the changes were recorded in history at the time they took place. Irish demographic sources fulfill both of these conditions admirably: a national census of population has been conducted on a regular basis since 1821 (with the 1841 Census being the first reliable count for most purposes);* and the compulsory registration of vital statistics began on a nationwide basis in 1864. Although repeated references will be made to the political and economic history of Ireland to point out important nonquantitative changes, and to Irish fictional literature and travelers' accounts to illustrate certain Irish life styles, the fundamental sources of evidence for the interpretations drawn in this book will remain the accurate, detailed but little analyzed archives of Irish demographic sources. The time period I cover ends

---

* The 1821 Census probably understates the actual population because of the "determined hostility" experienced by the enumerators; the 1831 Census probably overstates the actual population because many enumerators were paid on the basis of the population enumerated. The 1841 Census was the first for which Census Commissioners were appointed. *Census of Population of Ireland, 1926*, Vol. X, pp. 3, 4.

with the 1966 Census, the last volume of which was published in May of 1970. In spite of the continuous data available about Irish population trends over the last 125 years or so, there is a gap between works primarily concerned with the nineteenth century[2] and articles describing Ireland's population as it exists in the mid-twentieth century.[3] No book previous to this one has attempted such an analysis of Irish social and population change of the past century.

Since a major objective of this book is to focus on those aspects of Irish life which appear unusual or unique, no claim is made for the comprehensiveness often attempted in national demographic histories. The closest approach to such a demographic history of Ireland is found in the fundamental data presented in the Statistical Appendix, and in the brief final chapter where the various changes are presented chronologically to emphasize their mutual relationships. Nor is a claim made that a single theoretical perspective explains all of the various topics under study. Instead the Irish patterns will be used to examine the universality of certain "middle-range theories" about migration, marriage, and fertility. In some matters Ireland is unusual simply for being the most extreme example of a particular pattern.

The relevance of Ireland as a social science test case directly relates to the contemporary concern with social and population change in the economically less developed nations of Asia, Africa, and Latin America. The issue is whether these nations will repeat the patterns of change experienced by the presently industrial countries, or whether a new set of theoretical expectations must be drawn up to deal with changes that are and will be qualitatively different from the European, the American, and the Japanese patterns. The Irish were among the last Western European nations to industrialize, yet they were the second (after the French) to bring their birth rate under control. Ireland achieved in the past what is today desired by many developing nations — a predominantly agrarian population with low rates of natural increase resulting from low birth and death rates. An understanding of how the Irish accomplished this demographic feat improves our judgment for estimating whether and how present-day developing countries might also bring their rates of population growth under control.

The emphasis on testing middle-range theories has determined the general organization of the book and of each chapter. With the exception of the second chapter, which briefly presents some essential historical information, and the last chapter, which summarizes and relates historical trends, each of the other chapters focuses on a certain middle-range theory or group of theories. Although each chapter could be read as a separate entity, there is some rationale to their sequential ordering. Female emigration is better understood with some knowledge of Irish mortality patterns; marriage patterns have been influenced by emigration trends; fertility by both marriage and emigration, and so forth. In order to give an overview of these interrelationships from a theoretical rather than a chronological perspective, the rest of this chapter will be spent in a brief, nonstatistical statement of the basic issues and interpretations touched upon in each chapter.

Mortality and Relative Living Standards

It appears to be common sense that a low level of mortality is indicative of a high standard of living, especially if one considers the conditions associated with gradual decline in mortality in Europe during the nineteenth and early twentieth centuries. The sudden decline in the death rates of many developing countries after World War II, however, has cast doubt on the universality of such thinking. The success of modern public health measures in agrarian societies leads us to ask whether the current low death rates of most of the world's less developed societies are anomalous, or on the other hand, whether mortality rates are indeed reliable indicators of living standards. Ireland makes an interesting test case for this question since it experienced periodic famines in some areas into the 1870s, and it is commonly assumed that these famines motivated much of the emigration from Ireland. Speaking of the great 1845–48 famine and emigration, for example, one historian has commented: "The famine emigration, the exodus from Ireland, in which hundreds of thousands of Irish, with fever on the one hand and starvation on the other, fled from their country because to remain was death, is historically the most important event of the famine."[4] The picture given is of multitudes of individuals voting with their feet for lower rather than higher mortality levels, and simultaneously for higher rather than lower living standards.

Unfortunately no direct data are available which would permit us to see whether death rates were in fact lower in the Irish sections of American and English cities than in Irish rural areas during famine times. The available evidence presented in Chapter Three suggests on the contrary that death rates were *higher* in American and English cities than in the rural areas of Ireland, possibly even during famine times. Since the Irish persisted in moving from Irish rural areas to the less healthy urban areas abroad, one can reasonably conclude that they were either unaware of such mortality differences, or if knowledgeable, they found certain urban advantages compelling: they were willing to accept less healthy conditions in order to gain opportunities in an urban setting to improve other important elements of their living standards. The decline in general living standards and opportunities during famine times may have been as great a motivating force for emigration from Ireland as hunger and the threat of disease and death. (Some specific examples of what these other living standard considerations were during the 1845–48 famine will be given in Chapter Three.) Since mortality is usually higher in the urban rather than the rural areas of European nations, the Irish acted like most European rural-urban migrants in considering urban economic and social opportunities more important than the relatively better health conditions of their rural homes. In this one respect at least, the low mortality levels and the lack of industrial opportunities in the present-day agrarian societies are not anomalous, but rather have important precedents in the rural areas of Western societies.

Although death rates do not reliably indicate economic or social opportunities between areas, they may still serve as indicators of a group's relative social status within a specific area, especially if rural and urban populations are considered separately. The assumption that social status determines one's access to the societal resources for good health is so widely accepted that it appears self-evident, in need of no empirical test. The usual absence of information about social status in official death registration statistics also discourages studies in this area; this is the situation for Ireland, where detailed death statistics are tabulated only by age, sex, residence, cause of death, and recently also by conjugal status. While the linkage between mortality and socioeconomic status is not testable by the available Irish data, another interesting status differential is — the relative status of females.

Illustrations of the subordinate status of females, especially single females in Irish rural areas, are often found in Irish short stories, plays, and novels. The dominance of males over females is not unique to the rural Irish, of course, but the question remains whether the subordinate status of rural Irish women was sufficiently extreme to result in relatively higher mortality. Several comparisons of mortality by sex, nationality, rural-urban residence, age, and cause of death all indicate that the subordinate status of Irish females did indeed increase their mortality levels from what they might otherwise have been. The pattern of excess female mortality was especially marked in the decades before the 1940s, and among rural females from early childhood until marriage, and then after the childbearing period. In sum, the patterns of mortality in Ireland exemplify the fact that between geographic areas low mortality rates do not necessarily reflect high social or economic opportunities, while at the same time demonstrating that within the same area differential mortality rates can indicate significant differences in social status.

Female Emigration and the Movement from Rural to Urban Areas

One of the famous "laws of migration" formulated by E. G. Ravenstein in the 1880s was that females are more migratory than males over short distances.[5] Ravenstein's insight remains valid today for rural-urban migration in areas inhabited by Western Europeans and persons of Western European culture — in those countries, with few exceptions, the proportion of females is greater in urban than in rural areas.* In contrast, generally in non-European

---

* There are proportionately more females than males in the urban than in the rural areas of all 20 countries of North and South America

societies, there are proportionately more males among urban than rural residents.[†] The close association between which sex predominates in urban areas and the cultural heritage of a nation is striking, and the explanation presented in Chapter Four focuses on rural-urban differences in the relative social status of females. For rural females in Western Europe the choice was not between rural unemployment or urban work as a domestic servant (a common explanation for the presence of more Irish females than males in many English and American cities), but rather a choice between the subordinate role of an unpaid helper in her own family or the freedom and independence which a paying job in a distant city promised. If employment opportunities alone determined the sex ratios of Western cities, then the higher pay, greater promotion prospects, wider occupational choice, and generally greater demand for male workers would have attracted more males than females from rural areas — the pattern seen in virtually all non-Western societies. Yet the opposite pattern prevails in the West.

The contrast in social status of females between rural and urban areas in the West, of course, is not the entire explanation of the pattern. The argument assumes that both sexes are equally free to migrate to urban areas, and this condition may be more characteristic of Western nations than the nations of Asia and Africa. Since the sex ratio of any emigration stream is mainly determined by the movement of unmarried persons or of persons moving without their families, the generally later ages of marriage and the higher proportions of single persons in Western societies also contributed to the number of individual single females able to leave rural areas. The polarity in the social status of females between rural Ireland and urban United States and England, the continuing mass emigration of Irish persons of both sexes for over

---

except Peru, and of all 28 European countries except Greece and five Eastern European nations (Albania, Bulgaria, Romania, Yugoslavia, and the U.S.S.R.). United Nations, *Demographic Year Book, 1955*, Table 7, pp. 185–197; *1962*, Table 9, pp. 304–315; *1963*, Table 5, pp. 162–230; and *1964*, Table 27, pp. 648–664.

[†] Only 8 of the 33 countries of Asia, the Middle East, and Africa listed in the U.N. sources have female numerical dominance in urban areas, and 4 of these 8 are distinctly Western European in background (Australia, New Zealand, Israel, and the Philippines). *Ibid.*

125 years, and the unusually high proportions of single people in the Irish population all make Ireland an excellent test case of this pattern of human migration.

The major factors explaining the greater preference of females for urban areas in Western societies are rarely found‘ together in non-Western societies. This illustrates the need for different theories of urbanism and urbanization about non-Western societies from those commonly accepted in the literature about Western societies.

Emigration and Agricultural Labor-Saving Techniques

While the sex ratio of the rural-urban migration stream, with few exceptions, is different for Western and non-Western societies, the impact of agricultural labor-saving techniques on rural-urban migration appears universal. An agricultural labor-saving device or method by definition reduces the number of man-hours required for a certain task and yields two options for any particular farmer: to work a larger area of land using the same amount of labor, or to reduce the amount of labor needed to work the land he presently controls. Both effects could result in increased numbers of underemployed and unemployed rural workers, who from a strict model of economic rationality would be strongly attracted to urban job opportunities. But such an explanation does not account for the fact that generally the greatest amount of rural out-migration during such transition periods comes from small farms which *did not* adopt the new techniques.

In Chapter Five a sociological explanation is suggested for this seeming economic anomaly: the widening contrast between the improving conditions available on the larger farms worked with the newer techniques and the unchanging life style available on the smaller farms worked with the older, less efficient techniques. The link between population change and agricultural labor-saving methods is today of great importance to the futures of several large, developing nations because a major transition to such techniques appears to be beginning, and in fact is being counted on to avert famine in these countries during the 1970s and 1980s. Called by some the "Green Revolution," the success in increased food production which is hoped for might also bring increased frustration to the poorer farmers unable to afford the new methods, and increased pressures for rural-urban migration among these farmers' sons.[6]

Once again Ireland is an ideal test case for the study of the sociological effects of technological changes in agriculture because the large-scale transition from nineteenth to twentieth century farming methods did not take place there until after World War II. Changes in the composition of the Irish rural society during the transition period are easily and reliably studied since data on age, sex, and occupation are available by size of farm since 1926. In addition to these methodological considerations, Ireland is an important test case because it is more like present-day developing countries in some important attributes than many other Western societies. Ireland was almost three-fourths rural when land reform was successfully implemented after the turn of the century; it was more than two-thirds rural when political independence was won from Britain in 1921; and today it still has a high proportion of its population living in rural areas (51 per cent in 1966). Furthermore, evidence presented in Chapter Five suggests that Ireland experienced an earlier transition in agricultural technology during the middle part of the nineteenth century. Ireland at that time was even more similar to many of the developing nations today: almost half of the holdings being worked were five acres or smaller in 1841, marginal lands had long since been pressed into agriculture, only a small portion of the rural population was able to put aside reserves for the future, and the majority of the rural population had become dependent for their subsistence on annual good crops of a single staple food.

Although a century apart in time, the two great transitions in agricultural labor-saving techniques in Ireland were accompanied by declines in the total rural population. The sociological processes through which the technological changes were linked to demographic changes were similar in both cases and seem relevant to all societies in similar circumstances. In countries with a fixed amount of arable land all of which is being worked, relatively little mass out-migration, and a rapid rate of natural increase (Ireland before the 1840s and many developing nations today), the introduction of agricultural labor-saving techniques is resisted by small farmers and landless laborers who cannot afford to adopt the new methods but who would, nevertheless, be seriously affected by their adoption by larger farmers. A rapid acceptance of new labor-saving techniques can occur, however, during a rise in rural out-migration (as was the case in most Western societies during urbanization), or during a combination of out-migration and widespread famine and epidemic (as in Ireland during the late 1840s). Seen from this perspective of Irish history, the famines and epidemics predicted by some observers for certain developing nations within the next two or three decades possibly could act to speed up the acceptance of modern agricultural labor-saving techniques. Whether this actually happens in any particular nation, of course, probably depends on political and economic factors.

Protestant Emigration

The migrations in recent decades of hundreds of thousands of persons of European stock from colonies to their home countries following the breakdown of European colonialism and the emergence of the new nations of Asia, Africa, and Latin America are of more historical significance than the numbers of migrants alone would indicate. In many of these countries, Europeans accounted for a large proportion of the technical, commercial and administrative skills and their departure meant a reduction, at least temporarily, in the quantity and quality of certain goods and services. In some countries the Europeans were forced to leave for racial, political, ethnic, or religious reasons; but in other countries they left in large numbers even though they could have remained. This second pattern, the voluntary emigration of minority group members during periods of growing nationalism, is the topic of Chapter Six, with the Protestant emigration from Ireland being the case in point.

Because many students of Irish and English history do not customarily view Protestant emigration from Ireland in this connection, the first part of Chapter Six is spent documenting the fact that such an event did in fact occur. One of the ironies of Irish history is the point that had the Protestant population remained constant after the 1920s, the long-standing decline in the Irish population would have been reversed and small net gains would have been recorded in the 1936 and 1946 Censuses. Coming soon after the granting of Irish independence in 1921, such slight population increases would have been considered "no small achievement during the short period of self-government."[7] But the population of Ireland declined between 1926 and 1946 in spite of the slight increase in the Catholic population because of a one-quarter decline in the Protestant population. This great decline had been preceded by a one-third decrease in the number of Protestants in Ireland between 1911 and 1926, and was succeeded by proportionately greater declines among Protestants than Catholics through 1961 — the most recent Census to inquire about religion.

Evidence is presented in Chapter Six to show that the discrepancies in patterns of population change between the two major religious groups in Ireland were not due to relative changes in fertility or mortality, but were in fact due to the greater emigration of Protestants.* Furthermore, it is estimated that the large outmovement of Protestants from Ireland was composed primarily of native-born persons rather than Protestants born in England, Scotland, or other foreign countries. They, like the European colonials who had been born in India, Indonesia, or the Congo, may have been native-born citizens but still they voluntarily emigrated during periods of rising nationalism. Why?

No single factor explains the voluntary emigration of Protestants from Ireland after the granting of independence, but two major sets of reasons are most salient. First are two economic reasons: because of their closer connection with the industry and commerce of the nation before independence, the Protestants would have been more directly affected by economic stagnation or decline after independence; and because the level of their skills

---

* Another reason for the decline in the number of Protestants would be conversion to Catholicism. But Geary and McCarthy have pointed out that "while we have no statistics on the matter, we believe that changes in religious affiliation on the part of individuals had little effect on the trends." R. C. Geary and M. D. McCarthy, "Addendum No. 2," *Commission on Emigration and other Population Problems, 1948–1954,* "Reports," p. 201.

was relatively higher than that of Catholics, Protestants would have had more to gain by emigrating from a slowly to a more rapidly developing society — a version of the familiar "brain drain." Without playing down these economic matters, emphasis also is placed in Chapter Six on documenting four sociological factors: First, the old elite was replaced by a new nationalist elite, which resulted in a greater loss of social status for Protestants than for Catholics. Second, the passage of new sumptuary laws reflecting the ethnic or religious values of the nationalists was more disliked by Protestants than by Catholics (for example, laws restricting divorce, banning the sale of contraceptives, creating censorship of published materials and films, and ordering compulsory Irish language examinations in schools and for civil service positions). Third, continued political and economic conflicts between Ireland and the United Kingdom kept alive interpersonal conflicts and reduced the rate of assimilation of Protestants into the predominately Catholic Irish nation from what it otherwise would have been. And fourth, although the Irish government explicitly guaranteed the rights and privileges of religious minority groups, some Protestants may have feared that future Irish governments would not. These six economic and sociological factors do not exhaust all of the possible reasons why proportionately more Protestants than Catholics left Ireland after Irish independence, but they go far toward explaining the Irish case specifically, and generally in understanding the links between nationalism and minority group migration in developing nations.

Postponed Marriage and Permanent Celibacy

Some believe that the Irish experience is of little relevance to achieving population control in today's developing countries because the Irish made such extreme use of postponed marriage and permanent celibacy — important elements of the Malthusian concept of moral restraint. Yet the Irish were not unique in their marriage patterns; they were instead the best example of the general Western European pattern of a relatively late age at marriage and the prevalence of a high proportion of never-married persons in all age groups. As the most extreme case, Ireland becomes the most severe test of theories explaining the willingness of individuals to forgo the sexual and familial satisfactions of early and universal marriage for the social and economic advantages of remaining single.

Other scholars have a difficult time seeing Ireland as an important case study of population control because the Irish have the highest marital fertility rate of any Western country. It seems paradoxical that the Irish should be the best example of population control through marriage practices and at the same time the worst example of population control through acceptance of a small completed family size. A solution to this seeming paradox must stress the interrelationship between the Irish patterns of emigration, marriage, and fertility: because the decision to marry precedes the act of having legitimate children, a knowledge of Irish marriage patterns is necessary for an understanding of the high Irish marital fertility.

My basic assumption is that the processes by which rising material aspirations interacted with the "stem family system" were the same in Ireland as in other Western European countries; what is unusual about Ireland is the unique combination of fundamentally common Western social processes. Although versions of the stem family system may have been prevalent in Europe and Japan before industrialization, they appear to be rare among present-day developing nations. Like the "joint family system" of India and China, the stem family was an extended family in the sense that several generations lived in the same household. But unlike the joint family, in which all sons inherited part of the family wealth or held the wealth communally, in the stem family system *only one* child inherited control over the family holding. Upon reaching adulthood, the other children either remained on the home farm as unmarried, unpaid helping hands, or they left home. In my opinion, the stem family system was and is the essential social institution which motivated and permitted individuals to remain permanently single, or to marry at a relatively late age.

While the stem family system explains the way in which a late age at marriage and high rates of permanent celibacy can become an accepted part of a society, the family system itself does not explain *changes* in the age at marriage and the proportion that is single. To do this, we must combine a knowledge of the workings of the stem family system with an awareness of the aspirations and living conditions of the people involved. In Chapter Seven, the links between changes in agricultural technology and the stem family are traced.

Changes in agricultural technology, while important, do not compose the entire explanation for changing ages at marriage and proportions permanently single. The extreme degree of postponed marriage for which Ireland is famous today is the result of increases in the age at marriage which took place between 1871 and the 1930s, a period of relatively little consolidation of holdings and of no fundamental change in agricultural technology. Furthermore, explanations based on rural conditions do not directly help us to understand the similar patterns of late marriage and permanent celibacy among the urban Irish. The discussion of this issue in Chapter Seven is based on four elements of the stem family system which persisted in urban areas, and which operated in rural areas independently of changes in agricultural technology: the acceptance by parents of the responsibility for helping to establish their offspring in socially accepted positions in life; an awareness of the personal link between one's own decisions about marriage and one's chances of realizing a certain material standard of living; a belief that an unmarried status for an adult did not reflect individual deviance in sexual matters (for example, being single was not taken to mean was sexually frigid, homosexual, or perverted); and a willingness to postpone marriage until one had achieved a certain social status for oneself even if this meant the possibility of permanent celibacy.

Up to now one widely accepted explanation of the extremely late ages of marriage and high rates of permanent celibacy among the Irish has not been mentioned — the sexual puritanism of Irish Catholicism. The reason for this is my belief that the sexual puritanism of contemporary Irish Catholicism was the result, and not the cause, of the unusually high proportions of single persons in the Irish population. My argument is given in detail in Chapter Seven, but the major points are: by the mid-nineteenth century increasing proportions of Irish men and women decided to postpone marriage primarily for economic and social status reasons;

they wished to avoid emotional entanglements with the opposite sex and such temptations were more easily resisted with the help of a strong moral code; and in spite of official Roman Catholic doctrine which encourages marriage among lay persons and considers sexual union within marriage as sacred, the Irish desired and received from their clergy a very strong emphasis on the dangers and sinfulness of sex among single persons.

High Marital Fertility

The unusually high marital fertility of the present-day Irish is often thought to be due to their being a predominantly Roman Catholic nation. The argument usually has two major parts: abortion and the more effective methods of birth control are considered sinful in Catholic doctrine and devout Catholics are thus unable to effectively limit their fertility; and the Catholic emphasis on marriage for procreation, and on the large family ideal, result in Catholics being less willing to use even the acceptable birth control method of periodic or permanent abstinence until after having had several children. As an explanation of the extremely high Irish marital fertility, this argument contains a major flaw: there are other countries in Europe with as high or even higher proportions of Catholics in their population, but with unusually low marital fertility. Either the Irish are more devout Catholics than, say, the Belgians or the French (an opinion one sometimes hears expressed in Ireland), or there are other conditions existing in Ireland which have led the married Irish to desire and to have relatively large families. My interpretation in Chapter Seven entertains both of these possibilities, and suggests that the selective effects of the extreme degree of emigration from Ireland, and permanent celibacy and late marriage among those who remained, are the major reasons for the persistence of the large ideal family size among the married population of Ireland.

The basis for emphasis on the selective effects of emigration and marriage patterns on fertilty is the unusual way in which fertility has declined in Ireland during the past half century. Between 1911 and 1961 the greater the age of the wife at marriage, the greater the decline in completed family size. For example, comparing women married from 25 to 29 years in the 1911 Census with women of the same duration of marriage in the 1961 Census, the number of children ever born per woman declined by one-quarter for women married in their early twenties (from 7.5 to 5.5), and by one-half for women married in their late thirties (from 3.5 to 1.8).[8] This finding is not something to be routinely expected, at least on the basis of the English experience. Between 1911 and 1946 in England the age of the wife at marriage made no difference in the percentage decline in fertility.* Even though the younger brides would have had much larger families than the older brides for biological reasons alone, in Ireland they appear to have been less interested in limiting their family size. In what ways were the younger brides different from the women who waited until their thirties to marry?

First of all, women who remained in Ireland and who married in their early twenties were but a small fraction of their original cohorts. Most women chose either to emigrate, to postpone marriage until their thirties or to remain permanently single. Between 1861 and 1966 the proportions of all 10- to 14-year-old girls who survived, were still in Ireland, and married by their early twenties were only from 9 to 18 per cent of the original cohorts.[9] Since we have explained much of emigration from Ireland, postponed marriage, and permanent celibacy in terms of the social and economic gains involved, we are led to conclude that those individuals who remained in Ireland and married early in life cared least about such aspirations. Being released from this major constraint on fertility, it is not surprising that the Irish who married early in life had relatively large families.

The selective effect of emigration and marriage is also important for understanding the degree of religious orthodoxy among married Irish Catholics. Catholics who married in their twenties in Ireland conformed with their Church's encouragement of early marriage, but persons who postponed marriage until their thirties or who remained permanently single had ignored this

---

* In each age group between 20 and 34 years of age at marriage, the decline was about 47 per cent. D. V. Glass, "Malthus and the Limitation of Population Growth," in *Introduction to Malthus*, D. V. Glass (ed.), p. 36.

particular aspect of their Church's teaching. Having shown themselves independent of Church encouragement of early marriage, more late than early marriers in Ireland also adopted a small family ideal. Speaking only about the area of sex and family life, I believe proportionately more orthodox Irish Catholics are found among the married population, especially the early married, than among permanently single lay persons or the Irish abroad.

Curiously, the persistence into the mid-twentieth century of a large desired family size among many Irish makes the study of the acceptance of a small desired family size much easier in Ireland than in many other European countries: the contrasts are wider and more apparent between those Irish who did accept a small family size and those who did not. Furthermore the availability and quality of data relevant to the question are excellent because fertility questions were asked in the 1911, 1946, and 1961 Irish Censuses and have been published in cross-tabulations by such important variables as religion, occupation, rural-urban residence, and age at and duration of marriage.

What lessons can be learned from the Irish patterns of marriage and fertility which might be of some help in studying the less developed nations of Asia, Africa, and Latin America? If nothing else, the Irish clearly show that the personal motivation to limit one's fertility is much more important than the birth control technology available. For example, by the end of the nineteenth century England was much more highly urbanized and industrialized than Ireland, yet the English crude birth rate was also much higher than that of the Irish: the contrast ranging from an English rate of 35.4 and an Irish rate of 26.2 during the 1870s through the first decade of the twentieth century, when the English rate was 26.3 and the Irish was 22.4.[10] Ireland demonstrates that a nation does not necessarily have to be urban, industrial, or well supplied with contraceptive supplies to have a low crude birth rate.

Can presently agrarian societies also achieve low crude birth rates without first industrializing, or at the very least without providing abortion and contraceptive methods on a mass scale? Considering the importance of the family system in explaining the Irish acceptance of an extreme degree of postponed marriage and permanent celibacy, the question can be answered only for specific countries and only after examining the norms within each country concerning the proper age at marriage and the relative acceptance of never-married adults. In at least some non-Western societies we should find that, as in Ireland, age at marriage is variable and is linked to the social status one wishes to achieve or maintain. Once such pre-existing family norms are understood and documented in any given society, the groundwork has been laid for the formulation of governmental policies aimed at increasing the age at marriage through strengthening or modifying traditional practices. By encouraging what is thought to be "moral" behavior, rather than by trying to replace existing family norms with alien practices, such policies should be acceptable and effective at least to some degree. But it should be remembered that even in those societies where a late age at marriage is practiced, marriage patterns *alone* will not produce a crude birth rate as low as that of Ireland today unless the age at marriage and proportions single become as extreme, or more extreme, than Ireland's (depending on the age/sex compositions involved).

Does the persistence of a large family ideal in Ireland mean that a desire for several children will persist regardless of the economic consequences? Was Malthus correct in arguing that people will turn their surplus wealth into more offspring? Support for this thesis cannot be obtained from my interpretation of high Irish marital fertility. I argue that the Irish responsible for the large families of Ireland were not representative of their cohorts. They were atypical on those very factors usually given to explain the small family sizes of other European countries. Furthermore, the historical situation of Ireland itself was unique in that emigration from Ireland resulted in a declining population for over a century. Ireland had an escape valve for the children of large families which is not available for most less developed countries today. The conditions producing high marital fertility in Ireland today were unusual and extreme. Malthus may indeed have been correct about persons' desires for childrearing generally, but his thesis cannot be proved by the Irish of the past century.

CHAPTER II

Conditions in Nineteenth-Century Ireland

IRISH historical circumstances were unique and of course will never be repeated in Ireland or any other society; nevertheless they formed the setting in which the more general social and demographic processes mentioned in Chapter One took place. I shall focus attention in this chapter on four major areas: the relationship between Protestants and Roman Catholics, the question of land ownership, the competition between Irish and English economic interests, and the association between Irish nationalism and Roman Catholicism. These complex and interrelated topics cannot be covered in one chapter without the serious danger of oversimplification and exaggeration. But it would be perhaps even more misleading to attempt to understand Irish demographic patterns without being aware, to at least some degree, of the important social, political, and economic conditions existing in Ireland during the nineteenth century.

Protestants and Roman Catholics

In Ireland, as in several other European countries, laws once existed that discriminated against individuals on the basis of their religious affiliation. Ireland's case was somewhat unusual in that the laws in question discriminated against Roman Catholics even though the great majority of the Irish population was Catholic. In

the 1861 Census, the first to inquire about religion, 89 per cent of
the population of Ireland (26 Counties), was Catholic, 9 per cent
was Protestant Episcopalian (Church of Ireland) and Methodist,
and the remaining 2 per cent was composed of Presbyterians,
Baptists, Jews and others (Appendix Table 4). Irish Catholics lost
much of what status they had before the eighteenth century with
the passage of a series of acts between 1695 and 1746 known as
the Penal Laws. As J. C. Beckett has commented in what is considered to be one of the best one-volume histories of Ireland: "the
essential purpose of the Penal Laws . . . was not to destroy Roman
Catholicism, but to make sure that its adherents were kept in a
position of social, economic, and political inferiority."[1] Under
the Penal Laws all Roman Catholic bishops were banished from
Ireland (although some remained in hiding, and a fifty-pound
reward was offered to anyone turning in a "popish bishop"). Lay
Catholics were not permitted to inherit property from one another, purchase land, vote in elections, hold national or local government positions, become lawyers or act as grand jurors, have more
than two apprentices in their trade (except for linen-weaving), or
even own a horse worth more than five pounds.* Some of the
Penal Laws were not effectively enforced, especially those relat-
ing to the Catholic clergy and the ability of some Catholics to
send their children abroad for their education. The laws concerning ownership and inheritance of property, access to certain occupations, and governmental officeholding, on the other hand, were
put in force and almost destroyed the Roman Catholic gentry.[2]

Toward the end of the eighteenth century and the beginning
of the nineteenth, the letter of the Penal Laws was gradually abro-
gated, but their spirit continued in other laws which, while not
overtly persecuting Catholics because of their religion, had the
purpose of maintaining the power and privileges of Protestants
over Catholics. In 1793, for example, the vote was given to Cath-

---

* Edmund Curtis, *A History of Ireland*, 6th ed., pp. 281, 284–285. Presbyterians and other Dissenting Protestants were also subject to restrictions
but these were far fewer and lighter than those imposed on Catholics. For
example, Dissenters could purchase land, inherit property, engage in any
business or profession, vote, and sit in Parliament (p. 287).

olic tenants with holdings which had an annual interest of at least 40 shillings.[3] But because secret balloting was not introduced until 1872, Catholics voted not as they wished but as their Protestant landlords dictated (with few notable exceptions).* To do otherwise was to court eviction. The office of the director of the Bank of Ireland was opened to Catholics in 1793, but because all bank officials were Protestant very few Catholics were hired even as clerks for several decades (in 1844 only three of the 220 clerks employed by the Bank in Dublin were Catholic).[4] Catholics were given the right to sit in Parliament by the Catholic Emancipation Act of 1829, but the same act considerably reduced the number of Catholics eligible to vote by raising the qualification from 40 shillings to 10 pounds. The practice of tithe-proctors, police, and soldiers (who themselves were often Catholic) collecting the money required to support the Church of Ireland directly from tenants, who were predominantly Catholic, was replaced in 1838 by a tithe rent-charge collected from landlords. While this did eliminate one source of face-to-face conflict, landlords were empowered to increase rents to cover the added cost of the tithe and "all that the tenants got out of it was the knowledge that they were paying for what they considered heresy only at second hand."[5]

During this period the contrast between Ireland and the United States in freedom from religious discrimination was well known to the Irish, and it would have been surprising if it had not acted to encourage emigration. The precedent had been set during the eighteenth century, when the imposition of the Penal Laws on Irish Protestant Dissenters resulted in many going to North America, where they took a considerable part in the revolt of the colonies and the establishment of the United States. By 1776 perhaps one-sixth of the population of the American colonies was Irish, most having come from the province of Ulster.[6] The cost of passage across the Atlantic was a major reason why more Pro-

* The most famous "revolts" of Catholic tenant-voters against their Protestant landlords occurred in the 1826 general election and in the election of Daniel O'Connell to Parliament in 1828. J. C. Beckett, *The Making of Modern Ireland*, pp. 301–302.

testants than Catholics left Ireland for North America at this time. Being relatively more prosperous, proportionately more Dissenters than Catholics could afford the long and expensive transatlantic voyage, and so the less costly passage to England, Wales, and Scotland determined the destination of most Catholic emigration from Ireland during the eighteenth century and the first few decades of the nineteenth. But not all Irish Catholic immigrants in England became permanent residents; many stayed only long enough to earn the cost of passage to the United States and Canada.

Once having arrived in the United States, many Catholic immigrants sent money back to their relatives in Ireland so that they could emigrate directly to America without first having to go to England, except perhaps to actually embark on the voyage. By 1847 annual remittances from America amounted to 200,000 pounds (or one million dollars at the prevailing rate of exchange); these rose to 1,439,000 pounds ($7,195,000) in 1853 and averaged at least one million pounds (five million dollars) between 1848 and 1900 for a total of at least 260 million dollars during the second half of the nineteenth century.[7] Almost all of this money (called "America money"), came from immigrants, but as early as 1827 a small part began coming from employers seeking cheap labor.[8] The America money paid for at least three-quarters of all Irish emigration to the United States between 1848 and 1900, and without it Irish Catholic mass emigration across the Atlantic would not have been possible.[9] But because more than half of the America money was used by the Irish remaining in Ireland to pay rent and to improve living conditions, the net result of the America money was to make emigration less than it might otherwise have been and to direct the emigration stream away from the geographically closer but less attractive English urban areas to American towns and cities.[10] Irish Catholics not fortunate in having a generous relative in America still went to England, Wales, and Scotland, with many continuing on to the United States, Canada, and other English-speaking areas overseas.

Eventually several laws were passed which gradually increased the political power of Catholics in Ireland and reduced religious conflict: the Municipal Corporations Act of 1840 reformed a corrupt local government system in urban areas and made possible the election of Catholics to office in boroughs which had been under exclusive Protestant control (Catholics had been eligible to hold office in municipal government since 1793, but very few had actually held office and in Dublin none had).[11] The act passed in 1869 to disestablish the Church of Ireland greatly reduced religious tensions and ended the tithe rent-charge (although rents were not necessarily reduced). By the end of the nineteenth century the franchise had been widened and the Local Government Act of 1898 "helped to complete the process of transferring local powers from the class of large landowners to the predominantly Catholic populace."[12]

In spite of the Penal Laws and prolonged discrimination against Catholics, a very small Catholic middle class and aristocracy did survive (some through pretended apostasy or through the protection of influential Protestants), and it was able to reassert itself after the purely penal elements of the laws were eliminated between 1778 and 1829.[13] Unfortunately for the Catholic lower classes, the middle-class and aristocratic Catholics were more interested in avoiding friction with the Protestant ascendency and in maintaining their own privileges than in attempting to improve the lives of the peasantry and the poor.[14] For the great majority of the Catholic population, to be born poor was to remain poor as long as one remained in Ireland. The opportunity to improve one's social status either by self-denial or frugality was almost nonexistant for most Catholics. The exact proportion of Protestants in individual occupations is not available until the 1926 Census, but even by that late date Protestants were still disproportionately represented in the better jobs (Table 1).* The chances for pro-

* Earlier censuses used a classification system which did not distinguish between employers, managers, or workers but grouped all together under headings such as "Persons working and dealing in textile fabrics: woolen cloth manufacture," or "Persons engaged in commercial occupations; dealers in money: bank service." Some occupations were listed separately, and these show higher proportions of Protestants than does Table 1. In the 26 Counties in 1891, for example, 54 per cent of all barristers and solicitors, 45 per cent of all commercial travelers, and 44 per cent of all brokers, agents, and factors were non-Catholic compared with 38, 39, and 32 per cent respectively in 1926. *Census of Ireland, 1891,* "Report," Table 19, pp. 114–121; and Vol. III, "Province of Ulster" (County tables for occupation by religion).

motion in some fields were also better for Protestants than for Catholics; for example, 35 per cent of bank clerks but 52 per cent of bank officials were Protestant.

Throughout the nineteenth century and into the beginning of the twentieth, the social and economic discrimination experienced by Irish Catholics in a country where they constituted the

TABLE 1. Number and Percentage Protestant in Certain Occupations Among Males, Ireland, 1926*

Occupation	Number		Percentage Protestant
	All Males	Protestant	
Bank officials (not clerks)	960	495	52
Employers, mgrs., and foremen of printers, bookbinders, photographers	291	125	43
Navigating, engineering officers	744	309	42
Heads of commercial sections of businesses	372	154	41
Insurance clerks	518	205	40
Chartered accountants	373	150	40
Brewery clerks	543	208	38
Analytical chemists	258	96	37
Solicitors, barristers	1,348	486	36
Bank clerks	2,344	821	35
Watch and clock makers, repairers	711	244	34
Auctioneers, valuers	669	229	34
Church officials (not clergymen)	593	203	34
Commercial travelers	3,088	1,011	33
Employers and managers of metal workers (not shoe-forging)	551	182	33
Civil engineers, surveyors	976	314	32
Insurance officials (not clerks)	596	181	30
Employers, mgrs., and foremen of textile workers	364	111	30
Dentists	505	139	28
Farmers with over 200 acres	4,937	1,342	27
Employers, mgrs., and foremen of makers of drinks	426	114	27
Medical doctors	1,843	361	20
Total occupied 12 years and over	963,768	67,852	7

SOURCE: *Census of Population of Ireland, 1926,* Vol. III, Part I, Table 17, pp. 114–129.

* Protestant Episcopalians, Presbyterians, and Methodists; all occupations in which 33 per cent or more of employed males were Protestant, and selected occupations in which 20 to 32 per cent were Protestant.

great majority of the population was a major motivation for emigration. (Actual changes in population by religion between 1861 and 1961 will be discussed in chapter Six.) The Irish immigrant in the United States also faced religious prejudice and social discrimination, but legal discrimination on the basis of religion which characterized Ireland for more than a century was unknown in the United States. In large part because of the efforts of the colonial Irish Dissenters, the American government guaranteed freedom of religion and specifically separated church and state. The Irish emigrant to the United States is rarely characterized as a religious refugee, perhaps because there were so many other reasons for him to leave Ireland; but during the nineteenth century religious discrimination was present, and no doubt for some it was the chief reason for their decision to leave their homeland.

Land Ownership

Cutting across the religious issue was the matter of land ownership. Although there were some exceptions, by the beginning of the nineteenth century virtually all of the landlord class was Protestant, because of the Penal Laws and the economic disabilities suffered by the Catholics. On the other hand, the great majority of the tenant farmer class in the 26 Irish Counties was Roman Catholic (as was the landless laboring class). The relationship between landlord and tenant in Ireland was different from that which had developed in England. Instead of a system of mutual rights and obligations along English lines, the Irish tenant was legally and socially in a weak position in dealing with his landlord.* Some Protestant landlords in Ireland were enlightened in their dealings with their tenants, but many landlords did not manage their estates themselves, and derived their income instead through agents who collected rents from the tenants. Often these agents were Catholic, and it is well to remember that the exploitation of the tenant farmer class was not entirely a Protestant enterprise.

* In some parts of what is now Northern Ireland, the landlord-tenant relationship was more like that of the English.

As many slum landlords do today, many eighteenth and nineteenth century Irish landlords tried to get as much rent from as many tenants as possible. When Catholic tenants with 40 shilling holdings were given the vote in 1793, landlords were further encouraged to increase the number of tenants, for by doing so they increased their political influence. The Catholics, on their part, took advantage of the willingness of landlords to accept them as tenants and subsisted on potatoes, oats, cabbage, and milk while growing cash crops and animals (mainly pigs) to pay the rent. Both classes of people were willing to fragment holdings into progressively smaller units, but the process could not go on forever.

As increasingly larger proportions of the tenant population worked holdings of just a few acres, progressively more families did not produce enough for the rent, the tithe of the Church of Ireland (until 1838), the support of their own clergy, and their own subsistence. Since the combined cost of rent and clerical tithe did not decrease, the level of living of the tenant did; increasing numbers became dependent upon the potato for their main food staple. A description of the dirt hut of an Irish peasant gives an impression of what life was like: "Without windows, and in many cases without a chimney, its ventilation was always bad, and not improved by the fact that the whole family, including the pig, generally slept in its one room. . . . Sunk low against a damp hillside or a bog which grew up around it, it could neither be dried nor heated by the fire of wet peat which was all the peasant could afford. Even this poor fuel was not always available. . . . Dirt, cold, and bad air made the cabin a breeding ground for disease, and facilitated the spread of epidemics."[15]

When the level of nutrition worsened following a poor potato crop, resistance to disease was lowered. As Thompson and Lewis have commented in general about persons suffering from chronic undernourishment: "Because they were already greatly weakened by an inadequate diet they died prematurely, and at times of great epidemics they would always be the first to succumb."[16] Although it is well known that nutritional deficiencies of different types cause rickets, scurvy, beriberi, pellagra, night blindness, and kwashiokor, there is evidence that malnutrition also contributes to such diseases and disorders as some birth defects, tuberculosis, anemia, edema, and possibly others.[17] Typhus and dysentery were recurring aspects of nineteenth-century Irish life, and when the potato failed throughout the nation, or when two or more successive crops were poor, epidemics were accompanied by starvation; the more extensive famines of the nineteenth century occurred in 1800, 1807, 1816, 1822, 1839, 1845–48, 1863 and 1879.[18]

Because the first population decline was recorded in the 1851 Census, and because the 1845–48 famine was one of the most extensive in Irish history, there was and is a tendency to assume that the 1845–48 famine initiated mass emigration from Ireland. In a standard population text of the 1930s, for example, Carr-Saunders implies that the 1845–48 famine initiated not only Irish mass emigration but also low Irish fertility: "Then came the [1845–48] famine. Since that time the population has steadily declined owing to the combination of heavy emigration with a low birth rate."[19] This perspective is still with us, as shown by Beckett's comment in his relatively recent book (1966): "The [1845–48] famine not only halted the process of growth, but completely reversed it: the decline continued steadily, and by the beginning of the twentieth century the population of Ireland was only about half of what it had been on the eve of the famine."[20]

While it is true that a decline in Ireland's population did not occur until 1851, the actual beginning of mass emigration took place about three decades earlier. The outflow of poor persons, as distinct from the emigration of middle-class farmers and artisans which had begun during the eighteenth century, apparently began after the potato failure and typhus epidemic of 1817 and increased after the 1822 famine.[21] Between 1825 and 1844 the reported number of emigrants from Ireland (32 Counties) was 672,000 and the actual number was probably higher.[22] Between 1845 and 1870 at least three million persons left the 32 Counties, and 1.1 million emigrated between 1871 and 1891.[23] By 1891, 39 per cent of all Irish-born persons in the world were living outside of Ireland.[24]

Mass emigration from Ireland increased during and immediately following potato crop failures, but the question remains why more Irish did not eat their cash crops and animals during these periods. The answer is simple: if they ate their cash crops they would not be able to pay the rent. Since they had no money, they could not buy other food. As an English historian commented about the 1845–48 famine: "The Irish problem at the time of the famine was one of destitution rather than food shortage. There was sufficient food in Ireland to feed the population, if they had been able to buy it."[25] Or as an Irish historian put it: "The extraordinary spectacle of Irishmen starving by thousands in the midst of rich cornfields was thus witnessed. One case, typical of many others, is recorded of a man's dying of starvation in the house of his daughter, who had in her haggard a substantial stack of barley, which she was afraid to touch, as it was marked by the landlord for his rent."[26]

Destitute as small tenants were, if they chose not to emigrate they could do nothing but continue working their small holdings, paying their rent, and hoping that epidemic and starvation would pass them by. Although tens of thousands began emigrating after the 1820s, not everyone wanted to go to England and an even smaller number were able to go directly to America until remittances from the United States increased after the 1830s. Landlords, on the other hand, eventually became dissatisfied with having a large number of subsistence farmers on their land and wished to replace them with a more prosperous class of farmers who would pay their rents more steadily, avoid the danger of depleting the soil, and be less likely to become paupers dependent upon the ratepayers.[27] Not only had the Catholic Emancipation Act of 1829 removed the political value of small tenants, but reduced charges on shipping after 1826 had made the exportation of butter to England feasible; as one landlord said in 1827, "We now discover dairy cows are more profitable than cottager tenants."[28] The repeal of Foster's corn laws in 1846 (acts passed in 1784 which gave Irish grain preferential treatment in the English market) was still another event motivating landlords to evict tenants and convert tilled land into pasture.[29] The Encumbered Estates Act of 1849 facilitated the transfer of estates from bankrupt landlords to landlords generally even less interested in the welfare of their tenants and more concerned with converting the subsistence holdings into profitable commercial farms through the process of eviction.[30] The legal power of landlords over their tenants was at its zenith with the passage of the Deasy Act in 1860, which made the eviction process even easier for landlords.[31]

Countering the tendency of landlords to evict were the murders, burnings, cattle mutilation, and other forms of agrarian terrorism directed against the landlord, his agents, and persons who might move into an evicted tenant's holding. The terrorist organizations were local, but many went under the names of the Whiteboy Association and the Ribbonmen. As evictions increased after the 1830s so did the intensity of agrarian terrorism. In the words of one contemporary writer, "But for the salutary dread of the Whiteboy Association, ejectment would desolate Ireland."[32] Evictions and terrorism increased during and immediately after the 1845–48 famine, and to enforce the rights of the landlord class Parliament passed twelve coercion acts between 1847 and 1857 suspending the few liberties enjoyed by tenants.[33]

Resistance to eviction considerably increased following the formation of the Land League in 1879 by Michael Davitt. This organization not only improved upon traditional actions against landlords and persons moving into holdings from which someone had been evicted (the term boycotting comes from the name of the person — Captain Boycott — against whom it was first used), it also provided legal assistance for the evicted. The League quickly became the most widely supported movement since the days of Daniel O'Connell and within four months of its founding Charles Stewart Parnell agreed to become its president while Davitt continued as principal organizer. Irish immigrants in the United States and Canada contributed over one million dollars to the movement between 1880 and 1883, without which the League could not have sustained its legal activities.[34] The British government responded by outlawing the League and imprisoning Parnell and its other leaders in 1881, but they were released in 1882 to keep militant extremists from gaining control.[35] The movement was renamed the National League and new techniques of resistance were soon shrewdly used to gain the maximum amount of publicity and remind the British public of conditions in Ireland.[36]

The League's efforts were successful and seven land acts were passed between 1885 and 1889 laying the groundwork for the transfer of ownership from landlord to tenant.[37] Land acts had been passed before, the first being part of the disestablishment of the Church of Ireland in 1869. But while the first several land acts were important for the precedent they set, they did not result in much tenant ownership because of a lack of capital among tenant farmers (the 1881 Land Act required the tenant to pay one-quarter of the purchase price before taking ownership). The actual transition did not take place until after the government provided sufficient loans to the tenants to help pay the purchase price of their holdings. The early land acts did permit some transfer of ownership (the proportion of farmers owning their own holdings rose from 3 to 12 per cent between 1870 and 1895), but it was not until after the acts of 1903 and 1909 that a major change took place (the proportion of farmer-owners rose to 29 per cent in 1906 and to 64 per cent in 1921).[38]

With this brief review of the reasons for eviction and the ways in which tenants were able to resist, we can better understand some of the links between eviction and emigration during and following periods of famine and epidemic. This is an important matter because 83 per cent of the half million persons officially reported as having been evicted between 1849 and 1882 were evicted during two periods of extensive famine and immediately after, 1849–55 and 1876–82 (Table 2). Evictions were more numerous during famines for at least two reasons: tenants who ate their cash crops and animals could not pay their rent, and resistance to eviction decreased among those tenants who were thinking about emigrating anyway. (Crop failures by themselves would have increased the attractiveness of emigration by widening the gap between actual and desired standards of living.)

Contrary to what one might expect, the number of persons officially reported as having been evicted made up a small minority of all reported emigrants between 1849 and 1882 (Table 2). The high proportion of evicted persons to emigrants in the 1849–55 period was partly due to the fact that emigrants to England,

Wales, and Scotland were not included in the emigration data of this period but were included for the later periods. Although the figures for evictions and for emigration probably understate actual events, the general conclusion is clear: the great majority of emigrants during this time did not wait to be evicted before deciding to leave Ireland. The high rents demanded by many landlords and their refusal to lower or forego rents during times of bad harvests, the ruthlessness of both the terrorist and the landlord's agent in punishing those thought to be supporters of the opposite side, the pressures from nationalist organizations to contribute funds, and the lack of hope for meaningful change all contributed to emigration.

It was not until after the beginning of the present century that the Protestant landlord class was replaced by a class of small owner-farmers (predominantly Catholic in the 26 Counties), and

TABLE 2. Persons Evicted as a Percentage of the Total Emigration from the Whole of Ireland (32 Counties), 1849 to 1882.

Period or Year	Number of Persons Evicted [a]	Number of Emigrants [b]	Evicted Persons As a Percentage Of Emigrants
1849–55 [c]	350,841	1,333,697 [d]	26
1856–60	22,089	415,419	5
1861–65	33,314	467,304	7
1866–70	13,419	382,532	4
1871–75	14,805	364,137	4
1876–82	70,279	427,349	16
Totals	504,747	3,390,438	15

SOURCES: For eviction figures, John A. O'Brien, "The Vanishing Irish," in John A. O'Brien (ed.), *The Vanishing Irish*, London: W. H. Allen, 1954, Table 3, p. 25; for emigration figures, *Commission on Emigration and Other Population Problems, 1948–54*, "Reports," Statistical Appendix, Tables 26 and 28, pp. 314, 318.

[a] From the official reports made to Dublin Castle by the Royal Irish Constabulary.

[b] Except for the 1849–55 period, these are returns of the Registrar General based on particulars furnished voluntarily by emigrants and collected by the police at each of the principal Irish ports. These figures include emigration to Great Britain, but still should be considered as understatements of the actual number.

[c] Seven-year period.

[d] This figure *does not* include emigration to Great Britain; it represents persons of Irish nationality embarking at ports in Ireland and Great Britain for overseas destinations. It probably understates the actual overseas emigration from Great Britain of Irish nationals.

the landlord-tenant conflict was brought to an end. But the passage of land laws and the transfer of ownership did not improve the life of the landless farm laboring class. Until as late as 1930, when wages and conditions of work were fixed by law, the farm laborer and his children hired themselves out to farmers once each year for their lodgings, board, and a lump sum. Families were separated when the farm laborer's children worked for a different farmer, living conditions were worse than the tenant farmer's, and the hours worked and days off depended on the good will of the farmer.[39] The opportunities for exploiting farm laborers were as great after the tenant farmers gained ownership of their holdings as they were before.

Another large group of persons untouched by the land legislation was the urban population. Contrary to the urban growth experienced in other European countries, the urban population of Ireland was smaller in 1901 than it had been in 1841 (Appendix Table 3). Although Dublin's population had increased, its size was not an indicator of its prosperity: 29 per cent of the city's residents in 1913 were living in accommodations officially classified as slums.* What happened in Ireland during the nineteenth century that arrested urban development?

Irish and Engish Economic Interests

The decline in the urban population of Ireland between 1851 and 1901 was in large part a consequence of the unsuccessful competition of most Irish industrial enterprises with their English counterparts. In addition to discrimination against Irish goods on the part of some English industrialists, the provisions of the Act of Union of 1801 gradually established free trade between the two countries and by 1825 the transition was virtually complete. Free trade did not necessarily have to damage Irish industry, but because of the difference in industrial development between Ire-

---

* Quarters described as unfit for human habitation, so decayed as to be soon unfit for human habitation, or structurally sound but not in good repair. Eire, *Report of Inquiry into the Housing of the Working Classes of the City of Dublin, 1939–43*, pp. 15, 28, cited in Alexander J. Humphreys, *New Dubliners: Urbanization and the Irish Family*, p. 50.

land and England at this time, every Irish industry did in fact decline and many were eliminated except those which were competitive, such as brewing, distilling, shipbuilding, and the linen trade.[40] Under the Act of Union Ireland became part of the United Kingdom of Great Britain and Ireland. Politically, the control of Irish affairs moved from Dublin to Westminster; economically, Ireland gave up duties protecting her native industries from English competition in return for continued preferential treatment of Irish agricultural products in the English market.

The Act of Union brought about one condition in Ireland which implies the reverse of economic development: "industry's excess population was being compelled to transfer to agriculture."[41] Non-agricultural workers in Ireland (32 Counties) declined from 1.7 million to 1.6 million between 1821 and 1841, while during the same 20-year period agricultural workers increased from 2.8 million to 3.5 million.* (The proportion of the labor force occupied in agricultural pursuits increased from 40 per cent in 1821 to 53 per cent in 1841.) The reversal of Irish economic development was one reason for the increased emigration of artisans and commercial persons from Ireland to the United States. As William Forbes Adams has pointed out, "The decline of industry in one country and its amazing growth in the other made the shift of the city dwellers even more logical and natural than the movement of farmers, laborers, servants, and fishermen."[42]

In addition to dissolving customs barriers, the Act of Union also damaged Irish industry by making it more difficult to accumulate investment capital in Ireland. A provision of the Act was that Ireland was to bear two-seventeenths of the total expenditure of the United Kingdom. Whether this proportion was fair or not, the fact remains that between 1801 and 1817 the national debt of Ireland rose by 250 per cent compared with 50 per cent for Britain. When the exchequers of the two nations were joined in 1817, Ireland was relieved of separate responsibility for the debt

---

* J. R. Bellerby, *Agriculture and Industry Relative Income*, Table 23, p. 154. While the direction of change is clear between 1821 and 1841, the figures for 1821 should be considered less reliable than those for 1841.

incurred since the Union, "but the heavy financial strain imposed during the interval had drawn much-needed capital out of the country, and had weakened her economy at a critical period."[43] Another major drain on Irish financial resources was the practice of absentee landlordism — always present in Ireland but greatly increased after the center of Irish government moved from Dublin to England. The exact value of absentee rents is not known, but estimates ranged from two to six million pounds a year between 1810 and 1842.[44] The combination of exorbitant rents and absentee landlordism meant that few tenants or landlords contributed capital for the industrial development of Ireland after the Union.

Although free access for English manufactured goods and lack of investment capital were the two most important reasons for Ireland's industrial decline following the Act of Union, they were not the only causes. One of the more important secondary reasons was the chaotic Irish banking system of the time, and the discrimination of the Protestant bankers against Catholics attempting to expand their business operations following the abrogation of the Penal Laws.[45] Another secondary but frequently mentioned reason was the lack of coal and iron deposits in Ireland. While this did place Ireland at a disadvantage, the added cost of importing raw materials from England was not a bar to success, judging from the development of the shipbuilding industry in Belfast. The cost of transporting coal and iron from England to Ireland was only a small fraction of the total manufacturing cost of almost any item.[46]

The economic relationship between Ireland and England after the Union was that of an agricultural colony and the manufacturing home country. Even though absentee landlordism drained much of the wealth produced by Irish agriculture out of Ireland into England, in terms of total grain exports Irish agriculture did benefit from the relationship. Toward the middle of the nineteenth century, however, foreign grain became cheaper than Ireland's. Pressures built up in England to end the preferential treatment of Irish grain and permit the free entry of grain, regardless of origin, into English markets. The English Prime

Minister, Robert Peel, decided at the end of 1845 that Corn Laws should be repealed and was able to accomplish this in the summer of 1846.[47] Although Peel based some of his arguments for repeal on helping to feed the Irish experiencing the 1845–48 famine,* the more important result was to end Ireland's favored position in the English market. Much Irish land was shifted from the production of grain to pasture, less agricultural labor was needed, and the pressures for eviction increased.[48]

An Irish economic historian has argued that whenever there was a conflict of interest between England and Ireland, England prevailed.[49] When Irish manufacturers wished to maintain protective tariffs and English manufacturers wanted open access to the Irish market, free trade was established between the two countries. The favored position of Irish agriculture in the English market was ended when it became cheaper for the English to buy their grain from foreign nations. Regardless of the rationalizations offered by the English for their actions, many Irish believed Ireland would be better off if it could regain some power to run its own affairs; and until that time emigration from Ireland kept its strong appeal.

Irish Nationalism and Roman Catholicism

The links between the religion of the vast majority of the Irish people, Roman Catholicism, and the movement to return political power over Irish affairs to Ireland have demographic importance on at least two counts: improving the opportunities and status for Catholics in Ireland through political means would have reduced the attractiveness of emigration from Ireland for Catholics; and to the degree that the religious and political institutions of Ireland reinforced one another, the ideology of Roman Catholicism would have a more pervasive influence — a potent factor especially in the area of policy concerning sex and family life. The close association between Roman Catholicism and Irish politicians in the United States, what Paul Blanshard has called

* It is interesting to note that Peel made his decision to repeal the Corn Laws during the first year of the 1845–48 famine, when there was every reason to assume that the famine would not extend beyond one year.

"Irish Catholic Power,"[50] has led many Americans to believe that
the same pattern prevailed in Ireland between the Church and
Irish nationalists. In England it was once popularly assumed that
the Irish "electorate was entirely under the thumb of the priesthood."[51] The reasons why many Americans and English believed
the Catholic clergy dominated Irish politics stem from the time of
the Penal Laws and from Daniel O'Connell's organization of
parish priests to collect the "Catholic rent" of the 1820s. The
Penal Laws drove Catholic priests and people into close association
and virtually destroyed the Catholic middle classes and aristocracy, which might otherwise have acted as an intellectual elite for
Irish Catholics. O'Connell was the first politician to use the organization of the Catholic church to reach Catholics throughout the
country.

But even though O'Connell and the Catholic clergy worked
cooperatively, O'Connell did not hesitate to denounce the Pope's
representative and reject the Pope's recommendation on an important political issue in 1814 (the Vatican had given its approval
for English veto power over papal appointments for Ireland).[52]
O'Connell's action demonstrated that he was willing to put his
nationalism before his Catholicism, thus setting the model for later
nationalists. From this time the Vatican was inclined to distrust
the objectives of Irish nationalism.[53] The Young Ireland movement of the 1840s, while not antireligious, was insistent on keeping religion out of politics and putting nationalism above sectarian
differences.[54] The Young Ireland attitude was adopted by the
Fenians (most of whom were Catholics), whose leaders continual-
ly argued that the "people must learn to draw a clear line between
ecclesiastical authority in spiritual and in temporal matters."[55] The
Fenian movement was strongly opposed by the Catholic church,
yet it found widespread support, especially among farm laborers
and urban workers, even after the failure of its 1867 rising.[56]

The continuing conflict between the Irish Catholic hierarchy
and the Fenian activist minority widened to include the tenant
farmer class during the land war. Michael Davitt was a Fenian,
and his first agrarian demonstration was organized with the help
of Fenians in Mayo in 1879.[57] The Catholic hierarchy deplored
force and urged its followers to better their condition by keeping

within the law; in this spirit a Catholic Archbishop (John Mc-Hale), a respected moderate nationalist, denounced Davitt's meetings during the early stages of the Land League.[58] But the movement grew and gained wide popular support not only among the Catholic laity but among many parish priests as well. In 1882 the British government was able to get the Pope to send a letter to Irish bishops condemning a "national tribute" started for Charles Stewart Parnell and forbidding Catholics to subscribe, but the letter had little effect.[59] In April of 1888, Pope Leo XIII issued the famous Rescript which condemned the Plan of Campaign and boycotting as illegal, and forbade clerical participation in either. The Rescript split the Catholic clergy, with the more militant parish priests defying the Vatican and with most of the Irish Catholic hierarchy supporting the Pope.[60] The British government included parish priests in the provisions of the coercion acts, and the militant core of the Irish priesthood "continued to defy the criminal as well as canon law, whenever their consciences so dictated."[61] Because of their refusal to end their involvement in the land war after the Rescript, many parish priests received much publicity. But it should be remembered that the parish priests were following and not leading a movement begun and organized by Fenians and Parnellites.

In the midst of the controversy surrounding the Papal Rescript, the British government imprisoned several Irish members of Parliament for their participation in the land agitation. By August of 1888, 21 members had "received prison terms ranging up to six months with hard labor, and by the end of the year 11 more were facing prosecution."[62] Support of the Rescript by the Irish Catholic hierarchy linked it with the British government in suppressing Irish efforts to change their situation. This could not help but convince increasing numbers of Catholics of the wisdom of the Fenians' arguments for the separation of the church from politics.

The next stage in the conflict between the Irish Catholic hierarchy and Irish nationalists occurred when Parnell was cited as correspondent in a divorce verdict in 1890. At first, members of his parliamentary party enthusiastically reaffirmed their support of his leadership, while English Nonconformists demanded that "Parnell must go," and the "hierarchy in Ireland stood by in embarrassed silence."[63] It was only *after* the English Prime Minister (Gladstone) came out against Parnell, to placate the English Nonconformists, that the Irish hierarchy declared that Parnell was no longer morally fit to lead the party. In spite of the pressure of the English Liberal party and the Irish Catholic hierarchy, Parnell refused to resign and 27 of the 70 members of the Irish party continued to support him.[64] The death of Parnell in 1891 did not resolve the feud between the Parnellites and the Anti-Parnellites in Ireland. Even though the Catholic hierarchy followed rather than led the movement to remove Parnell from leadership, anticlericalism was characteristic of the Parnellite movement. Symbolic of the relation between the hierarchy and the Parnellites was the clerical ban on attendance at Parnell's funeral in Dublin. In spite of the ban, over 100,000 persons attended, but not a single priest.[65]

The hierarchy not only opposed the Fenians, the Land League, and the Parnellites, it also disassociated itself from the movement for Irish ethnic distinctiveness. In 1893 the Gaelic League was founded to promote Irish as the national language and to revive Irish customs, dancing, literature, and, in cooperation with the Gaelic Athletic Association, Irish sports. Although founded by a Protestant (Douglas Hyde), the League quickly developed into a popular national movement and hundreds of branches formed throughout the country.[66] Part of the movement aimed at introducing the Irish language as a compulsory subject in the nation's schools. The Scottish and English segments of the Irish population naturally opposed this idea, and so, ironically, did the Catholic hierarchy: in 1909 a professor of Gaelic was dismissed from the Catholic seminary at Maynooth for too fervently supporting compulsory Irish.[67] Once again it appeared to Irish Catholics that their hierarchy was siding with the English against Irish interests.

Whatever political influence the hierarchy had retained by the beginning of the twentieth century was further diminished when it opposed the Sinn Fein political party after the Easter Rising of 1916. Sinn Fein supporters believed in establishing an independent Irish republic by civil war if necessary. In May of

1918 the British government proclaimed Sinn Fein as an illegal organization and imprisoned its leaders.[68] The Catholic clergy denounced Sinn Fein both in and out of church, but: "Diatribes from pulpits could not divert the republicans from their course, nor deprive them of public sympathy, not even when reinforced with the Church's most formal condemnation (excommunication); although the weight of the Church was thrown against them, it appeared to influence public opinion little."[69]

Just how little influence the Church had in Irish politics at this time was shown by the results of the 1918 general election. Sinn Fein won 73 parliamentary seats, the Unionists won 26 (all in Ulster), and moderate home rulers won only 6. What the hierarchy could not accomplish by words the British government tried to accomplish by force; in January of 1919, 34 of the Irish members of Parliament were in prison and one had been deported, all for belonging to Sinn Fein.[70] That same month, in spite of the combined efforts of the hierarchy and the British government, 25 members of Sinn Fein who had been elected to parliamentary seats met in Dublin and, adopting a provision constitution, proclaimed themselves the lawful government of Ireland. The establishment of a second government in Ireland directly led to the Anglo-Irish war of 1919–21.

Regardless of the English orientation of the Irish Catholic hierarchy at this time, most Irish Protestants remained convinced that Irish Catholics were dominated by their clergy. This belief was especially strong among the Presbyterians of Ulster, whose slogan was "Home Rule is Rome Rule." They argued that existing differences between the Catholic hierarchy and the Irish nationalists would be resolved and forgotten once Ireland achieved self-government. Even though the answer to this argument had to await future events, the Protestants' belief that it eventually would happen dictated their political actions at the time. (The effect of subsequent events on the religious composition of the Irish emigration stream will be taken up in Chapter Six.)

The achievement of Irish independence in 1921 climaxed a series of changes which reduced the reasons for Irish Catholic emigration from Ireland. The disestablishment of the Church of Ireland, the gradual breakdown of exclusive Protestant control

over many industries and professions, the transfer of farm ownership from Protestant landlord to Catholic tenant, and the rise of
Irish nationalism all contributed to the decline in the number of
emigrants per 1,000 population from 12 during the 1890s to about
9 during the first quarter of the twentieth century (Appendix
Table 2). With the granting of Irish self-government the emigration rate dropped still more, to about 6 emigrants per 1,000 population between 1926 and 1946. After the break with Britain was
accomplished and accepted by the majority of the public in England and Ireland, the English gradually ceased to consider the Irish
as potential traitors to the Crown and the Irish increasingly accepted the advantages to emigration (and possible future re-
migration) offered by the geographic proximity of the two islands.
The end of British political domination of Ireland resulted in a
greatly increased attractiveness of Britain to potential Irish emigrants, and Britain became the destination of the great majority
of emigrants who had been born and raised in an independent
Ireland.

CHAPTER III

Mortality and Relative Living Standards

A LTHOUGH there is a need for a comprehensive study of Irish mortality which would include such topics as general mortality trends in the nineteenth and twentieth centuries, or mortality and population composition, the discussion of mortality in this chapter will be limited to the ways in which mortality statistics might possibly be used to indicate relative living standards. Even though Irish mortality data are available only by age, sex, residence, cause of death, and recently by marital status,* two questions can be at least partially answered. Did Irish mortality contribute to Irish emigration? And do mortality differences by sex in Ireland indicate the relative social status of the sexes?

Mortality and Migration

The most direct connection of mortality with migration is simple and straightforward: assuming persons migrate to improve their standard of living, migration should flow from high to low

---

* The publication of mortality rates by marital status began in the mid-1950s. For both sexes in 1961 single persons had the highest rates, then widowed persons, then married persons. Ireland, *Report on Vital Statistics, 1961,* Table 13, p. 16; *1964,* Table 2, p. 3.

mortality regions. The question here is whether mortality alone is a reliable indicator of "living standards." A more involved linkage of mortality with migration can be called the "flight from famine" theory. Under conditions of relatively low mortality and high fertility there would be a rapid rate of population growth but not necessarily any strong pressure for out-migration. Only when mortality suddenly increases, as during a famine period, would migration pressures also increase. The combination of high mortality and high out-migration eventually could reduce the pressure of the population on available resources, mortality conditions would improve, and consequently there would be less reason to migrate. In this way periods of high mortality also would be associated with episodes of heavy out-migration.

The flight from famine theory is often proposed to explain Irish emigration during and after the 1845–48 famine. Cecil Woodham-Smith has commented that "famine emigration" was the most important historical event of the 1845–48 famine.[1] While there is no doubt that some people left only to avoid starvation and disease, and others left as a result of the death of a spouse, or of their parents, or friends, it is an oversimplification to assume there was no other reason for increased emigration after 1845, and to assume that all emigrants left for the same reason. The inadequacy of the flight from famine theory as the sole explanation of Irish emigration at this time is shown by the increase in emigration after crops returned to normal in 1849.* There were 801,000 emigrants reported between 1845 and 1849 and 1,037,000 reported

---

* A blight destroyed the potato crops of 1845, 1846, and 1848, while the crop of 1847 was for the most part untouched. The 1849 crop failed in some regions, but the famine itself was over. J. C. Beckett, *The Making of Modern Ireland: 1603–1923*, p. 342. Although more persons died in the 1845–48 famine than in any other Irish famine, an estimated 800,000 in the 32 Counties, in relative terms the 1741 famine was just as serious. At that time an estimated 400,000 persons died in the 32 Counties in a population of 3.1 million (compared with a population of 8.2 million in 1841). Daniel Coghlan, *The Land of Ireland*, p. 106; T. W. Freeman, *Ireland: Its Physical, Historical, Social and Economic Geography*, p. 110; I am using K. H. Connell's figures to estimate the 1741 population, K. H. Connell, *The Population of Ireland, 1750–1845*, Table 4, p. 25.

† The figures are from the Reports of the Colonial Land and Emigra-

between 1850 and 1854.[†] According to a rigorous interpretation of the flight from famine theory, once the famine was over the emigration should have declined. The delayed response in Ireland, as in other European countries in similar circumstances, was not because high mortality persisted but rather because the famine experience was the final "convincer" added to a set of conditions which encouraged emigration. The decision to emigrate, once made, was only the first step in accumulating funds or requesting money from abroad and making the necessary arrangements to emigrate. But during this delay, the famine-related reasons for emigration should have lessened, for there was, at least in Ireland after the 1845–48 famine, less pressure on available resources because of the great and sudden decline in population: there were 1.4 million fewer persons in the 26 Counties in 1851 than there were in 1841, a decline of 22 per cent (Appendix Table 1).

There were several reasons why emigration from Ireland increased rather than decreased after the end of the 1845–48 famine. Because of religious discrimination, exorbitant rents, industrial decline, evictions, and the conflict between landlords and the agrarian terrorist organizations, mass emigration from Ireland was well under way by the 1830s (see Chapter Two). On the "push" side, pressures for eviction increased after the repeal of the Corn Laws in 1846 and the passage of the Encumbered Estates Act of 1849. To aid the landlord class in combating agrarian terrorism, twelve coercion acts were passed between 1847 and 1857 suspending existing civil rights.[2] As a result, evictions increased and 66 per cent of the 505,000 persons officially reported as having been evicted between 1849 and 1882 were evicted between 1847 and 1855 (Table 2).[3] Hopes for any political change in the existing situation lessened with the death of Daniel O'Connell in 1847 and the suppression of the Young Ireland rising of 1848. On the "pull" side, the attractiveness of emigration to America greatly

---

tion Commissioners; they do not include migration from Ireland to England, Scotland, and Wales; and they probably understate the actual number of emigrants. See Ireland, *Commission on Emigration and Other Population Problems, 1948–1954*, "Reports," Statistical Appendix, Table 26, p. 314.

increased following the discovery of gold in California in 1848.* The ability to go directly to the United States (rather than first migrating to England to earn passage across the Atlantic), was greatly increased as remittances from previous emigrants to the United States rose from about one million dollars in 1847 to $7,195,000 in 1853.[4]

Because of the emphasis often placed on famine as a cause of Irish emigration during the mid-nineteenth century, there is a tendency to assume that mortality conditions were better in the English and American towns and cities of the time. This point of view assumes that the rural Irish moved from high to low mortality areas and also assumes that mortality is a reliable indicator of "living standards." The measure of mortality selected to test this idea should meet three requirements: it should indicate mortality at all ages and not just those of peak ages of emigration, since entire families did emigrate during and after famine times in Ireland, and a young adult's decision to emigrate may have resulted from the death of his parents or a reluctance to raise his own children under high mortality conditions when an alternative was available; it should control for possible differences in the age-distribution of different areas at the same time, or of the same population at different times; and it should be easily understood, a single figure rather than a series of figures. The expectation of life at birth suits all of these requirements; it is the number of years on the average a person could expect to live if he spent his entire life at the age-specific mortality rates prevailing at any specified time. It is not to be taken as a projection since actual mortality rates change; it is instead a comprehensive measure of mortality which controls for the possible effect of different age distributions.

The expectations of life by sex and rural-urban residence fortunately are available for Ireland and part of England for the period just before the Great Famine (Table 3). These figures must

---

* Emigration to the United States from other European countries also reached a peak following news of the California gold discoveries: Great Britain and Scandinavian countries in 1849, and Germany in 1854. Brinley Thomas, *Migration and Economic Growth: A Study of Great Britain and the Atlantic Economy*, p. 94.

be interpreted with caution, for there may have been a greater under-reporting of deaths in rural than in urban areas, and the urban rates may have been boosted by rural persons coming into the city to die. Nevertheless, the contrast between rural and urban areas makes it reasonable to conclude that mortality conditions actually were better in rural Ireland than in Irish towns, Manchester, or Liverpool in 1841. Rural Irish immigrants in London would have moved from relatively worse to better mortality conditions only if we assume they enjoyed the average London life expectancy. A more realistic assumption would be that the Irish living in the slums and tenements of London experienced the same or a worse rate of mortality as that of Manchester and Liverpool.

TABLE 3. Expectation of Life at Birth in Years by Sex in Rural and Urban Areas of the Whole of Ireland (32 Counties) and England, 1841.

City or Region	Males (A)	Females (B)	(B–A)
Ireland [a]			
Dublin	24	28	+4
Irish civic districts	24	24	0
Irish rural districts	30	29	−1
England			
Manchester	24	NA [b]	NA
Liverpool	25	27	+2
London	35	38	+3
Surrey [c]	44	46	+2

SOURCES: Census of Ireland, 1841, "Report," pp. lxxx–lxxxii; W. Farr, Vital Statistics (ed. N. A. Humphreys), London, 1885, p. 454, cited in D. V. Glass, "Some Indicators of Differences between Urban and Rural Mortality in England and Wales and Scotland," Population Studies, XVII:3 (March 1964), Tables 1 and 2, pp. 264, 265.
([a]) The expectations of life were calculated from reports collected during the 1841 Census of over one million deaths in Ireland during the ten-year period preceding the census.
([b]) NA: Not available.
([c]) Considered an "illustration of rural conditions" in England.

There is every reason to accept the conclusion that mortality conditions were worse in urban than in rural areas in 1841 because the same pattern still existed during the first part of the twentieth century, when errors from under-registration were negligible. Mortality conditions were worse in Glasgow than in Scotland as a whole, worse in English urban areas than in English rural areas, and generally worse in English and Scottish urban areas than in Ireland (Table 4). The higher urban death rates mainly were due to higher infant mortality rates and a greater incidence of deaths due to infectious and parasitic diseases. In Ireland in 1901, for example, there were 150 deaths of infants under one year of age per 1,000 live births in urban areas, compared with 74 in rural areas; in the same year the death rate from infectious and parasitic diseases was almost three times higher in urban than in rural areas.[5]

TABLE 4. Expectation of Life at Birth in Years by Sex in Ireland (1910–12), Glasgow and Scotland (1920–22), and Rural and Urban Areas of England and Wales (1911–12).

City or Region	Males (A)	Females (B)	(B–A)
Glasgow	48	51	3
Scotland	53	56	3
English County Boroughs [a]	48	52	4
London	50	54	4
England and Wales	51	55	4
Other English urban districts [a]	52	56	4
English rural districts [a]	56	60	4
Ireland	54	54	0

SOURCES: *Censuses of Population of Ireland, 1946 and 1951,* "General Report," Table 51, p. 68; D. V. Glass, "Some Indicators of Differences between Urban and Rural Mortality in England and Wales and Scotland," *Population Studies,* XVII:3 (March 1964), Tables 1, 2, and 4, pp. 264–266.
    [a] Including the Welsh.

The fact that infectious and parasitic diseases were much more common in urban than in rural areas becomes important when asking whether the specific cause of death was of any significance in motivating emigration from Ireland during famine times. During the 1845–48 famine, and probably in all Irish famines, the major cause of death was not starvation but disease, particularly typhus, dysentery, and scurvy.[6] A reduction in the quality of diet lowers resistance to disease long before a simple lack of calories results in death by starvation.[7] Furthermore, typhus is carried by the louse (a fact not known at the time), and a crowding together of persons either in urban slums or in emigrant ships increased the chances for infection. So many emigrants died from disease on ships sailing to North America during the 1845–

48 famine that the vessels were often called "coffin ships," and epidemics were common following the arrival of Irish immigrants, in Canadian and American cities, regardless of quarantine regulations.[8] For many persons, the cause of death would have been the same whether they remained in rural Ireland during famine times or went to the towns and cities of England and the United States. We can only speculate whether the Irish rural areas actually lost their advantage in life expectancy over the Irish neighborhoods of English and American cities during times of famine in Ireland. What we do know is that the advantage of rural over urban areas in Ireland persisted until at least 1960–62 (Table 5). The actual gap between the two regions was greater than that shown because the national expectation of life averaged the rural and urban regions. In 1935–37 a separate expectation of life for Irish rural areas is available, and it shows a difference of 7.4 years for males and 4.0 years for females between rural and urban areas (compared with the difference between the national and urban figures for the same time of 5.1 years for males and 2.6 years for females).[9] Yet in spite of the rural advantage in mortality conditions, internal migration in Ireland went from rural to urban areas and not the other way around.

Migration from Ireland continued to the United States and to England even though the expectation of life was, for several decades, better in Ireland. Among males the national life expectancy was greater in Ireland than in England between at least 1871

TABLE 5. Expectation of Life at Birth in Years by Sex for the Total and the Urban Populations of Ireland, 1935–37 to 1960–62.

	Males			Females		
Period	Total Population (A)	Urban Population (B)	(A–B)	Total Population (A)	Urban Population (B)	(A–B)
1935–37	58.2	53.1	5.1	59.6	57.0	2.6
1940–42	59.0	54.4	4.6	61.0	58.4	2.6
1945–47	60.5	56.8	3.7	62.4	60.5	1.9
1950–52	64.5	62.3	2.2	67.1	66.7	0.4
1960–62	68.1	66.5	1.6	71.9	71.8	0.1

SOURCES: *Ireland, Commission on Emigration and Other Population Problems, 1948–1954*, Tables 78, 81, pp. 106–8; *Statistical Abstract of Ireland, 1950*, Tables 13, 14, pp. 17, 18; *1953*, Tables 17, 18, pp. 28, 29; *1964*, Tables 27, 28, pp. 37, 38; *1968*, Tables 27, 28, pp. 37, 38.

TABLE 6. Expectation of Life at Birth in Years by Sex in Ireland, The United States, and England and Wales, 1850 to 1960–62.

Approximate Period [a]	Males			Females		
	Ireland	United States [b]	England, Wales	Ireland	United States [b]	England, Wales
1850	NA	41.8	39.9	NA	44.9	41.8
1870–72	49.6	NA	41.4	50.9	NA	44.6
1880–82	49.4	NA	43.7	49.9	NA	47.2
1890–92	49.1	NA	44.1	49.2	NA	47.8
1900–02	49.3	48.2	48.5	49.6	51.1	52.4
1910–12	53.6	50.2	51.5	54.1	53.6	55.4
1925–27	57.4	57.8	55.6	57.9	60.6	59.6
1935–37	58.2	60.6	60.2	59.6	64.6	64.4
1945–47	60.5	65.1	66.4	62.4	70.3	71.5
1960–62	68.1	67.5	68.0	71.9	74.4	73.9

SOURCES: *Censuses of Population of Ireland, 1946 and 1951,* "General Report," Table 51, p. 68; L. I. Dublin, A. J. Lotka, and M. Spiegelman, *Length of Life: A Study of the Life Table,* rev. ed., New York: Ronald Press, 1949, Table 17, p. 60; Ireland, *Commission on Emigration and Other Population Problems, 1948–1954,* Statistical Appendix, Table 23, p. 311; *Statistical Abstract of Ireland, 1965,* Table 27, p. 37; *Statistical Abstract of the United States, 1965,* Table 59, p. 53; England and Wales, *Annual Abstract of Statistics, 1964,* Table 36, p. 38.

([a]) Specific dates and periods were: Ireland, 1870–72, 1881–83, 1890–92, 1900–1902, 1910–12, 1925–27, 1935–37, 1945–47, 1960–62; U.S.A., 1850 (Md.), 1900–1902, 1909–11, 1920–29, 1930–39, 1946, 1960; England and Wales, 1838–54, 1871–80, 1881–90, 1891–1900, 1901–10, 1910–12, 1920–22, 1937, 1950–52, 1961–63.

([b]) White population in reporting area.

and 1926, and greater in Ireland than in the United States from at least 1901 to 1911, and again in 1961 (Table 6). Among females the Irish life expectancy was greater than the English between 1871 and 1891, and greater than the American in 1911. The great improvement in life expectancy in Ireland between 1946 and 1961 was accompanied, ironically, by the highest rates of emigration out of Ireland since the 1880s (Appendix Table 2).

The more healthful living conditions in Ireland become even more apparent when Ireland is compared with the urban areas of Britain or the United States. Among males around 1911 the Irish life expectancy at birth was three years longer than that of all English and Welsh males, but six years longer than that of males living in English and Welsh County Boroughs (Table 4). Comparing Ireland with the United States during the 1930s, the life expectancy of rural Irish males was 1.4 years longer than that of all American males, and 3.8 years longer than that of urban American males (Table 7). In other words, even though the life expectancy of all Irish males was 0.9 years less than that of all American males, the rural-urban contrast favored the rural Irish males by almost four years. Among females a similar pattern, though less pronounced, existed comparing Ireland with England, or comparing Ireland with the United States.

TABLE 7. Expectation of Life at Birth in Years by Sex and Rural-Urban Residence in Ireland, 1935–37, and the United States, 1930.

Country and Residence	Females (A)	Males (B)	(A–B)
Ireland			
All areas	59.6	58.2	1.4
Urban	57.0	53.1	3.9
Rural	61.0	60.5	0.5
United States [a]			
All areas [b]	62.7	59.1	3.6
Urban	61.0	56.7	4.3
Rural	65.1	62.1	3.0

SOURCES: Ireland, *Commission on Emigration and Other Population Problems, 1948–1954*, Tables 79, 81, pp. 106, 108; L. I. Dublin, A. J. Lotka, and M. Speigelman, *Length of Life: A Study of the Life Table*, rev. ed., New York: Ronald Press, 1949, Tables 77, 79, pp. 324, 332.
[a] White population in reporting area.
[b] 1929–31.

Within some American cities the average level of mortality of the Irish was worse than that of the citywide figure, further widening the already large contrast in the health conditions between the rural origins and the urban destinations of most Irish migrants. The relatively high mortality of the Irish in some American cities and states in 1920 is illustrated in Table 8. The death rates are arranged by the country of birth of the mother of the decedent, and so include both the immigrants and the children of female immigrants. The mortality rates have been adjusted to eliminate the influence of possibly different age distributions in the various groups. The Irish death rate from all causes was several points higher than that for the other groups in the table; and the Irish death rate from tuberculosis of the lungs was about double that recorded for the others. The unusually high mortality of the Irish in urban America at this time, especially their high mortality from tuberculosis of the lungs, prompted the author of the census report to make the following speculation which has particular relevance to our present concerns: "A guess may be hazarded that the excessive death rate of the Irish . . . as compared with their relatively low mortality in Ireland, is due in part to their sudden transition from a predominantly rural environment, in a climate conducive to outdoor living, to a country which they are — for some reason — settled chiefly in large, densely populated cities."[10]

TABLE 8. Age-Adjusted Death Rates from All Causes and from Tuberculosis of the Lungs by Country of Birth of Mother of Decedent in Five Registration Areas, United States, 1920.*

Death Rate and Registration Area	Country of Birth of Mother				
	Ireland [a]	Italy	Germany [b]	United States	England, Wales, Scotland
Adjusted rate per 1,000 persons from all causes					
New York City	18.1	14.0	13.0	13.7	13.4
New York State	17.5	13.9	12.6	12.1	13.0
Philadelphia	16.6	NA	12.0	13.1	NA
Pennsylvania	16.6	14.1	12.8	12.2	14.0
Chicago, Illinois	16.5	NA	11.9	11.4	NA
Adjusted rate per 100,000 persons from tuberculosis of the lungs					
New York City	195	99	96	94	76
New York State	184	96	97	77	78
Philadelphia	173	NA	96	80	NA
Pennsylvania	150	71	89	71	86
Chicago, Illinois	106	NA	61	47	NA

SOURCE: Niles Carpenter, *Immigrants and Their Children, 1920*, Washington, D.C.: U.S. Government Printing Office, Census Monograph VII, 1927, Tables 91, 93, pp. 198, 200–201.
(*) Includes acute miliary tuberculosis.
([a]) 32 Counties.
([b]) Includes German Poland.

We are led to an interesting conclusion: with the possible exception of famine periods, Irish mortality did not contribute to Irish emigration. As rural-urban migrants in Europe did generally, the Irish moved from more healthful rural areas to less healthful urban areas. The living conditions relevant to mortality may have been better in rural Ireland, but the social status of Irish Catholics, opportunities to improve their lives economically, and perhaps many other elements of what they believed constituted a desired standard of living were perceived as being better in the less healthful cities abroad. Even during famine times mortality probably was a much less important reason for emigration than is generally believed, especially after considering the many other reasons the Irish had for leaving Ireland. There is even some doubt whether mortality levels were in fact worse in Irish rural areas during famine times than in the slums of London, Liverpool, Boston, or New York. Mortality did increase in Irish rural areas but it also increased in the Irish sections of English and American cities with the mass influxes of disease-carrying immigrants.

Mortality and the Relative Social Status of the Sexes

Even though mortality rates cannot be taken as indicators of economic or social opportunity, they may reflect the relative social status of persons within the same community. If food, shelter, clothing, and medical care are unequally divided, then this practice should show up in unequal mortality rates. The mortality rates of the religious and occupational groups in Ireland would be relevant to this question; unfortunately, such data do not exist. As we have said, the available data deal only with sex, age, region, cause of death, and marital status. Were there social practices which favored one sex in the allocation of vital resources to the extent that they affected mortality rates? My assumption is that if such practices were important enough to have influenced mortality rates, they also should have been readily apparent both to the Irish themselves and to foreign observers of Irish culture. Before presenting the patterns of mortality by sex for Ireland, I shall briefly give a few illustrations of the way some writers have seen the relative social status of the sexes in Ireland.

It has been said that Ireland is divided by a boundary even more pernicious than that between the North and the South — the boundary between the sexes.[11] Arensberg and Kimball described the situation as it existed in County Clare in 1932: "Men and women are much more often to be seen in the company of members of their own sex than otherwise, except in the house itself. . . . They go to mass, to town, or to sportive gatherings with companions of their own sex. Till recently and even now in remote districts, a conventional peasant woman always kept several paces behind her man, even if they were walking somewhere together."[12]

The act of a female walking behind the male was symbolic of the inferior position of females generally in Irish rural society. Women and children did not eat their meals until after the men and older boys had had their fill,[13] a practice which systematically made the more nutritious food and larger helpings available to the favored sex. The practice of males getting the better food, and more of it, apparently also prevailed among the urban working classes. Sean O'Casey mentioned the custom in his play *The Shadow of a Gunman*. A married couple were described: "He is a man of forty-five, but looks, relatively, much younger than Mrs. Grigson. . . . He has all the appearance of being well fed; and, in fact, he gets most of the nourishment, Mrs. Grigson getting just enough to give her strength to do the necessary work of the household."[14] The exploitation of females by males was one of the major motifs of O'Casey's *Juno and the Paycock*. At one point Juno says to her husband: "Shovel! Ah, then, me boyo, you'd do far more work with a knife an' fork than ever you'll do with a shovel! If there was e'er a genuine job goin' you'd be dh'other way about — not able to lift your arms with the pains in your legs! Your poor wife slavin' to keep the bit in your mouth, and you gallivantin' about all the day like a paycock!"[15]

The subordination of daughters in many Irish families was severe. Although things had changed considerably by the late 1950s, an observer was still able to describe the status of teenage girls in the rural areas of Limerick in the following way: "When a daughter reaches sixteen, if she remains on the farm, she must do a full day's work, and too often her life is one of unrelieved drudgery. . . . [Girls] are favoured neither by father nor mother and accepted only on sufferance. This is, perhaps, too strong a conclusion, and it would be better to say they are loved but not thought of any great importance. In general, the girl is subservient to all other members of the family and shares no confidences with either her parents or her brothers. Her only right is to a dowry if she marries with her parents' consent."[16]

In contrast to the daughter, the son in the Irish family system was given preferential treatment. Although sons were in a subordinate position to their father, they were above everyone else in the household in the way they were treated by their mother. The preference of the mother for her sons over her daughters is shown by an attitude, found both in rural and urban areas and among all social classes, that daughters were expected "to provide the sons with special service and comforts."[17] As a 26-year-old Dublin woman told an observer in the early 1950s, in front of her mother and brothers (who agreed with her comments): "If I am sitting in the easy chair there and Matt or Charley come home, I am expected to get up and give them the chair. They just say 'Pardon me' and up I get. . . . There is no use fighting against it. I used to, but I soon found out which way the wind blew — we have to wait on the boys from sole to crown. I do not mean that the boys do not do anything for us. Matt, for example, will always fix my bike. But Mammy is just a slave to them, a willing slave, and we are expected to be, too. And that is general. That's the common attitude."[18]

Although females were subservient to males both in rural and urban Ireland, there were two practices prevalent in rural areas which especially favored males in the allocation of vital resources. On almost all Irish farms the income from the sale of animals and cash crops was kept by the husband, who was under no obligation even to tell his wife how much he had. He was bound by custom to provide for his wife and family, but only after looking after his own personal needs and those of the farm and livestock.[19] Under this system the wife and children were liable to suffer if the husband overindulged himself in drinking and gambling, was otherwise irresponsible, or if he was willing to have his family lead a spartan existence so that he could buy more land or livestock. As in the matter of eating priorities, there was the chance that the wife and children would be supported by leftovers, with the sons getting the largest share.

The second rural practice which favored males was the matter of division of labor. Generally men took care of the fields and the animals when they were in the fields, while women were responsible for feeding the animals when they were in the barn, milking the cows and processing the milk, and taking care of the vegetable garden, in addition to the usual duties of cooking, housework, and child care. Whether the initial division of labor was equal or not (since the latter half of the nineteenth century only a small proportion of Irish agricultural land was tilled, most of it being in pasture),* the more important point is that women were expected to help do the men's work, but men would be ridiculed for helping with the women's work.[20] Women were usually called out into the fields during turf cutting, during the planting, cultivation, and lifting of potatoes, and during haymaking time when the pitching, raking, and some building of haycocks was left to the women.[21]

The situation of females in urban areas was much better, at least in so far as the family income and expected workload was concerned. According to Humphreys, the Dublin family of the early 1950s was a partnership arrangement with both spouses agreeing how to spend their income, and with many wives actually being responsible for the money.[22] Very few married women were employed outside their homes; at each census between 1926 and 1966 about 5 to 6 per cent of married women were working.[23] Even though few rural or urban wives were employed, the workload of the two groups differed considerably. The urban housewife was expected only to keep house, cook, and care for her husband and children. The great amount of farm work which the rural wife did was in addition to her normal duties as a mother and wife, but it was not considered to be work done outside the home.

On the basis of these comments and impressions, one could reasonably conclude that males were dominant in Irish society, and that they controlled many of the resources needed for good

---

* It is generally agreed that pasture requires less labor than plowed land. The highest proportion of agricultural land ever recorded as plowed was in 1851 when it was 29 per cent; this dropped to 18 per cent in 1881, and to 13 percent in 1926. Ireland, *Agricultural Statistics, 1847–1926,* "Report and Tables," Dublin, 1928, p. lx.

health in the rural areas. When we turn to the mortality statistics, the relatively worse position of Irish compared with American or English females becomes apparent. The relevant comparison here is the difference between the sexes in Ireland contrasted with the difference between the sexes in other countries. For example, the excess of female over male life expectation between 1871 and 1946 was less in Ireland than in England; females lived from three to five years longer than males in England but only 0.1 to 1.9 years longer in Ireland (Table 9). The greater longevity of females in all three countries was in large part a biological phenomenon. Females generally could be expected to have lower mortality rates, since males have higher mortality rates during foetal life,[24] and also in a number of species other than the human.[25] The greater physical soundness of females has been attributed to genetic causes, specifically the fact that the male possesses only one x-chromosome while the female possesses two.* The possible impact of environmental factors on the adult mortality of the sexes was virtually controlled for in a careful study of the mortality of

TABLE 9. Excess of Female over Male Life Expectation at Birth in Years in Ireland, the United States, England and Wales, 1850 to 1960-62.*

Approximate Period	Ireland	United States [a]	England and Wales
1850	NA	3.1	1.9
1870–72	1.3	NA	3.2
1880–82	0.5	NA	3.5
1890–92	0.1	NA	3.7
1900–02	0.3	2.9	3.9
1910–12	0.5	3.4	3.9
1925–27	0.5	2.8	4.0
1935–37	1.4	4.0	4.2
1945–47	1.9	5.2	4.7
1960–62	3.8	6.9	5.9

SOURCE: Calculated from Table 6.
(*) For specific dates and periods see note a, Table 6.
([a]) White population in reporting area.

* The female thus has two parallel sets of genes while the male does not since the segments of his x-chromosome do not exactly match those of his y-chromosome. The chances for a deleterious or lethal gene finding expression in the phenotype of an individual are therefore greater among males than females. G. Herdan, "Causes of Excess Male Mortality in Man," *Acta Genetica et Statistica Medica*, Vol. 3 (1952), pp. 351–375.

teaching Catholic monks and nuns: in these establishments the females continued to have a better mortality record than males.[26] The effect of social factors is to widen or narrow the biological advantage enjoyed by females.

Just how unusual was the relatively low excess of female over male life expectancy in Ireland? Before 1900 on a world-wide basis it probably was not unusual for males to have even greater longevity than females, and the present pattern of lower female mortality at every age became typical in the West only after the 1920s.[27] In addition to the decline in maternal mortality, another environmental factor explains the widening advantage enjoyed by adult females in Western nations, especially in recent decades: this is the greater increase in cigarette consumption among males.[28] A case has been made that environmental factors also account for the greater longevity of males and females in Ceylon, India, and Pakistan — specifically maternal mortality and the preferential treatment given to males at almost all ages.[29] The remainder of this chapter will attempt to show that the Irish case is an excellent Western illustration of the linkage of male dominance with relatively high female mortality. Irish mortality patterns by sex were not unique; where Ireland was unusual for a European nation was in the persistence into the mid-twentieth century of the social customs sustaining male dominance.

A consideration of some other countries in which the excess of female over male life expectancy at birth was less than one year at some time eliminates many possible explanations of the phenomenon which might be peculiar to Ireland alone (Table 10). The sexual puritanism of Irish Catholicism, for example, might be thought to contribute to the subordinate status of single females (although the strong veneration of the Virgin Mary in Ireland could be argued to enhance the status of married women). Yet an even worse pattern of female mortality existed in Northern Ireland during the first decade of the twentieth century, and this region is predominantly non-Catholic.

One trait which all nine of these countries may have shared was the extreme degree of the male dominance which is often found in rural societies: male dominance carried to such an extent that it considerably reduced the advantage in longevity which females normally would have expected for biological reasons. For example, the greater loss of expected female longevity in the rural

TABLE 10. Countries with an Excess of Female Over Male Life Expectation at Birth of Less than One Year at Various Times.*

Country and Period or Year	Expectation of Life in Years Female (A)	Male (B)	Excess (A–B)
Northern Ireland			
1890–92	45.7	46.3	−0.6
1900–02	46.7	50.7	−4.0
1910–12	51.0	54.2	−3.2
1925–27	56.1	55.4	0.7
Bulgaria			
1900–05	42.2	42.1	0.1
1905–06	42.9	43.7	−0.8
1925–28	46.6	45.9	0.7
India			
1891	25.5	24.6	0.9
1901	24.0	23.6	0.4
1911	23.3	22.6	0.7
1931	26.6	26.9	−0.3
China (Rural)			
1929–31	34.6	34.8	−0.2
Ireland			
1881–83	49.9	49.4	0.5
1890–92	49.2	49.1	0.1
1900–02	49.6	49.3	0.3
1910–12	54.1	53.6	0.5
1925–27	57.9	57.4	0.5
Italy			
1876–87	35.5	35.1	0.4
1891–1900	43.2	42.8	0.4
1901–10	44.8	44.2	0.6
1910–12	47.3	46.6	0.7
Union of South Africa Colored Population			
1935–37	40.9	40.2	0.7
Japan			
1899–1903	44.8	44.0	0.8
1908–13	44.7	44.2	0.5
Ukraine			
1895–98	36.2	35.3	0.9

SOURCES: *Censuses of Population of Ireland, 1946 and 1951,* "General Report," Table 51, p. 68; L. I. Dublin, A. J. Lotka, and M. Spiegelman, *Length of Life: A Study of the Life Table,* rev. ed., New York: Ronald Press, 1949, Tables 85–90, pp. 344–53.
* Out of 39 countries listed in the second source.

areas of both Ireland and the United States is shown in Table 7, but the Irish pattern was much more extreme. The excess of female over male life expectancy was 3.4 years more in the urban areas of Ireland, compared with 1.3 years more in the urban areas of the United States. The advantage in mortality enjoyed by females over males in urban areas existed in Ireland as early as 1841. Even though the life expectancy of both sexes was lower in the less healthful cities, the excess of female over male life expectation was five years greater in Dublin than in Irish rural areas (where females actually had a lower life expectancy than males, Table 3). The advantage of the Irish urban over rural areas in female compared with male mortality has continued to at least 1960–62, when females at birth had an expectation of life 5.3 years longer than males in urban areas, but only 3.8 years longer than males in the nation as a whole (Table 5).

Even though the loss of expected female longevity was a predominantly rural phenomenon, it also occurred among young urban persons in Ireland during both the nineteenth and twentieth centuries. Although no detailed analysis of the 1841 Census data on mortality would be warranted because of probable differences in the amount of under-reporting of deaths in various subcategories, the general pattern of mortality by age, sex, and rural-urban residence was striking and was similar to that existing a century later (Table 11). The mortality rate of females was greater than that of males generally after early childhood in the rural areas, and between the ages of about 10 and 34 years in urban areas both in the 1830s and in 1931. This finding is consistent with the impression given of the subordinate status of daughters in Irish families both in rural and urban areas, and of the additional disadvantages experienced by females at almost all age groups in rural areas.

The long term trends in relative Irish mortality by age and sex between 1864 and 1967 are given in Table 12. With the possible exception of the first several years after the compulsory registration of vital statistics began in Ireland in 1864, there is little reason to believe that the under-registration of deaths was greater for one sex than the other. In some male-dominated societies there is a greater under-registration of female deaths, and if

TABLE 11. Estimated Average Annual Death Rates for 1831–41 (32 Counties), and Death Rates for 1931 (26 Counties), by Age, Sex, and Rural-Urban Residence.

Period and Age-group in Years	Deaths per 10,000 of the Same Age and Sex				Female Death Rates as a Percentage of the Male	
	Rural Areas		Urban Areas		Rural	Urban
	Males	Females	Males	Females		
1831–41						
5 and under	371	364	417	414	98	99
6–10	73	80	96	105	110	109
11–15	46	56	49	61	122	124
16–25	156	153	169	171	98	101
26–35	141	165	204	205	117	100
36–45	160	181	274	254	113	93
46–55	225	218	342	295	97	89
56–65	384	408	475	450	106	95
66–75	509	512	578	540	100	93
1931						
Under 5	162	142	341	279	88	82
5–9	20	18	36	26	90	72
10–14	14	18	20	23	128	115
15–19	26	29	34	37	112	109
20–24	39	42	48	48	108	100
25–34	43	54	52	57	126	110
35–44	53	67	88	78	126	89
45–54	93	104	178	132	112	74
55–64	238	238	373	317	100	85
65 and over	746	693	878	773	93	88
All ages	139	143	160	149	103	93

SOURCES: *Census of Ireland, 1841,* "Report," p. lxxxiv; Saorstat Eireann, *Annual Report of the Registrar General, 1931,* Table 19, p. 29.

this had happened in Ireland during the 1860s and early 1870s the effect would have been to understate the actual degree of excess female mortality. The most dramatic aspect of the data is the sudden improvement in relative female mortality between the 1940s and the 1950s. This may have been due to a great change in the social status of females, but it also may have been due to improvements in medical care and public health measures which benefited females more than males (Table 6), and to the increased urbanization of Ireland (Appendix Table 3). For the period before 1950 the greater female than male mortality is obvious, especially among older children and young adults — age-groups which include very few persons who are not living as sons and

TABLE 12. Female Age-Specific Death Rates as a Percentage of the Male in Selected Age Groups in Ireland, 1864–1967.

Period	Under 5	5–9	10–14	15–19	20–24	25–34	35–44	55–64
1864–70	90	102	112	96	79	92	95	95
1871–80	91	106	120	102	83	91	90	95
1881–90	90	109	129	115	89	96	96	98
1891–1900	89	109	134	122	92	93	96	101
1901–10	88	113	140	123	95	92	99	101
1911–20	88	114	129	112	94	94	98	98
1921–30	86	104	120	115	98	105	105	98
1931–40	84	101	113	111	108	113	105	94
1941–50	81	89	109	109	111	113	100	86
1951–60	77	87	85	77	83	87	91	73
1961–67	79	79	73	50	54	72	77	62

SOURCE: Calculated from, Ireland, *Report on Vital Statistics, 1967*, Table 9, p. 11.
Note: Original death rates were expressed as average annual deaths per 1,000 of the corresponding population classified by age and sex, and were carried to two decimals.

daughters in their parents' home. The relatively lower ratio of female to male mortality for children under five is probably due to two things. The greater male mortality expected for biological reasons is higher among infants and young children than among older children; and sex differentials may have been less important in the way infants were treated since the adult males of the Irish family had little to do with the everyday care of children of either sex until after early childhood.[30]

The reasons for this rise in the ratios among teenagers after the 1870s, and among older women between 1921 and 1950, are a matter of speculation. There may have been some selective migration of the healthier rural women, but I am not aware of any data which could serve to negate or verify this hypothesis. It is as logical to argue that the healthy rural women would have had less reason to emigrate than their less fit sisters since they would have been better able to cope with the physical demands made upon them. If there had been some under-registration of female deaths during the first few years of compulsory registration of vital statistics in the 1860s and early 1870s, part of the increase in female mortality recorded would have been due to more accurate statistics. An interesting conjecture is the impact of the changing land laws on female mortality.[31] Although the laws were eventually designed so that no more money was needed to purchase a holding than one had been paying for rent, and that the legal cost of transfer was met out of public funds,[32] the fact remains that the decade of greatest transfer of land ownership was also the decade of highest excess female mortality among young women: at this time among persons aged 10 to 14 years the female death rate was 140 per cent of the male. Could there have been other expenses associated with land ownership which resulted in some of the more land-hungry farmers buying fields with money taken away from the support of their families? The subsequent rise in relative female mortality among older persons a decade or so later may have been due, at least in part, to the aging of this cohort. The males of this generation perhaps felt less of an obligation to share their incomes with their wives; the females may have demanded less, having been raised to expect very little (that is, the females who did not choose to migrate to urban areas).

When the age-specific mortality rates of females are higher than those of males, there is no doubt that the females have lost some of their biological advantage over males in longevity. Females also may have lost some advantage in those age-groups where the ratio of female to male deaths, while less than 100, is nevertheless relatively high compared with other countries. In the mid-1930s, for example, the Irish pattern was quite different from that of the United States and England (Table 13). Although the source used for the table compared ages from 25 to 69, there is no reason to assume that the American and English proportions in the younger age-groups were higher than the very high Irish proportions recorded in Ireland at this time (Table 12). The United States and England were roughly similar in their proportions of female to male death rates; the greatest discrepancy was 11 percentage points in the 25 to 29 years age-group. But both countries contrasted with Ireland. While the Irish proportions at no time fell below 91 per cent, the American proportions at no time rose above 81 per cent. In each of the five age-groups the discrepancy between the Irish and English proportions was at least 20 percentage points.

The loss of female advantage in mortality in several age-

TABLE 13. Deaths per 10,000 in Certain Age Groups by Sex in Ireland, 1935–37, England and Wales, 1939, and the United States, 1939.

Age Group	Ireland		England and Wales		United States [a]	
	Male	Female	Male	Female	Male	Female
25–29	41	49	26	24	26	21
35–39	53	57	37	30	42	33
45–49	91	85	80	58	93	64
55–59	188	175	195	123	205	140
65–69	407	370	445	316	441	331
Female death rates as a percentage of the male						
25–29	120		92		81	
35–39	108		81		79	
45–49	93		72		69	
55–59	93		63		68	
65–69	91		71		75	

SOURCE: W. A. Honohan, "Irish Actuarial Data," *Journal of the Statistical and Social Inquiry Society of Ireland*, Vol. XVII (1944–45), Table VI, p. 387.
([a]) White population in reporting area.

groups in Ireland is also shown by an international comparison of cause of death by sex and age. Although there may have been some differences in determining cause of death owing to dissimilarities in diagnostic procedures between England, Wales, and Ireland on the one hand and the United States on the other, the pattern is clear. For example, among persons aged 5-14 years in the early 1950s, mortality from infectious and parasitic diseases was much greater for Irish females than for Irish males or for both sexes in the United States and in England (Table 14). When the female rates were higher than the male for certain causes in England (two) or in the United States (one), the differences were small and of an entirely different order than the excess female mortality in Ireland.

The more rapid aging of Irish females as compared to males, commented upon in descriptions of the relative social status of the sexes, also shows up in international comparisons of cause of death by age and sex. Comparing Ireland with the United States, among older persons the mortality rates from anemias and from certain types of nervous and circulatory system disorders were higher among Irish females than males, while the reverse was true in the United States (Table 15). Although English females did have higher death rates than English males for some causes of death,

TABLE 14. Deaths per 100,000 Persons of the Same Sex and Aged 5–14 Years, Due to Certain Causes in Ireland, 1951, the United States, 1955, and England and Wales, 1955.*

Cause of Death	Ireland		United States		England and Wales	
	Females	Males	Females	Males	Females	Males
Tuberculosis of the respiratory system	4.5	0.7	0.1	0.1	0.3	0.1
Rheumatic fever	4.1	1.4	1.0	1.0	0.9	0.4
Ill-defined and unknown	3.8	2.2	0.4	0.7	0.0	0.0
Miscellaneous infectious and parasitic diseases	2.6	1.1	1.0	1.1	0.7	0.8
Chronic rheumatic heart disease	1.9	0.7	0.2	0.1	0.4	0.5
Scarlet fever and streptococcal sore throat	1.9	0.7	0.1	0.1	0.1	0.1
All causes	70.0	76.8	38.0	58.4	34.2	47.1
Female death rates as a percentage of the male:						
Tuberculosis	640		100		300	
Rheumatic fever	290		100		220	
Ill-defined	170		60		100	
Miscellaneous infectious	240		90		90	
Rheumatic heart disease	270		200		80	
Scarlet fever	270		100		100	
All causes	91		65		72	

SOURCE: United Nations, *Demographic Yearbook, 1957*, Table 17, pp. 494, 508, 516.

* Causes in Ireland in 1951 resulting in at least 1.0 more female than male deaths per 100,000 persons of the same age and sex. There was no cause of death in either England and Wales or in the United States where the female mortality rate was 1.0 higher than the male for this age group.

the differences generally were smaller than those of the Irish. Mortality statistics have confirmed the impression given by descriptions of Irish life that sons received preferential treatment both in rural and urban regions, and that males generally were favored in the allocation of vital resources in Irish rural areas. The less adequate diet given to females in many Irish families probably contributed to the lower resistance of females to infectious and parasitic diseases. Malnutrition and fatigue resulting from continued heavy workloads also probably explained at least part of the more rapid aging of Irish females.* Rural housewives in other

* There is evidence that fatigue resulting from continued hard physical labor, especially after 40 years of age, contributes to premature death. L. I. Dublin, A. J. Lotka, and M. Spiegelman, *Length of Life: A Study of the Life Table*, rev. ed. (1949), p. 233.

TABLE 15. Deaths per 100,000 Persons of the Same Sex and Aged 45–64 Years, Due to Certain Causes in Ireland, 1951, the United States, 1955, and England and Wales, 1955.*

Cause of Death	Ireland		United States		England and Wales	
	Females	Males	Females	Males	Females	Males
Vascular lesions affecting central nervous system	142.0	98.1	95.5	110.3	109.6	111.2
Hypertension without mention of heart	31.0	23.7	6.4	8.5	11.8	17.5
Chronic rheumatic heart disease	22.2	17.5	24.1	25.5	37.4	23.8
Anemias	19.4	12.3	1.4	1.7	3.1	2.1
Diabetes mellitus	13.4	9.9	26.1	18.5	8.2	4.5
Rheumatic fever	3.5	2.1	0.6	1.0	0.5	0.5
All causes	1,206.1	1,527.1	837.5	1,534.1	768.2	1,353.5

Female death rates as a percentage of the male			
Vascular lesions	145	87	99
Hypertension	131	75	67
Rheumatic heart disease	127	95	157
Anemias	158	82	148
Diabetes mellitus	135	141	182
Rheumatic fever	167	60	100
All causes	79	55	57

SOURCE: United Nations, *Demographic Year Book, 1957,* Table 17, pp. 494, 508, 516.

* Causes in Ireland in 1951 resulting in at least 1.0 more female than male deaths per 100,000 persons of the same age and sex. There were no other causes of death in either England and Wales or in the United States where the female mortality rate was 1.0 higher than the male for this age-group.

countries also experienced some loss of longevity for these reasons,[†] but compared with the United States and several northwest European countries in the twentieth century, the Irish pattern was extreme.

While mortality rates cannot be used as indicators of either the direction or the magnitude of the migration stream, nor as indicators of economic or social opportunities in different regions, they can be used as indicators of the relative social status of per-

---

[†] The higher death rates from tuberculosis, pneumonia, and influenza among rural than urban females in the United States has been attributed to the harder working life of rural housewives and the resulting greater fatigue and lower resistance. *Ibid.,* p. 78.

sons within the same community. The high female compared with male mortality was due, at least in part, to the subordinate status of females in rural areas, and of daughters in the Irish family system. Because the opportunities for improving one's social status were relatively much greater for females than for males away from their families, and in urban rather than in rural areas, we would expect migration to urban areas to appeal more strongly to Irish females than males (a matter to be taken up in the next chapter). The subordinate status of females in rural Ireland was also probably a factor contributing to the reluctance of many Irish women to marry rural men (Chapter Seven).

CHAPTER IV

Female Emigration and Movement from Rural to Urban Areas

PERHAPS the most striking characteristic of Irish emigration for more than a century has been its rural to urban direction. As I shall show, most Irish emigrants came from rural areas and went to the urban areas of Great Britain and the United States, two of the most highly industrialized nations in the world.* Access to these two countries was not only legally but also culturally easier for the English-speaking Irish than for rural migrants from other European countries. The attraction of urban living for many Irish was great since desired standards of living in Ireland were and are much influenced by American and British living standards, but the economic development of Ireland has lagged behind that of all other northwest European countries. As late as 1967 the per capita gross national product of Ireland ($910) was about half that of the average for the 14 countries of northwest Europe ($1,768), and 25 per cent lower than that of the second lowest ranking country, Austria ($1,210). At this time the American per capita gross national product ($3,760), was about

* Between 1870 and 1936–37 the United States and the United Kingdom together accounted for from 41 to 55 per cent of the world's manufacturing production. Brinley Thomas, *Migration and Economic Growth: A Study of Great Britain and the Atlantic Economy*, Table 31, p. 120.

four times Ireland's.[1] In perhaps no other European country was the gap between desired and actual standards of living wider than it had been for decades in Ireland; "in such circumstances it would be phenomenal if there were not emigration."[2] One important aspect of the rural-urban movement will be discussed in this chapter, which sex was more strongly attracted by urban living; and the next chapter will take up the impact made on the magnitude of the movement out of rural areas by the introduction of agricultural labor-saving devices.

Different patterns of rural-urban migration by sex in Western or non-Western societies account for much of the large and consistent differences in the sex ratios of their urban areas (Chapter One). The numerical dominance of urban areas by females in the West is best illustrated by Ireland because the relevant factors were so extreme there. The subordinate status of females in rural areas was unusually high in Ireland compared with other European countries (Chapter Three), yet rural Irish females generally were as free as males to leave their rural homes. The much better relative status of females in the urban areas of the two countries to which the great majority of Irish emigrants went, Britain and the United States, made the contrast in female social status an even more important reason for Irish female rural-urban migration — the movement in this instance extending beyond Ireland's borders. Among Western European countries around 1960, the comparison between the sex ratios was greatest in Ireland, where there were 24 more males per 100 females in rural than in urban areas (Table 16). This was quite different from that of England and Wales, where there were only 6 more males per 100 females in rural than in urban areas. Once again, however, while Ireland was different from the English pattern it was not unique; Northern Ireland and the five Scandinavian countries also had large dissimilarities in the sexual compositions of their rural and urban areas.

Because almost all migration from Irish rural areas since at least 1841 was also a movement out of Ireland itself, the sex ratios of Irish rural and urban areas have been strongly affected by trends in the sex ratio of the persons leaving Ireland. For the sake of clarity, however, we shall consider first the situation within Ireland before taking up the international migration.

TABLE 16. Contrasts in Rural and Urban Sex Ratios in Selected European
Countries, 1947–62.

Country and Exact Year	Males per 100 Females			
	Total Population	Rural Areas* (A)	Urban Areas* (B)	"Excess" males in rural areas (A–B)
Ireland, 1961	101	113	89	24
Denmark, 1960	98	114	93	21
Iceland, 1950	101	114	96	18
Sweden, 1960	100	112	95	17
Northern Ireland, 1961	95	106	89	17
Finland, 1960	93	102	86	16
Norway, 1960	99	108	93	15
Switzerland, 1960	96	102	91	11
Austria, 1961	87	93	82	11
Portugal, 1960	92	94	84	10
Luxembourg, 1960	98	102	95	7
Belgium, 1947	97	102	95	7
France, 1962	95	99	92	7
Scotland, 1961	92	97	90	7
England and Wales, 1961	94	99	93	6
Netherlands, 1960	99	103	98	5

sources: United Nations, *Demographic Year Book, 1963*, Table 5, pp. 162–230;
1964, Table 27, pp. 648–664.
* Definition of rural and urban areas varies from country to country.

Rural-Urban Migration by Sex Within Ireland

From a historical perspective, the first question to ask is whether the present-day contrast between the sex ratios of Irish rural and urban areas was always so extreme. And if there have been changes over time, precisely when did the current pattern emerge and what factors were associated with it? Because of the partition of Ireland, and due to varying definitions of a city's boundaries over the past 125 years, perhaps the best way to measure any general change is to consider the sex ratios of the four provinces of Ireland. The Dublin area is entirely in the province of Leinster, while two provinces, Connacht and Ulster (Part), are predominantly rural.* Three major trends are shown in Table 17 which are

* In 1926 the proportion of persons living in towns and villages, including "clusters of 20 or more houses," was 57 per cent in Leinster, 37 per cent in Munster, 16 per cent in Connacht, and 15 per cent in Ulster (Part). *Census of Population of Ireland, 1926*, Vol. I, Table 9, p. 19.

TABLE 17. Males per 100 Females in the Four Provinces and in the Total Population, Ireland, 1841–1966.

Year	Province				Total Population
	Connacht	Ulster (Part)	Munster	Leinster	
1841	100	97	98	96	97
1851	97	96	95	95	95
1861	99	97	97	96	97
1871	98	96	97	96	97
1881	98	96	98	97	98
1891	100	99	100	98	99
1901	100	101	100	99	100
1911	104	103	103	100	102
1926	106	107	104	100	103
1936	111	111	106	100	105
1946	110	110	104	97	102
1951	112	111	105	99	104
1961	110	109	103	96	101
1966	110	108	103	96	101

SOURCES: *Statistical Abstract of Ireland, 1964,* Table 5, p. 20; *Census of Population of Ireland, 1966,* Vol. I, Table 3, p. 3

of direct concern to our interests. First, during the past one hundred and twenty-five years the most urban province, Leinster, generally had the lowest sex ratio. Second, the sex ratios of all four provinces began to rise during the 1880s and continued to increase for several decades; in fact, in 1966 the sex ratios of Connacht and Ulster (Part) were still only two to three points lower than their historic highs of 1936 and 1951. Third, the sex ratio of Leinster plateaued earlier and fell sooner than that of the other provinces, thereby widening the gap between the most urban and the most rural provinces after 1901. In other words, the extreme pattern of the mid-twentieth century was not present in Ireland during the second half of the nineteenth century, when the differences in the sex ratios of the provinces were small, usually amounting to two or three points. The current pattern emerged after the turn of the century.

An explanation of these trends must take into account not only changes in the sex ratio of migrants, but also possible changes in the sex ratio at birth and mortality differences by sex. The increase in the proportion of males in the Irish population after 1881 was not due to changes in the sex ratio at birth because there were

106 male for every 100 female births in each decade between 1864 and 1920, and since 1920 the figure has been from 105 to 107.[3] An increase in female compared with male mortality after 1881, on the other hand, did contribute to the rise in the proportion of males in the Irish population. Among persons between the ages of 5 and 24 years, and from about 55 to 64 years, the relative mortality of females worsened between the 1870s and the first decade of the twentieth century (Table 12). For example, among persons aged 15 to 19 years there were 102 female to every 100 male deaths during the 1870s, and 123 between 1901 and 1910. The expectation of life at birth can be taken as a summary figure of the age-specific death rates. Between 1871 and 1891 the excess of female over male life expectancy at birth decreased from 1.3 to 0.1 years (Table 9).

The changing mortality trends closely match the rise in the sex ratios of the most rural provinces. Between 1871 and 1911 the sex ratio of Connacht rose from 98 to 104 and that of Ulster (Part) from 96 to 103. The period of highest numerical predominance of males in Connacht, Ulster (Part), and Munster, from about 1936 through 1951, was also a time of relatively high female mortality among persons aged 10 to 19 years, and the period of highest excess female mortality ever recorded among persons aged from 20 to 34 years: in the latter age-group between 1931 and 1950 female mortality rates were from 108 to 113 per cent of the male (Table 12).

In addition to its direct effect on the sex ratio, the worsening relative mortality of females also should have had an impact on female out-migration if we assume that relative mortality rates reflect differences in social status (Chapter Three). The growing attraction of out-migration for females at this time would have been further enhanced if there was also an increment in the freedom of Irish females to leave their rural homes. Since single persons generally can more easily leave their homes than married persons, especially single women compared with wives and mothers, the trend during the closing decades of the nineteenth century in the proportion single becomes relevant in understanding the rise in Irish sex ratios.

The increasing facility of Irish females to migrate is indicated by the rise in the proportion single between 1871 and 1911 of from 78 to 88 per cent among women aged 20 to 24 years, and from 38 to 55 per cent among women aged 25 to 34 years.[4] The exact rise in the proportion single among *rural* women in the 26 Counties before 1911 is not available by age-groups, but it may have been higher than the over-all figures would indicate judging from the situation in 1926 when the relevant data was first published. According to the 1926 Census, the proportion single was higher among rural than urban women both in the 20–24 age-group (89 compared with 84 per cent), and in the 25–29 age-group (65 and 58 per cent).[5]

The proportion single among females in Ireland remained high through 1951 when eight out of ten women in their early twenties, and not quite half of women aged from 25 to 34 years were still single. During the 1950s and early 1960s there was a sudden decline in the proportion single among Irish women in their twenties and early thirties. As in the case of mortality patterns by sex during the past century, the changes in the proportion single among women also fit the pattern of numerical male dominance in Irish rural areas: increasing between about 1871 and 1911, and then maintaining high levels until a decline began about 1951.

The coincidence of trends in mortality, marital status, and sex composition support the hypothesis that females were more highly motivated than males to leave rural areas, but as aggregate data they are not conclusive. They provide the general setting, nevertheless, for interpreting three pieces of information which, when considered together, do seem convincing. First, the proportion of males decreases in Ireland as the size of the urban area increases; the pattern as it existed in 1966 is given in Table 18. This would seem to indicate that Irish females not only went to urban areas but were also most strongly attracted to the largest cities, where the contrast in life style was perhaps greatest from their rural homes. Second, the sex ratios among *single* persons in rural and urban areas are even more extreme than those for all persons (Table 19). Since males generally migrate a few years later, and also marry later, I have compared women in their early twenties with men in their late twenties. In Irish urban areas since at least 1926, there have been about five or six single men for every ten single women in the specified age groups, while in rural areas there were as many, and at times considerably more, single men as women in the same age groups. If young Irish women were migrating simply to find a husband, they were going in the wrong direction. A more reasonable interpretation, and one which will be taken up in Chapter Seven, is that many Irish women preferred urban over rural life styles even if it meant the possibility of becoming a spinster. The rural-urban pattern by sex among persons aged 45 to 54 years confirms this thesis: since about 1961 in Irish rural areas there have been about 24 bachelors for every 10 spinsters (we have taken persons in the same age group since differences in age at marriage by sex or age at migration by sex are of minor importance at this stage in life). Urban areas are more preferred by females than males in Ireland, and among single people the difference increases with age.

TABLE 18. Sex Ratios by Type of District, Ireland, 1966.

Type of District	Number in Thousands		Males per
	Males	Females	100 Females
Dublin County Borough and suburbs, Dun Laoghaire Borough and suburbs	345.8	389.1	89
Cork, Limerick, and Waterford County Boroughs and their suburbs	101.6	111.6	91
Other towns of 1,500 population and over and their suburbs	227.2	243.7	93
Other towns and villages	127.9	131.9	97
Remainder of country	646.5	558.7	116
Total Population	1,449.0	1,435.0	101

SOURCE: Ireland, Census of Population, 1966, Vol. I, Table 13, pp. 146–147.

The third persuasive piece of evidence involves the change in the sex ratios of Ireland's four largest cities during World War II. Legal restraints were placed on the movement of Irish females to Britain during the war; for example, females could not go to Britain to work in factories unless they were over 22 years of age; and females under 22 were allowed to emigrate only if they were going to work as nurses, teachers, or midwives, or if they were

TABLE 19. Males per 100 Females Among Single Persons in Selected Age Groups in Rural and Urban Areas, Ireland, 1926–1966.*

| | Age Group in Years | | | |
| | Males, 25–29 Females, 20–24 | | Both Sexes, 45–54 | |
Year	Urban Areas	Rural Areas	Urban Areas	Rural Areas
1926	63	99	87	176
1936	62	112	82	185
1946	53	122	67	178
1951	64	136	66	184
1961	52	125	68	244
1966	45	100	68	241

SOURCES: Censuses of Population of Ireland, 1926, Vol. V, Part I, Table 14, pp. 84–85; 1936, Vol. V, Part I, Table 14, pp. 84–85; 1946, Vol. V, Part I, Table 16, pp. 96–97; 1951, Vol. II, Part I, Tables 13B, 13C, pp. 69, 72; 1961, Vol. II, Table 16, p. 221; 1966, Vol. II, Table 16, p. 233.
* Urban areas include places of 1,500 or more inhabitants.

going for training courses in those fields.[6] These restrictions were gradually lifted after the end of the war, and at the end of 1947 all legal hindrances to female emigration from Ireland were permitted to lapse.[7] Between the 1936 and the 1946 Census, the sex ratios of Dublin, Cork, Waterford, and Limerick declined by five to six points to unusually low levels (Table 20). This sudden dip was followed by an abrupt rise of three to four points between 1946 and 1951. Except for the wartime restrictions on female emigration from Ireland, it would be difficult to explain why this should have happened. But given the limitations it seems reasonable to conclude that many young women in this particular cohort found themselves confined to Ireland, and if they wanted to lead an urban life they would have to be satisfied with whatever jobs and accommodations they could find in Irish cities. The postwar rise in the sex ratios of the largest Irish cities would be expected, from this point of view, once international migration was again available to Irish females without legal hindrance.

The Rural-Urban Character of Irish Emigration

As mentioned at the beginning of this chapter, much of Irish emigration was a rural-urban movement which happened to cross international boundaries.[8] During the nineteenth century the

TABLE 20. Males per 100 Females in the Largest Boroughs of Ireland, 1926–66.

Year	Dublin and Dun Laoghaire	Cork	Waterford	Limerick
1926	88	90	90	93
1936	88	90	90	91
1946	83	84	85	86
1951	87	87	88	90
1956	86	88	87	90
1961	86	88	87	91
1966	88	91	90	92

SOURCES: *Statistical Abstract of Ireland, 1935,* Table 6, p. 5; *1938* Table 8, p. 12; *1950,* Table 8, p. 12; *1951,* Table 8, p. 20; *1957,* Table 8, p. 24; *1963,* Table 8, p. 21; *Census of Population of Ireland, 1966,* "Preliminary Report," Table 2, pp. 16–20.

decline of the total population of Ireland was due primarily to a decline of the rural population: between 1841 and 1891 the rural population decreased by 2.8 million while the urban population declined by 212,000 (Statistical Appendix, Table III). The actual migration out of Ireland from urban areas, of course, is understated by the decline of 212,000 since there was some movement from the rural areas into the Irish towns and cities. Irish urban areas, especially Dublin, began to grow after the political and social reforms instituted around the turn of the century (Chapter Two), yet the rural decline continued. By 1966 not quite half of the total Irish population lived in urban areas, and the Dublin area constituted one-quarter of the total national population. Taking the 125-year period between 1841 and 1966 as a whole, the rural population declined by not quite four million persons, while the urban areas grew by just over 300,000 persons.

Most Irish emigrants went to the towns and cities of the United States, England, and Scotland. Nine out of ten persons who left Ireland (32 Counties) between 1825 and 1925, and who did not go to England, Wales, or Scotland, went to the United States and Canada.[9] For the 26 Counties alone data are available for the 1876–1921 period, and during this time 84 per cent of Irish emigrants went to the United States, 8 per cent to England, Wales, and Scotland, 7 per cent to Australia and Canada, and only 1 per cent to all other countries.[10] After the Anglo-Irish war and the establishment of an independent Ireland in the years following World War I, the major stream of Irish emigration shifted from the United States to England and Scotland. While it is true that a quota was established in 1921 on Irish emigration into the United States, and in 1930 general restrictions were placed on the entry of persons without money or the promise of employment, these legal events were of minor importance in determining the destination of Irish emigration, because up through 1929 the relatively large Irish quota was never filled.[11] By the 1946–51 period, eight out of ten Irish emigrants were going to England, Wales, and Scotland.[12]

Once in the United States or in England, the Irish immigrants concentrated in the largest cities. As late as 1940, for example, nine out of ten Irish persons born in the 26 Counties and living in the United States were urban residents and more than half of these lived in five large cities: New York, Chicago, Philadelphia, Boston, and San Francisco.[13] Of the Irish (26 Counties) immigrants in England and Wales, one-third were living in Greater London, while among those in Scotland, two-fifths were residents of Glasgow according to the 1951 British Census of Population.[14]

The urban destination of most Irish immigrants into the United States at least between 1875 and 1926 is illustrated by the occupations they gave for themselves to the American immigration officers. Although the great majority of these immigrants came from rural homes, only a small fraction presented themselves as farmers or farm laborers (Table 21). On the other hand most, about eight out of ten until after the turn of the century, claimed to be common laborers or servants. The heavy urban occupational preference of Irish compared with German or Swedish male immigrants is exemplified by a special tabulation for certain states made from the 1920 United States Census (Table 22). While the great majority of the latter two groups were farmers, only a small proportion of the Irish were. The Irish were overrepresented in certain categories which made up part of the stereotype of the Irish immigrant held by many: the Irish railway laborer, the Irish salesman, and the Irish foreman. While the pattern for Irish males is distinct from the other groups listed in the table, it must not be inferred that the figures given necessarily present the precise national picture. Complete tabulations of the occupational status of various nationality groups for the entire population are not available, and these data refer only to those six states which in 1920 had the largest numbers of foreign-born persons employed in the occupations selected: Massachusetts, New York, Pennsylvania, Michigan, Minnesota, and Wisconsin. The reasons why so few Irish shared the desire of many other European immigrants in America at this time to own their own farm will be discussed in the following chapter. For now the point is that the occupations given by Irish immigrants upon entering the United States, and the occupational pattern of the Irish in six states of important immigrant influx, show that international emigration from Ireland had many of the same qualities as rural-urban migration within other nations. The question remains whether this similarity extended to the sex ratio of Irish emigrants; did females outnumber males among emigrants from Ireland after the 1880s (when the present extreme contrast between rural and urban sex ratios emerged within Ireland)?

TABLE 21. Percentage Distribution of Immigrants to the United States from the Whole of Ireland (32 Counties), by Occupational Group in Selected Years from 1875 through 1926.

| | Year Ended June 30 | | | | | |
Occupational Group	1875	1881	1891	1901	1911	1926
Common laborers	52	67	55	34	26	17
Servants	27	20	31	52	38	30
Skilled workers	13	7	7	8	19	22
Farmers	5	4	4	1	3	6
Farm laborers	0	0	0	3	9	13
Entrepreneurs	1	1	1	1	1	2
Professionals	1	0	1	0	2	3
Miscellaneous	1	1	1	1	2	7
Totals	100	100	100	100	100	100
Bases	19,446	39,232	34,621	24,192	33,575	33,170

SOURCE: Brinley Thomas, *Migration and Economic Growth: A Study of Great Britain and the Atlantic Economy*, Cambridge: The University Press, 1954, Table 82, p. 270.

International Emigration by Sex from Ireland

Fortunately for our purposes, precise figures for the sex ratio of emigrants from Ireland first become available with the 1871–81 intercensal period. The data deal with *net* emigration and so take into account any re-migration which may have taken place. The

TABLE 22. Per Cent Distribution by Sex of Five Groups of Foreign-born Whites Ten Years of Age and Over in Selected Occupations in Certain States, 1920.*

Sex and Occupation	Country of Birth				Mother Tongue
	Ireland	England, Scotland, Wales	Sweden	Italy	German
Males					
Steam railroad and blast furnace laborers	25	10	2	30	8
Carpenters	18	14	10	10	8
Coal mine operatives	18	41	4	50	8
Salesmen (stores)	16	10	1	5	8
Farmers	14	18	82	1	64
Foremen and overseers (manufacturing)	8	6	1	3	3
Physicians, surgeons	1	1	0	1	1
Total percentage	100	100	100	100	100
Base numbers	12,612	24,064	27,665	53,708	67,457
Females					
Domestic servants [a]	81	32	87	8	70
Semiskilled operatives (clothing, cotton factories)	10	46	5	86	13
Teachers (school)	4	6	2	3	8
Stenographers, typists	3	13	5	3	7
Telephone operators	2	3	1	1	2
Total percentage	100	100	100	100	100
Base numbers	22,161	9,869	2,952	11,187	10,667

SOURCE: Niles Carpenter, *Immigrants and Their Children, 1920*, U.S. Bureau of the Census Monograph VII, Washington, D.C.: U.S. Government Printing Office, 1927, Tables 129, 130, 131, 132, pp. 284–90.
* Massachusetts, New York, Pennsylvania, Michigan, Minnesota, and Wisconsin.
[a] Excluding chambermaids, cooks, ladies' maids, and nursemaids.

same procedure for calculating total net emigration is used to determine net emigration by sex except that the births, deaths, and census enumeration for each sex are considered separately. At first glance, there appears to be no long-term trend in the sex ratio of emigrants from Ireland; during some periods males predominate while at other times many more females than males left (Table 23). Upon closer inspection, however, a pattern does reveal itself. In those periods where more females than males emigrated, the sex ratio gradually declined between 1881 and 1951 before rising slightly in the 1961–66 period. Assuming for the moment that this is the general trend, then what would account for the male dominance of Irish net emigration during the periods 1891–1901, 1911–

26, 1936–46, and 1951–61? With the exception of the 1950s, the first three periods included major wars in which Britain was involved: the Boer War (1899–1902), World War I (1914–18), and World War II (1939–45). Realizing that many Irish men served in the British armed forces,* the occurrence of a major British war may have drawn more men out of Ireland than otherwise would have emigrated.

TABLE 23. Average Annual Net Emigration by Sex, Ireland, 1871–1961.

Intercensal Period	Males	Females	Males per 100 Females
1871–81	24,958	25,214	99
1881–91	29,257	30,476	96
1891–1901	20,315	19,327	105
1901–11	11,764	14,390	82
1911–26	13,934	13,068	107
1926–36	7,255	9,420	77
1936–46	11,258	7,453	151
1946–51	10,309	14,075	73
1951–56	21,657	17,696	123
1956–61	21,914	20,486	107
1961–66	7,523	8,598	87

SOURCES: Censuses of Population of Ireland, 1946 and 1951, "General Report," Table 17, p. 38; 1966, Vol. I, Table X, p. xix.

I have not been able to find information about the number of men born in the 26 Counties who served in the British armed forces either in the Boer War or in World War II, not even the number killed in action while overseas. But a strong case is made for the impact of a British war on the sex ratio of the Irish emigration stream by the data collected and published in the 1926 Irish Census concerning "special" emigration by sex between 1911 and 1926 (Table 24). Between 1914 and 1918, 27,405 Irish-born (32 Counties) men died on active duty outside Great Britain and Ireland while serving in the British armed forces. This figure understates actual Irish male emigration, of course, because deaths of

* The proportion of the British army which was Irish-born has not been published since the nineteenth century, but it probably has been sizeable. In 1871, 23 per cent of all British army officers and 25 per cent of British army soldiers had been born in Ireland (32 Counties). Census of England and Wales, 1871, Vol. IV, "General Report," Table 132, p. 133.

TABLE 24. Actual and Estimated "Normal" Sex Ratio Among Emigrants from Ireland between 1911 and 1926.

Type of Emigration	Males	Females	Males per 100 Females
Actual total net emigration	209,010	196,020	107
Special emigration			
Withdrawal of British Army	25,242	NR	
Emigration of British Army dependents [a]	2,190	6,570	
Disbanding of Royal Irish Constabulary [b]	6,460	NR	
Men born in the 26 Counties and killed as British soldiers in World War I [c]	19,720	NR	
Total special emigration	53,612	6,570	
Residual net emigration (estimated "normal" emigration)	155,398	189,451	82

SOURCE: Calculated from figures given in *Census of Population of Ireland, 1926,* Vol. X, pp. 11–12, 19.

NR: Not relevant.

([a]) Assuming one wife and three children (two daughters and one son), as the average family making up the total of 8,760 dependents mentioned in the source.

([b]) Assuming 80 per cent of the 8,079 enumerated in 1911 had emigrated by 1926.

([c]) Assuming 72 per cent (the proportion of the total 32 County population in 1911 which was enumerated in the 26 Counties), of the 27,405 Irish-born (32 Counties) soldiers who died on active duty outside Great Britain and Ireland between 1914 and 1918 were born in the 26 Counties. The figure of 27,405 does not include deaths of Irish-born officers.

Irish-born officers are not included, and thousands of men left Ireland to join the British forces and then remained abroad after the war was over. To estimate how many of the Irish-born war deaths had been men from the 26 Counties, I arbitrarily multiplied by the proportion of the total 32 County population in 1911 which was enumerated in the 26 Counties; this reduced the number of foreign military deaths to not quite 20,000, or about nine per cent of the total male net emigration from Ireland between 1911 and 1926.

The "special" emigration mentioned in the 1926 Census also included the withdrawal of the British army from Ireland following Irish independence, and the voluntary emigration of a large part of the men who had been employed by the British in the

Royal Irish Constabulary. The R.I.C. had been responsible for helping to enforce British law in Ireland, and fought on the British side during the Anglo-Irish war. Many of its members, though Irish-born, did not choose to remain in the newly independent Ireland. One of the first acts of the Irish government was to establish its own police force. I have assumed that 80 per cent of the 8,079 members of the R.I.C. in 1911 had joined the male emigration stream by 1926. While the number of R.I.C. family dependents is not known, the 1926 Census did estimate the total number, but not the sex, of dependents of British army personnel in Ireland. Since these dependents also left Ireland when the British army withdrew, they constituted part of the "special" emigration. In order to argue against my thesis by increasing the number of females in the "special" emigration, I took as an "average" army family one with three females and one male (wife, two daughters, and a son). This purposeful error in one direction should help offset any unintentional error committed in the assumptions underlying my estimates of male net emigration due to foreign military deaths, the withdrawal of the British army from Ireland, or the disbanding of the R.I.C.

The result of these calculations is a residual net emigration, or what might be considered the normal net emigration by sex, of about eight males for every ten females. This is only a rough estimate and nothing more should be drawn from it except the conclusion given in the 1926 Census: "Were it not for the abnormal migration [between 1911 and 1926], it is probable that there would have been a very considerable excess of females amongst the emigrants."[15] This would mean that during the first 35 years or so of the present century, under "normal" conditions, there would have been more female than male emigrants from Ireland.

The voluntary participation of thousands of Irish men in World War II (Ireland itself was neutral during the war), combined with the wartime restrictions on female emigration mentioned above, no doubt accounts for much of the unusually high sex ratio of emigrants for the 1936–46 period. For example, among persons receiving new travel permits, identity cards, and passports to go abroad for employment at the peak of wartime emigration between 1941 and 1943, men outnumbered women

268 to 100 (98,444 men and 36,723 women during the three-year period); but immediately after the war, during 1946 and 1947, the pattern was reversed and men were outnumbered by women 62 to 100 (23,340 men and 37,932 women).[16] An estimate of what was the "normal" sex ratio of emigration from Ireland between 1936 and 1946 can not be even roughly calculated, however, until at least the number of military deaths of Irish-born men is known.

The greater male than female emigration between 1951 and 1961 in large part was due to the sudden change in agricultural technique in Ireland at this time. This topic will be taken up in detail in the next chapter; for now it will suffice to point out that because more men than women are employed in agriculture, more males were affected by the rapid adoption of agricultural labor-saving techniques. The general picture is given by the decline between 1951 and 1961 of 91,000 in the male agricultural labor force (from 442,000 to 351,000), compared with a decline of 26,000 in the female agricultural labor force (from 68,000 to 42,000).[17] These great and rapid declines during the 1950s contrast with earlier intercensal periods during which little change occurred in agricultural technique. In 1926, for example, the male agricultural labor force was not quite five times larger than the female (549,000 compared with 121,000), but between 1926 and 1936 the decline recorded for these occupations was greater among females than males (15,000 as opposed to 11,000).[18]

The major transition to the new labor-saving methods was accomplished by the 1961 Census insofar as the demographic adjustments were concerned, and the sex ratio of net emigration from Ireland once again registered about nine males for every ten females between 1961 and 1966. The sex ratio of the early 1960s was somewhat higher than that of the late 1940s, and it reversed the long-term trend of a gradually declining sex ratio in those intercensal periods during which more females than males emigrated. Although the change was small, it is interesting to speculate that some of the change may have been due to a lessening during the early 1960s of two factors which previously had contributed to the greater number of females in the emigration stream. There was a decline in the proportion single among all females aged 25–34 years in Ireland from 46 to 31 per cent between 1951 and 1966 (Appendix Table 5), and there was a rise in the proportion of the total Irish population living in urban areas of from 42 to 49 per cent during the same fifteen-year period (Appendix Table 3). With a decline in the number of single persons in the population, and with more potential emigrants living in urban areas, the movement of single females from Ireland should have become relatively less important than it had been in the past.

It seems reasonable to conclude that since 1881 there were more female than male emigrants in every intercensal period except those characterized by British wars or a rapid change in agricultural technique. Furthermore, the proportion of females in the emigration stream seems to have increased between the close of the nineteenth century and the mid-twentieth century once the "special" emigration is accounted for. One reason for the increasingly greater proportion of females in the emigration from Ireland during "normal" times was probably the widening gap in degree of urbanization between Ireland and the United States (Table 25). I have selected the United States rather than England for the comparison because before the 1920s the great majority of Irish emigrants went to the United States. During the early 1860s there was no difference in the degree of urbanization

TABLE 25. Urbanization in the United States and in Ireland, 1840–41 to 1920–26.

Period	Percentage Urban[a] in the Total Population		(A–B)
	United States (A)	Ireland (B)	
1840–41	11	15	−4
1850–51	15	20	−5
1860–61	20	20	0
1870–71	26	22	4
1880–81	28	23	5
1890–91	35	25	10
1900–01	40	28	12
1910–11	46	29	17
1920–26	51	32	19

SOURCES: U.S. Bureau of the Census, *Historical Statistics of the United States, Colonial Times to 1957*, Series A 195–209, p. 14; Ireland, *Commission on Emigration and Other Population Problems, 1948–1954*, "Reports," Statistical Appendix, Table 3, p. 283.

([a]) Places of 2,500 or more inhabitants in the United States, and of 1,500 or more in Ireland, are classified as "urban."

between the two countries, and by the 1880s it was still only five percentage points greater in the United States. But in the following decades the United States rapidly industrialized, and the proportion of its population living in cities swiftly grew. By the 1920s just over half of the American population was urban, while about two-thirds of the Irish population still lived in rural areas or villages and towns of less than 1,500 persons. In contrast to the relative stagnation of Irish urbanization between 1881 and 1926 (up by 46,000 or 5 per cent), the American urban growth was extraordinary: up from 14 to 54 million between 1880 and 1920 (282 per cent).

The rapid growth of the urban population of the United States is only a crude indicator of the meaning this urbanization had in the minds of potential Irish emigrants in terms of real or perceived opportunities. In the field of employment, for example, the increased demand for female workers generally is reflected in the changing sex ratio of the total American labor force: down from 557 males for every 100 females in 1880 to 391 in 1920.[19] The occupational distribution by ethnic group and sex for the entire United States at this time is not available. But the pattern for six states with large proportions of foreign-born residents in 1920 is available, and the data for the Irish are given in Table 22. Most Irish female immigrants in the labor force, as most Swedish and German female immigrant workers, were employed as domestic servants. In contrast, most Italian and almost half of the British female immigrant workers were employed as operatives in clothing and cotton factories. The different occupational preferences of the various ethnic groups are marginal to our interests except for two points. First, most females, regardless of nationality, who wanted to work in non-farm jobs could not easily get any other type of work except as domestics or factory workers. Second, the range of occupations open to males was much wider, and the total demand for male labor in 1920 was still many times greater than for female. Both factors should have made emigration to the United States more attractive to males than females, a pattern found in many immigrant groups in the United States. But since the Irish emigration stream was composed of a large proportion of females, I believe the opportunities they thought were offered by life in the cities of the United States (and later of England and Scotland), involved more than just employment in a paying job.

The relatively greater emigration of females than males from Ireland after the 1870s was due to several factors, some of which are particularly important. When women were gaining in social status in Britain and in urban America around the turn of the century, through what is generally called the emancipation of women, the status of young single women in Ireland was worsening judging by changes in the age-specific mortality rates of the sexes. The desire to escape from an unusually severe degree of male dominance (by northwest European standards) probably increased among young Irish females at this time. At the same time the proportion of single persons in the Irish population suddenly increased, and this alone would have led to more females among all emigrants. Another important point was that the attraction of emigration to the United States for Irish females probably increased during the closing decades of the nineteenth century with the rapid urbanization of that country.

Even before the 1870s Irish emigration to the United States was unusual, compared with the emigration from other European countries, in its high proportion of females among all emigrants. Yet there was an extreme degree of male dominance in at least one of these other countries — Italy between the late 1870s and about 1911 (Table 10). Why the Italian emigration stream had so many males, of course, can only be answered in specific terms by studying Italian population trends. But it is possible to state in general terms why there were so many females in the Irish emigration stream: first, the urban areas of the United States were more accessible to English-speaking Irish females emigrating on their own than to potential female emigrants in non-English-speaking countries; second, almost all Irish rural-urban migration went to the United States before the 1920s and to Britain afterwards, while in other European countries the rural-urban movement, and hence the greater migration of females than males, was mainly internal and did not cross national boundaries; third, although there was extreme male dominance in Ireland, Irish single females were as free as males to migrate from their rural homes, and this may not have been true in other male-dominated societies; and fourth, the sex ratio of an emigration stream is mainly determined by the movement of unmarried persons and of married men migrating without their families, and the proportion of single persons in Ireland after the late 1840s, and especially after the 1870s, has been unusually high compared with other European countries.

CHAPTER V

Emigration and Agricultural Labor-Saving Techniques

BECAUSE so much of the total emigration from Ireland for over a century was also a movement out of Irish rural areas, the technical and economic changes which took place in rural Ireland are of prime importance in understanding Irish demographic trends. In previous chapters it was argued that an increasing gap between a desired way of life and one's actual level of living would increase the attraction of emigration for many, and comparisons between life abroad and in Ireland were discussed. In rural Ireland there was also at least one internal comparison which contributed to the aspiration gap: the contrast in style of life associated with farms of adequate size worked with the most productive techniques and that available on smaller farms worked with less productive methods. No internal gap need exist if all farmers in a certain region used the same methods, produced about the same amount per farm worker, and had holdings of roughly the same size. But if one of these farmers adopted methods which raised productivity per worker and then used some of his increased income to buy more land to further increase productivity per worker, then he would set an example of a more prosperous style of farming life. As his neighbors followed his example, a new minimum standard of living would develop based upon an increase in the minimum size of an "adequate" holding and a greater capital investment in equipment per farm worker.

Not all farmers, of course, would be equally able to increase their acreage or to buy new equipment. Generally speaking, the farmers least able to expand would be those with lower productivity per farm worker and those with smaller holdings. The cash surplus of a 15-acre holding is less than that of a 50-acre holding, all other factors being equal. With no decline or even a slower rise in the actual material level of living of the very small farmer, his way of life would seem increasingly less acceptable as his neighbor's standard of living rose. It is a matter of relative, not actual, wealth; of socially, not economically, defined standards.

Productivity per agricultural worker increases with the adoption of labor-saving techniques due to the increased ability to work more acres in the same amount of time. The productivity *per acre* might actually be higher under manual agriculture due to more intensive care of the crops, but the productivity *per man* is higher with labor-saving methods, given sufficient acreage. On the other hand, more land per worker is needed using labor-saving methods because part of the farm's productivity must pay the additional costs of the new machines and power supplies.[1] This logic applies both to the early transition from manual to animal-powered methods, and to the more recent shift from animal-powered methods to tractors and machines powered by electricity. It also explains why the minimum adequate size of a holding rises with the adoption of labor-saving methods.

Agricultural Mechanization and Emigration
in Nineteenth-Century Ireland

The earlier process of agricultural mechanization in Ireland involved the increased substitution of horses and horse-drawn implements for manual agriculture. In spite of recent modernization, in parts of Ireland today one can still see small holdings worked by manual methods using the spade, scythe, and wooden rake and pitchfork.* On many manually worked farms it is common practice to have some of the heavier work done by a

---

* Mogey described practices of manual agriculture in Northern Ireland during the 1940s which are almost identical to those I saw in Ireland in 1966 and 1967. John M. Mogey, *Rural Life in Northern Ireland*, pp. 41–52.

neighbor who owns a pair of horses or a tractor. In return the manual farmer pays for the mechanized assistance either in cash, or more usually, with his labor.

Under manual methods, desired farm size was determined at one extreme by the largest area the farm family was able to work, and at the other extreme by the smallest area which would provide for the needs of the family. During the early 1840s the desired size in Ireland ranged from 5 to 15 acres depending primarily on the soil, the crops or animals raised and the burden of taxes and rents for which the farmer was responsible.[2] The average desired size was about 10 acres. It is important to point out that a manual farmer and his family could not work a larger holding by themselves without using labor-saving techniques, and that they could not improve their standard of living with their existing holding except by increasing their productivity per acre. If their desired standard of living rose more rapidly than their productivity per acre, then their holding would seem increasingly less satisfactory. But because virtually all of the land suitable for agriculture had been claimed by landlords long before 1841, and because most landlords' estates had already been fragmented into very small holdings, the average farmer could achieve a higher standard of living only by giving up farming in Ireland. An increase in acres per farm worker in Ireland in the 1840s could only come through a decrease in the number of farm workers themselves.

In the early 1840s almost half of the holdings in Ireland were below the minimum size even for manual agriculture (Table 26). Many persons working these small holdings actually were part-time farmers who worked as laborers for larger farmers. They were only slightly better off than landless laborers, and probably were unable to set aside savings to tide them over periods of crop failure. Because of this, both they and the landless laborers were the most vulnerable of all rural social classes to disease and death during famines. The farmer with from 5 to 15 acres, on the other hand, enjoyed as high a standard of living as was possible in Ireland at that time under the limits of manual agriculture. A farmer in this category probably was able to accumulate a small surplus to see him through one or perhaps even more bad harvests and still be able to pay his rent and feed his family. His standard of living was very low, not only from the viewpoint of the mid-twentieth century, but reportedly also from the standards of rural England.* But the life of the Irish manual farmer with at least ten acres of good land did have its compensations. At least half of the population was worse off than he, since they held no land at all or only five acres or less. On the other hand, holdings large enough to support the horse-drawn, labor-saving techniques of the day were exceptional (only 1 out of 14 holdings was 30 acres or larger). In relative terms the ten-acre farmer in 1841 occupied what might be called a respectable, middle status position in spite of his absolute level of material poverty by modern standards.

TABLE 26. Percentage Distribution of Holdings Above One Acre, Ireland (32 Counties), 1841–1901.

| Year | Size of Holding in Acres | | | | Total | Number of Holdings (thousands) |
	1–5	5–15	15–30	30 and Over		
1841	45	37	11	7	100	691
1851	15	34	25	26	100	570
1861	15	32	25	28	100	568
1871	14	31	26	29	100	544
1881	13	31	26	30	100	527
1891	12	30	26	32	100	517
1901	12	30	26	32	100	516

SOURCE: *Agricultural Statistics of Ireland, with Detailed Report for the Year 1901*, p. 15 (cited in Arnold Schrier, *Ireland and the American Emigration, 1850–1900*, Minneapolis: University of Minnesota Press, 1958, p. 163).

The events of the late 1840s, however, greatly changed the character of Irish farming. It is a reasonable assumption that mortality rates were highest among those with less than five acres and among the landless laborers, and that this accounts for part of the large decline in the proportion of holdings of less than five acres between 1841 and 1851 (Table 26). But under normal conditions land made available through the death of the previous tenants

---

* The predominance of manual methods on Irish agriculture during the 1820s caused observers to comment that Irish agriculture was 100 years behind the English and Scottish. George O'Brien, *The Economic History of Ireland from the Union to the Famine*, p. 29.

would simply have been taken over by someone else who had no land before, or added to an existing holding to build toward the desired size of about 10 acres. This did not happen mainly because Irish landlords wanted to consolidate the small holdings into larger and more prosperous farms. Landlords not only consolidated land cleared by high mortality, they also forcibly cleared land through eviction. As pointed out in Chapter Two, the number of persons legally evicted amounted to 26 per cent of all Irish emigrants from Great Britain and Ireland between 1849 and 1855 (Table 2).

One aspect of the shift away from labor-intensive, subsistence farming on small holdings is indicated by the transition from tillage to pasture. The abolition of the Corn Laws in 1846 ended preferential treatment for Irish grain in British markets and resulted in a decrease in the amount of land tilled in Ireland to produce grain. The cash crop changed from grain to livestock for milk or meat production, depending on the region of the country. Because less labor was needed per acre when land was under pasture than when it was tilled (and most probably tilled by spade before 1846), both unemployment and emigration increased in the grain growing regions of Ireland.

Data first become available in 1851 which permit us to examine the association between a decline in area of tilled land and the decline in the rural population (Table 27). Regional differences were great, of course, but since we are interested in understanding overall *national* trends, the data has been arranged to group the small administrative areas (Poor Law Unions) by changes in area tilled and rural population regardless of which part of Ireland they happened to come from. Between 1851 and 1881 there was a strong and consistent association between the decline in tillage in an average Poor Law Union and the decline in its rural population. During the next thirty-year period, between 1881 and 1911, the association remained but it was considerably weakened. A proper ranking still existed, but while great variations were recorded in the average percentage decline in area tilled (from -5 to -44 per cent), there was little difference in the averages of decline in the rural population (from -23 to -27 per cent). By the 1911 to 1926 period, the weakened association

TABLE 27. Percentage Changes in the Rural Population and in the Area of Tilled Land in Poor Law Unions, Ireland, 1851–81, 1881–1911 and 1911–26.*

Period and Categories of Change in Area of Tilled Land	Number of Poor Law Unions in Each Category	Average Percentage Changes	
		Area Tilled	Rural Population [a]
1851–81			
0 to −20%	24	−8	−14
−20% to −30%	17	−26	−27
−30% to −40%	32	−36	−28
−40% to −50%	26	−45	−31
−50% and over	18	−58	−35
1881–1911			
0 to −10%	14	−5	−23
−10% to −20%	19	−15	−25
−20% to −30%	30	−24	−26
−30% to −40%	24	−35	−27
−40% and over	24	−44	−27
1911–26			
+10% to 0	30	+6	−7
0 to −10%	29	−4	−9
−10% to −15%	15	−13	−8
−15% to −20%	25	−16	−12
−20% and over	16	−24	−11

SOURCE: Saorstat Eireann, *Agricultural Statistics, 1847–1926*, "Report and Tables," Dublin: The Stationery Office, 1928, p. lxi.

* Poor Law Unions are areas used by the government for administrative purposes.

([a]) Population residing outside towns of 1,500 or more inhabitants.

between decline in tillage and decline in rural population virtually disappeared. The rate of population decline was about 8 per cent regardless of whether the average change in tillage was an increase of 6 per cent or a decline of 13 per cent; and the decline in the rural population was only slightly greater (11 to 12 per cent), in those Poor Law Unions which experienced a 15 per cent or greater decline in tillage. We can conclude that the period of greatest association between decline in tillage and decline in rural population was between 1851 and 1881, and that this strong association was directly related to the consolidation of small holdings of less than 5 acres into larger farms, especially holdings of 30 acres and over (see Table 26). After the 1880s changes from tillage to pasture were less important in explaining rural population declines since increasingly smaller proportions of land were in tillage. Less than one-third of Irish agricultural land was tilled in

1851, less than one-fifth in 1881, and less than one-seventh in 1926.[3]

Before 1851 the transition from tillage to pasture probably was extensive but unfortunately I have not been able to find data which would permit me to systematically examine just how extensive. The lack of data also hampers the study of another great agricultural change which was associated with the decline in the rural population — the change from manual to horse-drawn technology. The best that we can do is speculate on the way in which the change might have occurred, and how such a change would have been related to the great emigration from Irish rural areas which took place between the mid-1840s and the mid-1850s.

The adoption of horse-drawn methods affected every farmer to some degree regardless of the type of crop or livestock he produced. The advantages of horse-drawn implements over manual methods in general transportation, hay making, and grain cultivation need no comment. But the effect of the horse and the associated horse-powered machines on potato cultivation is interesting and significant: "It was reckoned that six men and two horses were sufficient to sow an acre of potatoes in drills and that thirty men were necessary to set them in the old lazy beds."[4] As long as most Irish rural persons preferred subsistence agriculture to emigration, they would continue to occupy, and to intensively work, the land needed for consolidation into farms large enough to support the horse-drawn technology. It was only after emigration became more attractive than manual agriculture for hundreds of thousands of rural Irish that the transition to horse-drawn methods could occur on a large scale.

The great emigration of the 1840s and early 1850s made possible the change to a more labor-saving agricultural technique. Although the 1845–48 famine was not the only reason for the exodus (Chapter Three), the high mortality rates of the late 1840s were also probably associated with the transition from manual to horse-drawn techniques. With the great reduction in the number of tenants with less than five acres (Table 26), the *relative* social status of the 5 to 15 acre manual farmer declined. To maintain his previous middle social status, the manual farmer would have to either enlarge his holdings to the point where horse-drawn methods were feasible or he would have to emigrate. To remain as a manual farmer during a period when a more prosperous class of farmers working larger holdings was being introduced, and when a simultaneous reduction in the old lower class was occurring, would have been downwardly mobile. Because the Irish techniques of manual agriculture were not appropriate for the large farms available to immigrants in the United States at this time, the Irish manual farmer was ill-prepared to begin farming in America. For many, this was probably a major reason why emigration from Ireland was also a movement out of agriculture.

The transition in Irish agriculture was well under way by the time the famine came to an end in 1848. As more passage money came from immigrants already in the United States and Canada, more manual farmers were able to give up their holdings and leave Ireland with their families. As landlords consolidated holdings into larger farms and established a more prosperous technique of farming which could not be achieved by manual farmers, even more manual farmers decided to emigrate. In some parts of Ireland so many tenants began leaving that landlords stopped evicting and began trying to coax their solvent tenants not to abandon their holdings.[5] The need for farm laborers decreased because farmers using the new methods could do more work in less time with fewer laborers. As unemployment increased among farm laborers, emigration became more attractive for them as it was becoming for the manual farmers.

Although thousands of persons may have decided to emigrate during the late 1840s, if they did not wish to go to Britain (because of political feelings on the part of the Irish and religious discrimination on the part of the English), they would have to wait for passage money to arrive from previous emigrants before going to North America. The reported number of emigrants from Ireland (not including persons who went to England, Wales, and Scotland), rose from 181,000 in 1848 to 255,000 in 1851.[6] By 1855 the suddenly greater emigration associated with the transition to labor-saving techniques was over and during that year and the next several years, emigration returned to about the same level that it had been during the early 1840s.

Because the distribution of holdings by size changed but little between 1851 and 1861 (Table 26), the great amount of emigration reported between 1852 and 1854 was probably composed more of previously evicted persons, farm laborers, and farmers' assisting relatives than of small farmers themselves. The roughly stable distribution of holdings by size of farm between 1861 and 1901 shows that only a relatively small amount of rural emigration was due to the consolidation of small holdings.* The consolidation of holdings after 1851, and, consequently, further adoption of horse-drawn methods became a very gradual process, for in most small farmers' families there was at least one person in each generation who was willing to remain on the home farm. This was essentially the situation in Irish agriculture up to 1946, when the second great transition began to take place.

Although nineteenth-century data needed for a rigorous verification of the process do not exist, the transition from manual to horse-drawn methods in Ireland seems to have involved four basic points:

1. Farmers with larger holdings made the most complete transition to the new techniques because of their greater ability to afford the initial investment and upkeep of the new machines, and their need for labor-saving techniques to accomplish the greater amount of work to be done on larger holdings.

2. The transition did not take place on holdings below a certain size, and the minimum "adequate" size holding rose with increased acceptance of the new methods.

3. As living standards rose, increased numbers of persons working smaller farms with relatively constant incomes became dissatisfied with their way of life; yet the smaller the holding one owned or was in line to inherit, the more difficult it was to accumulate either more land or better equipment.

4. The social acceptance of leaving agriculture for another occupation (and for most this also meant emigration from Ireland), reduced resistance to the spread of new techniques and

* This point was made by Meenan in reference to emigration during the first half of the twentieth century, but it also applies to emigration after the late 1850s. James Meenan, "Some Features of Irish Emigration," *International Labour Review*, 69:2 (Feb. 1954), p. 132.

made the modernization process more rapid than it otherwise would have been.

While the validity of these points for nineteenth-century Ireland remains a matter of speculation, the detailed, reliable, and comprehensive statistical data available in Ireland after 1926 permit a careful analysis of the processes through which the adoption of agricultural labor-saving techniques led to increased out-migration from rural areas.

Agricultural Mechanization and Emigration in Twentieth-Century Ireland

During the 1950s emigration from Ireland returned to levels characteristic of the closing decades of the nineteenth century (Appendix Table 2). Between 1951 and 1961 the estimated net emigration from Ireland was 409,000 persons — an amount equivalent to about one-seventh of the total population of Ireland in 1961 (2.8 million). Such heavy out-migration seems anomalous, however, because many of the explanations of nineteenth-century emigration were no longer applicable. For example, from a country of exploited tenant farmers, Ireland had become a nation of small farm owners. Political aspirations had been realized and the Irish had been running their own affairs in the 26 Counties for a quarter century. Part of the increased emigration probably was due to the change in direction of the emigration stream from the United States to Britain. The easy and relatively cheap passage to Britain compared with the more expensive passage to the United States made emigration a less permanent, and so less serious, decision in one's life. And due to a wartime labor shortage in Britain, Irish were increasingly employed in occupations which previously had been closed to them because of discrimination.[7] But one of the most important reasons for the increased emigration during the 1950s was quite similar to processes associated with the great emigration of the late 1840s — the widespread adoption of agricultural labor-saving techniques.

While the agricultural labor force declined in number by 17 per cent during the decade of the 1950s, the level of productivity *per farm worker* rose by almost 50 per cent (a rate much faster than that in industry).[8] Part of the increase in productivity per worker was due to higher yields per acre using more fertilizers and raising new varieties of crops and animals,[9] and part was due to the adoption of labor-saving techniques. The number of tractors rose from about 4,500 in 1946 to about 39,700 in 1961, and brought the number of farmers per tractor down from 56 in 1946 to 5 in 1961.[10] The great increase in the number of tractors paralleled the decline in the number of horses and ponies: from 452,000 in 1946 to 207,000 in 1961. While the exact proportion of all horses and ponies which were used for agricultural purposes in 1946 is known (78 per cent), this proportion cannot be calculated for any year after 1951 due to a change in definitions. During the first part of the twentieth century the number of horses and ponies used for agricultural purposes slowly increased from 260,000 to 355,000 between 1901 and 1946.[11]

Rural electrification also progressed rapidly after World War II. Before 1948, fewer than 1,000 of the 237,000 consumers of electricity from the nationally operated Electricity Supply Board were rural residents. By 1961 the number of rural consumers had increased by 255,000, or to about 41 per cent of all electricity consumers.[12] The proportion of private dwellings with electricity in rural areas rose from a negligible amount in 1946 to 71 per cent in 1961.[13] In addition to the benefits of more efficient and convenient lighting, heating and refrigeration, rural electrification made possible the use of such important labor-saving devices as electric water pumping systems and milking machines.

Greater adoption on larger holdings. The first of the four points assumes the most complete transition to the new techniques would be on larger farms since there was more work to be done, and the cost of the new machines could be better afforded. The smaller farmer would not buy a water pump, milking machines, or a tractor if he and his family could handle the work themselves within their daily routine. When the numbers of such machines are arranged by the size of holding, this assumption is borne out. In each case, the proportion of farms with the device increases with the size of the farm (Table 28). Of course, the size of the farm is only one factor in determining the need for a particular machine, other considerations being crops or animals raised, quality of the soil, region of the country, and the access to tractor service or electricity. But generally speaking, we can take tractors to indicate a labor-saving form of transport and portable power; milking machines to indicate modern, commercial dairy practices; and stationary electric motors for driving water pumps and other machines as an overall indicator of the shift away from methods based on human and animal muscle.

TABLE 28. Tractors, Stationary Electric Motors, and Milking Machines per 100 Holdings by Size of Holding, Ireland, June 1960.

	Size of Holding in Acres					
Item	1–30	30–50	50–100	100–200	200–Over	Total
Number of Holdings	144,083	62,056	54,209	22,884	7,076	290,308
Number of Tractors	4,699	6,364	13,181	12,266	6,809	43,319
Number of Stationary electric motors	2,188	2,512	7,672	8,643	5,204	26,219
Number of milking machines	204	798	3,865	4,059	1,527	10,453
Tractors per 100 holdings	3	10	24	53	96	15
Stationary electric motors per 100 holdings	2	4	14	38	73	9
Milking machines per 100 holdings	–	1	7	18	22	4

SOURCE: *Statistical Abstract of Ireland, 1964*, Tables 64, 70, pp. 90, 94.

The very small proportion of holdings with less than 30 acres which had any of the three machines shows that such small farms were left out of the transition to such labor-saving techniques. Virtually none had milking machines in 1960, only one in 50 had stationary electric motors, and one in 33 possessed a tractor. Farmers with such small holdings either had no economic use for such machines, or if they did, they had a difficult time accumulating enough capital to buy them. It was only among farms of 100 acres or more that over half of the holdings had tractors, or sizeable proportions of the other two machines. But such large farms accounted for only one-tenth of all holdings in Ireland in 1960. Most farmers in Ireland were in the situation of watching their neighbors on larger farms adopt new, more productive techniques, but of being unable to make the transition themselves. Rural cooperatives could have provided some types of agricultural machinery to the smaller farmers, but in spite of extensive efforts to organize cooperatives since the 1890s they succeded only for creameries and the sugar beet industry.[14]

The greater use of labor-saving machines on the larger farms resulted in higher total output per farm worker. In eight western counties in Ireland in 1960, the annual value of the output per worker increased from 238 pounds on holdings of 15 to 30 acres, to 537 pounds on holdings of 50 to 100 acres, to a peak of 1,056 pounds on holdings of 150 to 200 acres.[15] The gap in productivity per worker was extreme and no doubt known to the workers themselves. Although these data on productivity per worker by size of farm relate to only one part of Ireland, there is no reason to believe that the basic pattern was not roughly the same throughout the country. The increased total productivity and increased productivity per farm worker on the larger farms using the new techniques should have resulted in the second point — an increase in what was believed to be the minimum size holding which would provide an "adequate" standard of living.

Increase of the minimum "adequate" size holding. Perhaps the simplest and most direct way to measure changes in the minimum acceptable size of a farm in Ireland is to compare changes over time in the number of holdings in certain size categories. Because we are interested in national trends we shall deal with national averages; but it should be understood that what is considered a minimum "adequate" size farm will vary from county to county in Ireland. Presumably individual farmers would consolidate smaller units into farms closer to the desired size when given the opportunity, and this would result in a simultaneous decline in the number of holdings of sub-standard size.

In our discussion of nineteenth century consolidation patterns, the optimum size for a manually worked farm seemed to be about 10 acres, while that for a farm worked with horse-drawn techniques seemed to be at least 30 acres. In the 32 Counties between 1841 and 1901, holdings generally too small even for manual agriculture declined from 45 to 12 per cent of all holdings, while farms generally large enough to support horse-drawn methods (30 acres and over), increased from 7 to 32 per cent of all holdings

(Table 26). With the advent of more modern methods after World War II, we would expect the new minimum adequate size to become larger than 30 acres.

The years 1949 and 1960 were selected to compare the situation in the 26 Counties as it existed just before the great emigration of the 1950s, and just at the end of that decade. Although slightly over half of all holdings were of less than 30 acres in 1949, the 15 to 30 acre size was considered too small by many farmers judging by the 17 per cent decline recorded between 1912 and 1949 (Table 29). Farms in the next largest category, from 30 to 50 acres, were still thought to be desirable by enough farmers to have increased in number by 5 per cent over the same period. (The decline in the number of holdings over 200 acres was due to the breakup of some large estates and the redistribution of the land to small farmers by the government.) We can reasonably say that through the late 1940s, the minimum adequate size was at least 30 acres. The large proportion of all holdings which were below the minimum simply meant that the most common size was not the most desired. Some farmers may have been fully satisfied with the style of life provided by farms of 5, 15, or 25 acres, but many others had become resigned to a standard of living below their

TABLE 29. Estimated Number in Thousands, and Percentage Distribution of Agricultural Holdings by Size, Ireland, 1912, 1949, 1960, and 1965.

Year or Period			Size of Holding in Acres				
	1–15	15–30	30–50	50–100	100–200	200–Over	Total
1912	164.1	104.5	59.5	49.0	20.4	8.5	406.0
1949	88.8	87.0	62.5	51.3	21.8	7.3	318.7
1960	70.8	73.3	62.1	54.2	22.9	7.1	290.4
1965	68.0	68.8	61.2	55.2	23.3	7.0	283.5
Percentage change							
1912–49	−46	−17	+5	+5	+7	−15	−22
1949–60	−20	−16	−1	+6	+5	−3	−9
Percentage distribution							
1912	40	26	15	12	5	2	100
1949	28	27	20	16	7	2	100
1960	25	25	21	19	8	2	100
1965	24	24	22	20	8	2	100

SOURCES: Ireland, *Commission on Emigration and Other Population Problems*, "Reports," Table 28, p. 43; *Statistical Abstract of Ireland, 1964*, Table 70, p. 94; *1968*, Table 65, p. 87.

desired level because they consider emigration an even less attractive alternative. Subsistence farming, however unsatisfactory, was
at least familiar. Emigration presented unknown risks, and, in the
words of one Kildare man, "The devil I know is better than the
devil I don't."

Most relevant to the increased rates of emigration after 1951
was the drop in the number of holdings of from 30 to 50 acres
between 1949 and 1960. Although the decline was small (397
fewer holdings), it reversed the trend which had led to an increase
of almost 3,000 among farms of this size during the previous 37
years. Apparently some farmers were no longer satisfied with 30-
acre holdings and were either building them up or selling out as
farmers with less than 30 acres had been doing. If the 50-acre line
is taken as the new minimum size for an "adequate" holding, one
conclusion is inescapable: there were relatively *more* holdings
below the desired minimum size in 1949 (75 per cent), than in
1912 (66 per cent), in spite of the consolidation which had resulted in a decline of more than one-fifth in the total number of holdings over the 48-year period.

The increase in the minimum size of an "adequate" farm
during the 1950s should have resulted in the third and fourth
points.As desired standards of living rose, the level of living provided by a farm of less than, say, 30 acres should have become
increasingly less acceptable. And because it was most difficult for
the smallest farmers to accumulate capital to buy either more land
or new equipment, their hopes for improving their situation
should have lessened. Some were still willing to accept subsistence farming, of course, but for many others the attractiveness of
emigration as an alternative way of achieving a higher living
standard should have increased. Once emigration occurred on a
large scale there would have been increased opportunities for the
remaining farmers to add land to their existing holdings. This in
turn would have reduced resistance to the adoption of the new
techniques and accelerated the modernization process. From this
perspective, we would expect the greatest amount of out-
migration not from those farms which experienced the most extensive transition to the labor-saving techniques, but, on the contrary,
from those farms which failed to adopt the new methods.

Greater out-migration from smaller holdings. Because we are interested in the effect brought about by the rise in a minimum "adequate" holding to more than 30 acres, we shall group all holdings of less than 30 acres into one category. The decline in the number of male farmers working farms of less than 30 acres accelerated from 18 per cent between 1926 and 1946, to 35 per cent between 1946 and 1966 (Table 30). The only other category which experienced an increased rate of decline in the number of farmers was in the 200 or more acres group, and this was due primarily to the breaking up of large, private estates. The decline in the number of farmers with holdings of 30 to 50 acres between 1946 and 1966 contrasts with the 10 per cent increase in this group during the previous 20 years; it also is consistent with my hypothesis that increasing numbers of farmers became dissatisfied with farms of less than 50 acres. The 25,000 total decline in the number of male farmers between 1946 and 1961, however, accounts for only a small portion of the net emigration from Ireland of over 500,000 persons during that 15-year period. What other rural occupations were more highly attracted to out-migration during the change in agricultural methods?

If the third point concerning increasing dissatisfaction among many smaller farmers is correct, then we would expect some to

TABLE 30. Number of Male Farmers by Size of Holding in Ireland, 1926, 1946, 1961, and 1966.*

Year	Size of Holding in Acres [a]					
	1–30	30–50	50–100	100–200	200–Over	Total
1926	120,563	43,146	34,506	13,917	4,937	217,069
1946	98,971	47,403	38,322	15,592	4,794	205,084
1961	70,365	46,863	41,551	17,011	4,682	180,472
1966	64,660	46,916	43,854	16,893	4,368	177,452
Percentage change						
1926–46	−18	+10	+12	+12	−3	−6
1946–66	−35	−1	+14	+8	−9	−13

SOURCES: *Censuses of Population of Ireland, 1926*, Vol. II, Table 2, p. 2; *1946*, Vol. II, Table 2, p. 4; *1961*, Vol. XII, Table 2, p. 3; *1966*, Vol. IV, Table 2, p. 2.

* Persons whose principal occupation was farming their own holding. Persons who may farm a small holding but whose principal occupation was working on a larger farm, or was non-agricultural (for example, publican, shopkeeper, or doctor), were not included in this table.

([a]) Excluding those for whom area was not stated.

attempt to improve their living standards by reducing costs. And one major area for cost cutting would be the wages paid for hired agricultural workers. The smaller total income and smaller total work load generally characteristic of smaller farms would combine to make the position of a hired hand on such farms especially vulnerable. Should the farmer and his family decide to undertake the work usually done by the hired worker, they could, in effect, pay his wages to themselves. If the wages demanded by hired farm workers increased, the farmer would have even more reason to undertake the work himself. Wages of male agricultural workers in Ireland did increase, in fact, between 1953 and 1966 by 113 per cent.[16] One reason for the increased wages probably was the greater willingness of farmers using the more productive techniques to pay each worker somewhat more since he did not need to hire as many.

The impact of these forces combined with the general labor-saving impact of the new technology on the employment of male agricultural workers was great. The number of such workers declined by 59 per cent between 1946 and 1966, compared with a decline of 10 per cent between 1926 and 1946 (Table 31). As expected from my thesis, the decline was much greater on farms of less than 50 acres, and especially on those of less than 30 acres (unfortunately for my purposes, tabulations of the size of farm on which an agricultural laborer was employed were first made only in 1951). Unemployment and under-employment apparently were higher among these men, for the proportion unable to state the size of farm upon which they were regularly employed rose from 7 to 29 per cent between 1951 and 1966. The larger out-migration of younger men resulted in an increase in the proportion of men who were 45 years or older among all farm laborers from 29 to 40 per cent between 1946 and 1966.[17]

It is reasonable to say that farm laborers as a group did not benefit from the adoption of labor-saving techniques. The younger men who found the regular, higher-paying jobs on larger holdings were the exception, and for most men the transition meant a choice between under-employment or migration. They did not actively resist the change partly because emigration had long been accepted by many as an escape valve, and partly

TABLE 31. Number of Male Agricultural Laborers in 1926 and 1946, and by Size of Farm on Which Employed, 1951, 1961, and 1966, Ireland.*

Year	Area not Stated	Size of Farm in Acres					Total
		1–30	30–50	50–100	100–200	200– Over	
1926	NA	NA	NA	NA	NA	NA	125,161
1946	NA	NA	NA	NA	NA	NA	112,999
1951	6,163	7,349	10,559	23,036	20,841	16,332	84,280
1961	12,147	3,029	5,200	14,118	13,958	10,995	59,447
1966	13,357	1,919	3,523	9,843	9,527	8,126	46,295
Percentage change							
1951–66	+117	−74	−67	−57	−54	−50	−45

SOURCES: *Censuses of Population of Ireland, 1926*, Vol. II, Table 2, p. 3; *1946*, Vol. II, Table 2, p. 5; *1951*, Vol. III, Part I, Table 2, p. 5; *1961*, Vol. III, Table 2, p. 4; *1966*, Vol. IV, Table 2, p. 3.
* Including men both living in and living out.

because opportunities were relatively better for Irish immigrants in Britain after 1946.[18] It was fortunate that an acceptable alternative was open to many farm laborers, for they had little power to influence the changes that were going on. They were not the men who decided whether to introduce new machinery or to consolidate smaller holdings into larger units. They contributed only their labor and this became increasingly less effective in bargaining to protect their interests. The men who made the relevant decisions were the farmers and the farmers' assisting sons.

When techniques were adopted which made human muscle power increasingly redundant, farmers generally could be expected to care more about the employment problems of their own sons than of any farm laborers they might happen to have working for them; they would dismiss the laborer before turning out a son. In spite of their favored position, farmers' assisting sons decreased in number by over half between 1946 and 1966 (Table 32). The largest reduction occurred on farms of less than 50 acres, and especially of less than 30 acres; and the post-1946 declines on farms of 50 to 200 acres contrast with the sizeable increases recorded during the 1926 to 1946 period. The preference which did exist for sons over hired hands (given a willingness of the sons to remain), was greatest on farms of 50 to 200 acres judging from the much greater relative decline in farm laborers than sons on farms of this size, compared with smaller or larger farms.

TABLE 32. Number of Farmers' Assisting Sons and Sons-in-Law Aged 14 Years
and Over by Size of Home Farm, Ireland, 1926, 1946, 1961, and 1966.*

	Size of Home Farm in Acres					
Year	1–30	30–50	50–100	100–200	200–Over	. Total
1926 (a)	80,741	31,299	25,948	10,807	3,510	152,305
1946	54,984	31,580	28,327	12,004	3,533	130,428
1961	22,546	18,058	19,186	9,310	2,477	71,577
1966	15,010	13,722	15,997	7,470	1,910	54,109
Percentage change						
1926–46	−32	+1	+9	+11	+1	−14
1946–66	−73	−57	−43	−38	−46	−59

SOURCES: Censuses of Population of Ireland, 1926, Vol. II, Table 2, p. 2; 1946,
Vol. II, Table 2, p. 4; 1961, Vol. III, Table 2, p. 3; 1966, Vol. IV, Table 2, p. 2.
* Excluding those for whom area was not stated.
a Including 1,055 sons aged 12 and 13.

The impact of the post-1946 agricultural innovations on the
willingness of many farmers to keep at least one son or son-in-law
employed on the home farm can be measured, perhaps, by comparing the changes in the ratio of sons and sons-in-law to farmers
by size of farm. In 1926 there were remarkably consistent ratios
of from 73 to 78 sons and sons-in-law per 100 farmers on each
size of farm above 30 acres (Table 33). The smaller total amount
of work to be done and the smaller total income of the smaller
holdings are probably the two most important reasons for the
somewhat lower ratio (67) for farms of less than 30 acres. Given
the facts that there were some farmers who never married, some
married farmers who had no children, and some who had all of
their children either die or emigrate, the uniformly high proportions of assisting sons and sons-in-law can be interpreted to mean
that most farmers wished to have at least one son or son-in-law
remain to help with the work and to take control of the farm
when the farmer died or was no longer able to run the farm. In
1946 the ratio of 74 to 77 sons and sons-in-law persisted on farms
of 50 acres or larger, but a decline in the ratios had begun on the
smaller farms. After 1946 a great transformation occurred on
farms of all sizes. By 1966 there were fewer than 29 assisting
sons per 100 male farmers on holdings of less than 50 acres, and
no more than 44 per 100 male farmers on holdings of 100 acres
or more.

TABLE 33. Number of Assisting Sons and Sons-in-Law Aged 14 Years and Over per 100 Male Farmers by Size of Home Farm, Ireland, 1926, 1946, 1961, and 1966.

	Size of Home Farm in Acres					
Year	1–30	30–50	50–100	100–200	200–Over	Total
1926	67	73	75	78	71	70
1946	56	67	74	77	74	64
1961	32	39	46	55	53	40
1966	23	29	36	44	44	30

SOURCE: Calculated from Tables 30 and 32.

Given the higher aspirations of many farmers after 1946, and the increased ability of some to do much of the work themselves by using new technology, many apparently decided they no longer needed the help of a son, and also became less concerned with keeping an heir on the home farm. After 1946 increasing numbers of farmers, regardless of size of the home farm, permitted, encouraged, or forced their assisting sons to leave the home farm. The farmers' desires were only half of the story, however, since increasing numbers of sons began to believe that the home farm was no longer worth waiting for.

While we cannot impute motivation to farmers' assisting sons, we can consider the behavior of those for whom emigration is still an alternative but who also have remained on the home farm longer than the usual age for emigration. Sons on the home farm who are in their mid-twenties or younger may have no hopes for inheritance, and may be planning to emigrate, but simply have not taken the final step. On the other hand, sons on the home farm who are in their late thirties or early forties generally have made their decision to remain in Ireland and not to emigrate, whether or not they are in line to inherit the family farm. Changes in attitude concerning the relative desirability of emigration as opposed to waiting to inherit the family farm should be best indicated by the behavior of farmers' assisting sons between the ages of 25 and 34 years.

It is important to remember that the son who remains on the home farm helping his parents is most likely to inherit regardless of his birth order among his brothers. Because of the reluctance of the father to give up control until late in life, this sometimes happens to be the youngest son simply because he has the shortest wait between reaching adulthood and getting the farm. To simplify the discussion, I shall consider changes in the number of assisting sons and sons-in-law by age on only three sizes of farms: less than 30 acres; the transitional size of 30 to 50 acres; and 100 to 200 acres, generally large enough to support the new labor-saving techniques widely adopted after 1946. For assisting sons and sons-in-law aged 25 years and over we find what has now become a familiar pattern: between 1926 and 1946 their number increased on farms of greater than 30 acres, and declined on smaller farms (Table 34). Since the replacement of men by machines was not an important factor at this time, it is reasonable to assume that increasing numbers of young men left holdings of less than 30 acres because they felt such a farm was too small to provide a level of living comparable to that enjoyed by assisting sons on larger holdings.

The pattern which Table 34 reveals that is specifically relevant to judging the modification in attitudes of the most likely heirs is the much greater difference in the trends for sons in the 25–34 year age group before and after 1946, than for assisting sons in other age groups. For example, on farms of 30 to 50 acres between 1926 and 1946 the number of sons aged 25 to 34 years increased by 8 per cent, while their number declined by 67 per cent between 1946 and 1966: a total change of 75 percentage

TABLE 34. Percentage Changes in the Number of Farmers' Assisting Sons and Sons-in-Law by Age on Farms of Selected Sizes, Ireland, 1926–46 and 1946–66.

Period and Size of Home Farm	Age		
	14–24	*25–34*	*35–44*
1926–46			
100–200 acres	+8	+10	+2
30–50 acres	−2	+8	+2
1–30 acres	−38	−19	−24
1946–66			
100–200 acres	−30	−45	−45
30–50 acres	−53	−67	−49
1–30 acres	−69	−81	−70

SOURCES: Calculated from *Censuses of Population of Ireland, 1926*, Vol. V, Part II, Table 9, pp. 66–70; *1946*, Vol. V, Part II, Table 4A, pp. 10, 11; *1966*, Vol. V, Table 2A, p. 11.

points. The total change in trend on this size farm for younger sons was 51 percentage points (the absolute difference between −2 and −53), while for older sons it also was 51 percentage points (the difference between +2 and −49). The respective total changes for sons aged 14–24, 25–34, and 35–44 years were 38, 55, and 47 percentage points on farms of 100 to 200 acres, and 31, 62, and 46 percentage points on farms of 1 to 30 acres. I interpret the greater total change in trend for sons aged 25 to 34 years to indicate a greater reluctance after 1946 to become farmers, the change in attitude being most extreme on farms of 30 to 50 acres.

If 50-acre holdings were increasingly seen as inadequate after 1946, how did farmers' sons feel about inheriting farms of 30, 15 or 5 acres? Since it is more difficult to build up an adequate farm the smaller the holding one inherits, it is not surprising that the smaller the holdings the fewer the sons willing to remain in hopes of inheriting. On farms of less than 30 acres, the number of assisting sons aged 25 to 34 years declined by 81 per cent between 1946 and 1966. The figures given refer to all 26 Counties of Ireland, but a study of variations within the nation came to the same conclusion: the decline of farms of less than 30 acres in Connacht and Ulster (Part), suggests "that even in areas where the small holding predominates the occupants are not content with the living standard it affords."[19]

With the increased emigration of assisting sons who once would have remained in hopes of inheriting the home farm, greater numbers of holdings were worked by farmers who had no heirs willing to work the family holding. The sale and consolidation of holdings in this situation might be made by the farmer himself, but this was unlikely because of the age of small farmers in Ireland (76 per cent of farmers with holdings of from one to 30 acres were over 45 years old in 1946).[20] Consolidation of small holdings in Ireland was more likely upon the death of the farmer and the sale of the land by non-farming heirs. Given the limited opportunities to start new careers at the high average age of the small farmer, it is understandable that the farmers persisted in working their own small holdings even though they recognized their own relatively low productivity.

Amount of Net Emigration Accounted
for by Agricultural Mechanization

If we make two assumptions, we can roughly estimate the importance of agricultural mechanization as an explanation of Irish emigration at various times, and for each sex. First, we assume that a decline of one agricultural job represents one out-migrant from Irish rural areas. The loss of a job affected more individuals than the person holding the job at the time; it also reduced the employment opportunities for future generations of job seekers. Second, let us assume that the increase in non-agricultural jobs in Ireland was entirely utilized by new additions to the labor force. This would mean a choice between unemployment or emigration from Ireland for the person who lost his rural job, or who, such as the farmer's assisting son, was unwilling to continue in his rural job. The net result of these two assumptions would be that the loss of one rural job represents one emigrant from Ireland.

In addition to the 1951–61 period, I also selected the 1926–36 period for analysis because of that decade's relatively low emigration and the presence of more females than males in the emigration stream. The great importance of the agricultural changes discussed in this chapter in understanding male emigration from Ireland during the 1950s is shown in Table 35. Given our assumptions, 40 per cent of all male net emigration between 1951 and 1961 was due to the decline of rural occupations — especially those of farmers' assisting sons and of farm laborers. This high proportion was more than double that of the 1926–36 period. As expected from the argument of the preceding chapter, changes in rural employment opportunities were less important in explaining female emigration during either time period. Females were more concerned with general social status differences between the sexes in rural Ireland compared with those prevailing in the towns and cities of the United States or Britain.

Even though they occurred a century apart, the two periods of most rapid transition to agricultural labor-saving techniques in Ireland were characterized by unusually high rates of emigration. An important reason for the higher rates was the suddenly

TABLE 35. Decline in Selected Rural Occupations as a Proportion of Total Net Emigration by Sex, Ireland, 1926-36 and 1951-61.

| | Period and Sex (Numbers in thousands) | | | |
| | 1926-36 | | 1951-61 | |
	Male	Female	Male	Female
Estimated Net Emigration	72.6	94.2	217.9	190.9
Change in the number of				
Farmers' assisting				
sons, daughters [a]	−6.4	−8.5	−37.4	−15.4
Farm laborers	+2.1	−0.4	−24.9	−0.3
Farmers	−7.8	−2.0	−18.2	−6.8
Other assisting relatives	−0.8	−4.2	−7.0	−3.1
Total	−12.9	−15.1	−87.5	−25.6
Change in rural occupations				
as a percentage of net				
emigration:	18	16	40	13

SOURCES: *Census of Population of Ireland, 1926,* Vol. II, Table 2, pp. 2-3; *1936,* Vol. II, Table 2, pp. 4-5, Vol. IX, Table 18, p. 19; *1951,* Vol. III, Part I, Table 2, pp. 4-5; *1961,* Vol. III, Table 2, pp. 4-5; *1966,* Vol. I, p. xix.
[a] Including sons-in-law and daughters-in-law.

widened gap in way of life between large farmers using the new methods and small farmers using traditional methods. Because additional land was not available to most small farmers, and because small farmers could not afford to adopt the new methods without enlarging their holdings, the only way most small farmers could achieve the higher living standards was by giving up agriculture in Ireland. The emigration of small farmers made land available for consolidation into larger holdings which could successfully use labor-saving techniques. But this in turn reduced the need for persons who had provided labor under the old methods — specifically, farm laborers and farmers' assisting relatives. While the need for their labor decreased, their own personal desired standards of living increased just as the small farmers' had. And most of the farm laborers and assisting relatives, like most of the small farmers, could achieve the new standards of living only through emigration.

CHAPTER VI

Nationalism and Protestant Emigration

THE significance of Protestant emigration from Ireland during the first half of the twentieth century cannot be overstated: the population of Ireland would have increased slightly between 1926 and 1946 had it not been for the 24 per cent decline in the number of Protestants because the Catholic part of the population actually did increase (Table 36). Such a reversal of Ireland's long record of population decrease after the achievement of self-government would have been a major event in the nation's demographic history. Emigration trends by religion are not directly available, however, and this may explain why such an important aspect of Irish emigration has received little systematic study until now. The first part of this chapter is an attempt to show that the Protestant decline was in fact due to the out-migration of native-born Irish Protestants, and was not due to unusually high mortality or low fertility among Protestants, or to the movement of foreign-born (non-Irish) Protestants.* The special character of Protestant emigration will also be indicated by the fact that it cannot be interpreted as a rural-urban movement, the most common type of "normal" emigration from Ireland. The remainder of the

---

* It is generally believed that the trends were little influenced by individuals changing their religious affiliation.

chapter will consider the possible impact of the attainment of self-government on Protestant emigration. Apparently the transfer of political power from England to Ireland in 1921 reduced the reasons for Catholic emigration but at the same time increased the attractiveness of emigration for Protestants.

Different patterns of emigration for Irish Catholics and non-Catholics have existed for at least 200 years. Probably the first period of greater Protestant thán Catholic emigration took place after the imposition of the Penal Laws, when Protestant Dissenters migrated to the United States during the eighteenth century (Chapter Two). Proportionately greater Protestant than Catholic emigration also probably took place after the Act of Union of 1800 because of three interrelated facts: Irish industry declined after the Act of Union; because of their dominance of Irish industry, Protestants were more strongly affected by the industrial decline than Catholics; and because of their favored economic position, Protestants could better afford passage to the United States and Canada than could Catholics.[1] But since religion was asked for the first time in the 1861 Census and most recently, at the time of this writing, in the 1961 Census, I shall limit my analysis to that 100-year period.

Net Emigration by Religion

Even though the registration of births and deaths in Ireland does not include information about religion and hence precludes calculations of natural increase by religion, it is possible to estimate relative net emigration by religion among persons already born. If the number of persons of a certain age at one census is compared with the number ten years older ten years later, the difference would be due to mortality and to migration. If both religious groups in Ireland experienced the same age-specific levels of mortality during the ten years, then a greater rate of decline in one group would have been due to greater emigration from the nation. Data needed for such an analysis of cohorts by religion are not directly available for the 26 County area of modern Ireland from the censuses of 1911 and earlier; and an analysis of the 32 County area of the entire island before 1911 would not be useful for our purposes because of the high proportion of Protestants in the Six

TABLE 36. Population and Intercensal Change by Religion, Ireland, 1861 to 1961.

Year	Population (thousands)			Intercensal Change (thousands)			Intercensal Percentage Change		
	Total[a]	Catholic	Protestant[b]	Total	Catholic	Protestant	Total	Catholic	Protestant
1861	4,402.1	3,933.6	457.3	NA	NA	NA	NA	NA	NA
1871	4,053.2	3,616.4	418.3	−348.9	−317.2	−39.0	−7.9	−8.1	−8.6
1881	3,870.0	3,465.3	392.5	−183.2	−151.1	−25.8	−4.5	−4.2	−6.2
1891	3,468.7	3,099.0	357.9	−401.3	−366.3	−34.6	−10.4	−10.6	−8.8
1901	3,221.8	2,878.3	330.4	−246.9	−220.7	−27.5	−7.1	−7.1	−7.7
1911	3,139.7	2,812.5	313.0	−82.1	−65.8	−17.4	−2.5	−2.2	−5.3
1926	2,972.0	2,751.3	208.0	−167.7	−61.2	−105.0	−5.3	−2.2	−33.5
1936	2,968.4	2,773.9	183.5	−3.6	+22.6	−24.5	−0.1	+0.8	−11.8
1946	2,955.1	2,786.0	157.5	−13.3	+12.1	−26.0	−0.4	+0.4	−14.2
1961	2,818.3	2,673.5	130.1	−136.8	−112.5	−27.4	−4.6	−4.0	−17.4

SOURCES: *Statistical Abstract of Ireland, 1950,* Table 34, p. 31; *1968,* Tables 5, 6, 42, pp. 20, 53.
(a) Includes Catholics, Protestants, Jews, Others, and No statement.
(b) 1861–1946: Protestant Episcopalian, Presbyterian, Methodist, and Baptist.
1961: Church of Ireland, Presbyterian, Methodist, and Baptist.

Counties of what is today Northern Ireland. Our cohort analysis of changes by religion, then, is limited to the 1926–61 period.

To arrive at the percentage changes given in Tables 37 and 39, I took the decline in the number of persons in a given cohort between two census dates as a percentage of the total number in that cohort at the first census. In Table 37, for example, between 1926 and 1936 the number of all Catholic persons who had been born between 1901 and 1892 declined by 11 per cent (in 1936, these persons were 35 to 44 years old). Since this 11 per cent decline was less than the 13 per cent decline recorded for Protestants in the same cohort, and since we assume the same age-specific levels of mortality for both religious groups, the conclusion is that proportionately more Protestants emigrated.

Table 37 has been arranged to show the changes taking place during each intercensal period by the birth year of the cohort; it is best to read each of the three columns from the bottom up, from the youngest to the oldest ages. Between 1926 and 1936 the proportionately greater declines among Protestant children aged 10 to 14 years in 1936 (5 compared with 2 per cent), indicates that the emigration of entire families was somewhat more common among Protestants than Catholics. The same interpretation can be made for the greater decline among Protestants who were aged 15 to 19 years in 1936, although some of the older persons in this cohort may have emigrated on their own. The only cohort of those listed for which the Catholic decline was greater was among persons aged 25 to 34 years in 1936 — the cohort with peak emigration for economic reasons.

During the 1936–46 period the Protestant decline was greater in each cohort regardless of age. The greater emigration of Protestant children shows the continuance of relatively more family emigration among Protestants. But even in the cohorts with peak emigration for occupational causes, between 25 and 34 years in 1946, the Protestant decline was greater than the Catholic. For the ages between 20 and 29 in 1946 (persons who would have been in their late teens or twenties during World War II), the Protestant decline was especially marked. The larger decline among Protestants in those ages beyond the normal time for occupational emigration, among persons 35 to 54 years old in 1946, may reflect

TABLE 37. Intercensal Percentage Decline in the Number of Persons in Certain Age Cohorts Arranged by Birth Years of Cohort and Religion, Ireland, 1926–61.

Birth Years of Cohort and Religion	Intercensal Percentage Decline and, in Parentheses, Age of Cohort at End of Period		
	1926–36	*1936–46*	*1946–61*
1901–1892			
Catholic	11	12	NA[a]
Protestant [b]	13	16	NA
	(35–44)	(45–54)	
1911–02			
Catholic	24	10	NA
Protestant	22	15	NA
	(25–34)	(35–44)	
1916–12			
Catholic	14	19	NA
Protestant	16	26	NA
	(20–24)	(30–34)	
1921–17			
Catholic	5	22	18
Protestant	10	32	16
	(15–19)	(25–29)	(40–44)
1926–22			
Catholic	2	18	28
Protestant	5	28	24
	(10–14)	(20–24)	(35–39)
1931–27			
Catholic	NR	6	40
Protestant	NR	14	34
	(5–9)	(15–19)	(30–34)
1936–32			
Catholic	NR	2	45
Protestant	NR	5	40
	(0–4)	(10–14)	(25–29)
1941–37			
Catholic	NR	NR	41
Protestant	NR	NR	33
		(5–9)	(20–24)
1946–42			
Catholic	NR	NR	21
Protestant	NR	NR	20
		(0–4)	(15–19)

SOURCES: Calculated from *Census of Population of Ireland, 1926*, Vol. III, Part I, Table 13A, p. 99; *1936*, Vol. III, Part I, Table 13A, p. 103; *1946*, Vol. III, Part I, Table 11A, p. 32; *1961*, Vol. VII, Part I, Table 9A, p. 36.

[a] Due to the 15-year gap between the last two censuses to inquire about religion, the proper data for particular cohorts were not published in the 1961 Census.

[b] Church of Ireland, Presbyterian, Methodist, and Baptist.

a movement of individuals or families out of Ireland for non-economic reasons.

The larger decline among Protestants than Catholics between 1936 and 1946 was noticed by the Irish government statisticians who published the 1946 Census. Although the assumption of exactly equal mortality rates for both religious groups at all ages is not strong enough to warrant the calculation of precise emigration figures for both young and old persons, the authors of the 1946 Census did calculate net emigration rates by religion and sex for persons with relatively low age-specific mortality: individuals aged 10 to 34 years in 1936. Using the Irish Life Table for 1940–42, the authors subtracted the estimated number of persons who died in each cohort between 1936 and 1946 from the actual decline recorded in the censuses. The result was the estimated total net emigration and comparing this with the number of persons in the cohort in 1936, rates per 1,000 persons in 1936 were calculated (Table 38). Because a small number of non-Protestants were included in the non-Catholic category, the data refer literally to non-Catholics rather than to Protestants. For these particular cohorts, the emigration of non-Catholics was from 40 to 90 per cent greater than the Catholics. The greatest rate of emigration took place among young, non-Catholic men who were in their twenties during World War II, (men aged 15 to 19 years in 1936). Almost one-third of the non-Catholic men in this particular

TABLE 38. Estimated Net Emigration between 1936 and 1946 per 1,000 Persons in Selected Age Groups in 1936 in Ireland by Religion and Sex.

Age in 1936	Males			Females		
	Catholics	Others [a]	$\frac{B}{A}$	Catholics	Others [a]	$\frac{B}{A}$
	(A)	(B)		(A)	(B)	
10–14	147	251	1.7	154	237	1.5
15–19	203	309	1.5	160	215	1.3
20–24	184	261	1.4	113	148	1.3
25–34	73	121	1.7	38	71	1.9

SOURCE: Censuses of Population of Ireland, 1946–1951, "General Report," Tables 149, 155, pp. 164, 169.
[a] Church of Ireland, Presbyterian, Methodist, and Baptist accounted for 94.3 per cent of the total non-Catholic population in 1936.

TABLE 39. Intercensal Percentage Decline in the Number of Persons in Certain
Age Cohorts Arranged by Age Group at End of Intercensal Period and Religion,
Ireland, 1926 to 1961.

Age at End of Intercensal Period and Religion	Intercensal Percentage Decline and, in Parentheses, Birth Years of Cohort		
	1926–36	1936–46	1946–61
10–14 years			
Catholic	2	2	NA
Protestant	5	5	NA
	(1926–22)	(1936–32)	
15–19 years			
Catholic	5	6	21
Protestant	10	14	20
	(1921–17)	(1931–37)	(1946–42)
20–24 years			
Catholic	14	18	41
Protestant	16	28	33
	(1916–12)	(1926–22)	(1941–37)
25–29 years			
Catholic	NA	22	45
Protestant	NA	32	40
		(1921–17)	(1936–32)
30–34 years			
Catholic	NA	19	40
Protestant	NA	26	34
		(1916–12)	(1931–27)

SOURCE: Table 37.

cohort had emigrated by 1946 compared with one-fifth of the
relevant Catholics.

The pattern of relatively greater Protestant than Catholic
emigration reversed after World War II: between 1946 and 1961
the Catholic decline was larger in each cohort listed in Table 39,
which arranges the data by age group rather than by the cohorts'
years of birth. Because of the additional five years in the 1946 to
1961 period (religion was not asked in the intervening censuses),
if there had been no change in the rate of population decline the
total percentage decline would have been 50 per cent greater.
Actually the total percentage declines for Catholics in each age
group between 1946 and 1961 were more than double those of
1936 to 1946. In contrast, the percentage declines for Protestants
between 1946 and 1961 were in no case more than 50 per cent
higher than the already high 1936 to 1946 declines. While the

rate of population decline among Protestants was somewhat less after than before 1946, the Catholic rate of decline increased greatly. Changes in agricultural technique after 1946 account for much of this change, and will be discussed later under the more general topic of rural-urban emigration by religion.

The greater percentage decline for Catholics among certain cohorts after 1946 does not, at first glance, appear to be consistent with the larger percentage decline for the *total* Protestant than Catholic population after 1946 (Table 36). The seeming paradox is resolved by two other differences between the two religious groups — fertility and age composition. Once again our analysis is limited to the 1926–1961 period due to the difficulty of calculating for the 26 Counties child/woman ratios, and the proportion of women of childbearing age among all adults, by religion, from the information given in the 1911 and earlier censuses. Between 1926 and 1961 the fertility of Protestant women was from 60 to 75 per cent that of Catholic women, assuming levels of age-specific mortality were the same for both groups (Table 40). The number of births per 1,000 persons per year, the crude birth rate, would have been even lower for Protestants than indicated by the child/woman ratio, because the proportion of women of child-bearing age among all adults was also smaller among Protestants than Catholics. In other words, not only did Protestant women have fewer children, there were also proportionately fewer women in the Protestant population able to have children. The result

TABLE 40. Child/Woman Ratios and Women of Childbearing Age as a Proportion of All Adults by Religion, Ireland, 1926–61.

Year	Children 0–4 per 100 Women 15–44		Protestant Child/ Woman Ratios as a Percentage of Catholic	Women 15–44 as a Percentage of all Persons 15 and Over	
	Catholic	Protestant [a]		Catholic	Protestant
1926	47	31	66	30	28
1936	45	27	60	29	26
1946	48	36	75	29	25
1961	60	39	65	27	21

SOURCES: Calculated from: *Census of Population of Ireland, 1926*, Vol. III, Part I, Table 13A, p. 99; *1936*, Vol. III, Part I, Table 13A, p. 103; *1946*, Vol. III, Part I, Table 11, pp. 32–34; *1961*, Vol. VII, Table 9, pp. 36–38.
([a]) Church of Ireland, Presbyterian, Methodist and Baptist.

TABLE 41. Distribution of Population in Three Main Age Groups by Religion, Ireland, 1926–61.

Religion	Age in Years			
and Year	0–14	15–64	65+	Total
Number in thousands				
Catholic				
1926	817.9	1,687.0	246.4	2,751.3
1936	782.4	1,729.9	261.6	2,773.9
1946	789.6	1,708.6	287.8	2,786.0
1961	846.9	1,536.1	290.5	2,673.5
Protestant [a]				
1926	47.1	136.7	24.2	208.0
1936	35.6	123.4	24.5	183.5
1946	31.1	101.1	25.3	157.5
1961	27.2	80.0	22.9	130.1
Percentage distribution				
Catholic				
1926	30	61	9	100
1936	28	63	9	100
1946	28	62	10	100
1961	32	57	11	100
Protestant				
1926	23	65	12	100
1936	19	68	13	100
1946	20	64	16	100
1961	21	61	18	100

SOURCES: Calculated from: *Census of Population of Ireland, 1926*, Vol. III, Part I, Table 13A, p. 99; *1936*, Vol. III, Part I, Table 13A, p. 103; *1946* Vol. III, Part I, Table 11A, p. 32; *1961*, Vol. VII, Table 9A, p. 36.
[a] Church of Ireland, Presbyterian, Methodist, and Baptist.

was a much smaller proportion of children in the Protestant than in the Catholic population; 21 compared with 32 per cent of the respective groups were composed of children from 0 to 14 years of age in 1961 (Table 41).

At the other end of the life span the proportion of elderly persons was much higher among Protestants; and the proportion rose consistently between 1926 and 1961. In 1961 not quite one in five Protestants was 65 years or older, compared with about one in ten Catholics. If both groups had the same level of age-specific mortality, then the total number of deaths per 1,000 persons per year, the crude death rate, would have been higher for Protestants. This would have been due to their smaller proportion in the low mortality years of childhood, and their larger proportion in the high mortality years beyond 65. A combination of a lower crude birth rate and a higher crude death rate would have meant that natural increase was less among Protestants than Catholics, with the 1946–61 period having the greatest difference between the two religions. With a lower rate of natural increase, a smaller rate of emigration among Protestants still could have resulted in a greater percentage decline in their total numbers than was the case for Catholics; and this appears to have happened between 1946 and 1961.

Estimates of which religion had greater rates of emigration between 1861 and 1926 are necessarily rough due to a lack of readily accessible data; but such estimates can be made, nevertheless, if the differences in percentage decline between the two religious groups were exceptionally large. During the entire 65-year period, there was only one interval during which the percentage decline between the two groups differed by more than 4 percentage points: 1911–26, when the Protestant decline was 31 percentage points more than the Catholic (Table 36). Unless Protestant mortality suddenly increased to epidemic proportions, or unless Protestant fertility drastically declined (and there is no evidence of either having happened between 1911 and 1926), then the reduction by one-third in the number of Protestants in Ireland in just 15 years was due to extraordinarily high rates of emigration. Before concluding that this great decline was due to the emigration of Irish Protestants, a possibly confounding factor must be accounted for — the movement of non-Irish Protestants. After the 1921 Treaty, thousands of English, Welsh, and Scots persons who had been employed in Ireland by the British army, and in administration and business, returned to Britain.

Population Decline Among Native-Born Protestants

Because religion was not cross-classified by place of birth in Irish censuses, it is necessary to estimate the number of native-born Protestants by making assumptions about the proportion of foreign-born persons who were Methodists, Presbyterians, Baptists, or members of the Church of Ireland. If we assume that none of the foreign-born were members of these four major Protestant denominations in Ireland, then the figures given in Table 36 would refer only to native-born persons. But since it is virtually certain that some foreign-born persons were Methodist, etc., their numbers should be subtracted from the total Protestant figures given in Table 36. In order to include all possible proportions of foreign-born who were Protestant, while at the same time keeping the estimating process itself clear, I made only three assumptions: that none, half, or all of the foreign-born were Methodist, etc. (Table 42). Persons born in the Six Counties of Northern Ireland were considered Irish-born and hence not included in the foreign-born figures.

TABLE 42. Estimated Number of, and Intercensal Percentage Changes Among, Native-Born Protestants, Ireland, 1861–1961.

Year	Number of Foreign-Born [a] (thousands)	Estimated Number of Native-Born Protestants (thousands) [b]			Intercensal Percentage Change			
		A^e	B^d	C^e	A	B	C	Catholic [f]
1861	62	457	426	395	NR	NR	NR	NR
1871	81	418	378	337	−9	−11	−15	−8
1881	83	392	350	309	−6	−7	−8	−4
1891	85	358	316	273	−9	−10	−12	−11
1901	86	330	287	244	−8	−9	−11	−7
1911	100	313	263	213	−5	−8	−13	−2
1926	67	208	174	141	−34	−34	−34	−2
1936	65	184	152	119	−12	−13	−16	+1
1946	65	158	126	93	−14	−17	−22	+0
1961	72	130	94	58	−17	−25	−38	−4

SOURCES: Calculated from *Censuses of Population of Ireland, 1946 and 1961*, "General Report," Tables 149, 157, pp. 164, 171; *1961*, Vol. VII, Part I, Table 1A, p. 1; Part II, Table 1A, p. 78.
([a]) Excluding those born in Northern Ireland.
([b]) Church of Ireland, Presbyterian, Methodist, and Baptist.
([c]) Assuming *none* of the foreign-born are Church of Ireland, etc.
([d]) Assuming *half* of the foreign-born are Church of Ireland, etc.
([e]) Assuming *all* of the foreign-born are Church of Ireland, etc.
([f]) From Table 36.

For the 1911–26 period, ironically, it does not matter whether we assume all, half, or none of the foreign-born were Methodist, etc., since the estimated decline among native-born Protestants was the same in each case, 34 per cent. Assuming the same rates of natural increase among both foreign-born and native-born Protestants, this would mean that the two groups also had the same unusually high rates of emigration.

During all other intercensal periods between 1861 and 1961, the subtraction of foreign-born persons from the total Protestant population of Ireland results in higher percentage declines among Protestants. Before 1901 the resulting changes were moderate and in no case different by more than 3 percentage points from the Catholic, assuming half of the foreign-born were Methodist, etc. But beginning in 1901 the consideration of changes in the foreign-born population yields some instances of much greater estimated declines among native-born Irish Protestants than the figures for the total Protestant population indicate. Between 1946 and 1961, for example, the assumption that half of the foreign-born were Methodist, etc., increases the estimated decline for native-born Protestants from 17 to 25 per cent. The reader can make his own guess about the actual proportion of foreign-born persons who were Methodist, etc., but it may have been more than half judging from the fact that from 72 to 86 per cent of all foreign-born residents in Ireland between 1861 and 1961 had been born in England, Scotland, or Wales.[2] In any case, my general conclusions are: first, except for the 1911–26 period when there was no difference, in all other intervals the degree of emigration of native-born Irish Protestants is understated by the figures for the total Protestant population; and second, the understatement has increased since 1926, and was especially apparent between 1946 and 1961.

Rural-Urban Migration by Religion

The special character of Irish Protestant emigration after the turn of the century is also indicated by its divergence from the "normal" pattern of rural-urban migration. Once again rates of population change must be used because migration rates by religion are not available, and some of the observed differences between Catholics and Protestants could have been due to differences in natural increase rather than migration. But the magnitude and direction of the trends shown in Table 43 strongly suggest that the same general pattern would be presented by emigration rates were they available. A picture of normal rural-urban migration is presented for Catholics with declining rural and increasing urban populations. But a rural-urban movement cannot explain the decline of Protestants in both rural and urban areas. In fact, among Protestants the urban decline was *greater* than the rural decline between 1911 and 1926, and was the same as the rural decline between 1936 and 1946. It appears that the Protestant population decline was impelled by social factors operating both in rural and urban areas.

Protestant population decline in urban areas. The decline in the urban Protestant population, coupled with the increase among urban Catholics, reduced the proportion of non-Catholics among all urban residents from 16 to 6 per cent between 1911 and 1961.* Because of the difficulty in calculating figures for the 26 Counties for Protestants alone from the 1911 and earlier censuses, data for all non-Catholics are used. Furthermore, it would be difficult to estimate the proportion non-Catholic of all urban residents in the 1901 and earlier censuses because of changing town boundaries. But some idea of changes during the past century in the proportion non-Catholic in Irish urban areas can be gained by considering changes in the four largest cities (Table 44). Except in Dublin, there is a clear break between the period before 1911 and the time after 1926: before 1911 there were rela-

TABLE 43. Intercensal Percentage Changes in the Total, Rural, and Urban Populations by Religion, Ireland, 1911–61.

Period	Total Population		Urban Areas		Rural Areas	
	Catholic	Protestant [a]	Catholic	Protestant	Catholic	Protestant
1911–26	−2	−34	+8	−38	−6	−28
1926–36	+1	−12	+13	−8	−4	−14
1936–46	+0	−14	+6	−14	−3	−14
1946–61	−4	−17	+18	−9	−17	−24

SOURCES: *Census of Population of Ireland, 1926,* Vol. III, Part I, Tables 1B, 5B, pp. 1, 6; *1936,* Vol. III, Part I, Tables 1A, 1B, 5A, 5B, pp. 3, 8; *1946,* Vol. III, Part I, Tables 1A, 1B, 5A, 5B, pp. 1, 6; *1961,* Vol. VII, Part I, Tables 1A, 1B, 6A, pp. 1, 11.

[a] Protestant for 1911–26 means non-Catholic; for 1926, 1936, and 1946, Protestant Episcopalian, Presbyterian, Methodist, and Baptist; for 1961, Church of Ireland, Presbyterian, Methodist, and Baptist.

* The number of urban non-Catholics declined by half from 147,000 in 1911 to 73,000 in 1961. *Census of Ireland, 1911,* "General Report," Table 125, pp. 222–224; *Census of Population of Ireland, 1961,* Vol. VII, Part I, Table 6A, p. 11.

TABLE 44. Percentage Non-Catholic in Ireland and in the Four Largest Parliamentary Boroughs of Ireland, 1861–1961.

Year	Ireland	Boroughs			
		Dublin	Cork	Limerick	Waterford
1861	11	24	15	10	11
1871	11	23	15	10	11
1881	10	21	14	11	9
1891	11	20	14	10	9
1901	11	18	13	10	8
1911	10	17	12	9	8
1926	7	10	6	5	4
1936	7	11	4	3	3
1946	6	9	3	2	3
1961	5	6	2	2	2
Total population in thousands					
1861	4,402.1	263.8	102.5	56.8	28.8
1961	2,818.3	537.4	78.0	50.8	28.2

SOURCES: *Censuses of Ireland, 1871*, Table LXI, p. 116; *1891*, Table 135, p. 458; *1911*, Table 124, p. 221; *Censuses of Population of Ireland, 1926*, Vol. III, Table 8A, p. 10; *1936*, Vol. III, Table 7, p. 10; *1946*, Vol. III, Table 7, p. 8; *1961*, Vol. VII, Part I, Table 7A, p. 12; *Statistical Abstract of Ireland, 1950*, Table 34, p. 31; *1963*, Table 42, p. 53.

tively constant or slowly changing proportions of non-Catholics, while after 1926 the proportions suddenly declined. Cork Borough, for example, was 15 per cent non-Catholic in 1861, still 12 per cent in 1911, but only 2 per cent in 1961. And of that 2 per cent, a good portion, perhaps the majority, were not native-born Irish Protestants but rather foreign non-Catholics, considering the fact that in 1961 there were more foreign-born than non-Catholic persons enumerated in Cork County Borough.[3]

While Dublin also experienced a major decline in the non-Catholic proportion of its population between 1911 and 1926, the post-1911 trends were not simply a change from the status quo as was the case in the other large cities. Since at least 1861, when one in four Dubliners was not Catholic, the Catholic proportion of the Dublin population gradually increased during each intercensal period but one. The exception was the 1926–36 period, when the proportion of non-Catholics in Dublin increased from 10 to 11 per cent. After 1936 the gradual decline among non-Catholics began again, and by 1961 the proportion of non-Catholics in Dublin was about the same as for the nation as a whole — one in twenty.

The reasons for the decline in the urban Protestant population will be discussed later with my interpretations of Protestant
emigration generally. But at this point we can conclude that the
period of greatest decline in the non-Catholic proportion of Ireland's four largest cities was between 1911 and 1926, and that by
1961 the native-born Irish Protestants who were still living in
large Irish urban areas were probably concentrated in the Dublin
area.

Protestant population decline in rural areas. The percentage
decline in rural areas between 1911 and 1961 was greater, and in
some periods several times greater, among Protestants than among
Catholics (Table 43). The much greater decline among Protestants cannot be explained by economic considerations alone because they were generally better off financially than their Catholic neighbors. In 1926, for example, 27 per cent of all farmers with
holdings of over 200 acres were Protestant compared with only
5 per cent of all farmers with 15 to 30 acre farms.[4] Although we
are primarily concerned with national and not regional patterns,
it is interesting to note that Protestants were disproportionately
represented among owners of large farms regardless of the proportion of Protestants in the total rural population of the area. In
Ulster (3 Counties) where a higher proportion of the population
is Protestant, 19 per cent of the 15 to 30 acre farms were Protestant owned but so were 38 per cent of the holdings of over 200
acres. In Connacht the proportion Protestant among all farmers
was 2 per cent for those with 15 to 30 acres, and 23 per cent for
those with over 200 acres.

A more comprehensive measure of economic status is the
percentage distribution by size of farm *within* each religious
group (Table 45). In 1926 the proportion of farmers with holdings of 50 acres or more, generally the minimum size needed to
support modern, highly mechanized agricultural technology (see
Chapter Five), was 23 per cent among Catholics and 44 per cent
among Protestants. By 1961 important changes in agricultural
technology had occurred in Ireland, but the proportion of Catholic farmers with 50 or more acres had risen to just 33 per cent.
Among Protestants, in contrast, the proportion had reached 58
per cent. Because there were proportionately more Catholics with

small holdings, we would normally expect greater percentage declines among Catholic small farmers and their assisting relatives. And because proportionately more Protestant farmers were in a better position to afford buying extra land to enlarge their holdings, or buying the machines and supplies of the new, capital intensive techniques, we would normally expect greater percentage increases among Protestant than Catholic farmers with holdings of from 50 to 200 acres.

Neither expectation is supported by the facts, however. At each intercensal period between 1926 and 1961 the percentage decline among farmers with 50 acres or less was greater, and again, in some cases several times greater, among Protestants than Catholics (Table 46). Between 1926 and 1946, in fact, farmers with 30 to 50 acres actually *increased* among Catholics by 11 per cent, while decreasing among Protestants by 18 per cent. Protestants also experienced greater percentage declines among farmers' assisting sons, daughters, and other relatives between 1926 and 1946, although the differences between the two religions were not as pronounced as they were with the small farmers. Between 1946 and 1961 the percentage decline among farmers' assisting relatives was about the same for both Protestant and Catholic.

The greater decline among Protestant small farmers and farmers' assisting relatives might be interpreted as part of a shift toward labor-saving techniques and a consolidation of farms from smaller to larger units, which occurred earlier among Protestants

TABLE 45. Percentage Distribution of Farmers, Both Sexes, by Size of Farm and Religion, Ireland, 1926–61.

Farm size	Catholic				Protestant [a]			
in acres	1926	1936	1946	1961	1926	1936	1946	1961
200 or more	2	2	2	2	9	9	9	10
100–200	6	6	7	9	13	15	16	19
50–100	15	16	18	22	22	24	26	29
30–50	19	21	23	26	21	21	21	20
Less than 30	58	55	50	41	35	31	28	22
Total	100	100	100	100	100	100	100	100
Base (thousands)	246.0	238.7	231.1	196.3	18.5	16.9	15.3	12.4

SOURCE: Calculated from Table 46.

([a]) Protestant for 1926, 1936, and 1946 is Protestant Episcopalian, Presbyterian, and Methodist; for 1961, Church of Ireland, Presbyterian.

TABLE 46. Number and Intercensal Percentage Change Among Both Sexes in Major Agricultural Occupations by Religion, Ireland, 1926–61.

| | Number in Thousands | | | | | | | | Intercensal Percentage Change | | | | | |
| | Catholic | | | | Protestant (a) | | | | Catholic | | | Protestant | | |
Occupation	1926	1936	1946	1961	1926	1936	1946	1961	1926–1936	1936–1946	1946–1961	1926–1936	1936–1946	1946–1961
Farmers:														
200 acres +	4.3	4.3	4.4	4.1	1.6	1.5	1.3	1.2	0	+2	−7	−6	−13	−8
100–200 acres	14.0	14.9	16.0	16.9	2.5	2.5	2.5	2.4	+6	+7	+6	0	0	−4
50–100 acres	36.9	39.0	41.2	43.3	4.1	4.0	4.0	3.6	+6	+6	+5	−2	0	−10
30–50 acres	47.2	50.0	52.3	50.7	3.9	3.6	3.2	2.5	+6	+5	−3	−8	−11	−22
30 acres or less	143.6	130.5	117.2	81.3	6.4	5.3	4.3	2.7	−9	−10	−31	−17	−19	−37
Farmers' assisting sons and daughters (b)	194.7	180.8	151.7	75.6	11.3	10.3	8.0	4.1	−7	−16	−50	−9	−22	−49
Other assisting relatives	54.1	49.5	41.0	26.4	3.5	3.2	2.4	1.5	−8	−17	−36	−9	−25	−38
Agricultural laborers	122.8	124.6	111.4	57.9	3.5	3.1	2.2	1.4	+1	−11	−48	−11	−29	−36
Total	617.6	593.6	535.2	356.2	36.8	33.5	27.9	19.4	−4	−10	−33	−9	−17	−30

SOURCES: *Census of Population of Ireland*, 1926, Vol. III, Part I, Tables 18A, 19A, 20A, pp. 130–134; *1936*, Vol. III, Part I, Tables 18A, 19A, 20A, pp. 132–136; *1946*, Vol. II, Table 13B, pp. 198–199; *1961*, Vol. VII, Part I, Tables 11A, 11B, pp. 75, 77.
(a) Protestant for 1926, 1936, and 1946 is Protestant Episcopalian, Presbyterian, and Methodist; for 1961, Church of Ireland, Presbyterian.
(b) In 1961 including sons-in-law and daughters-in-law.

than Catholics. But such a conclusion would be wrong because an essential part of the process did not occur: an increase in the number of larger farmers. Between 1926 and 1961 the number of Protestant farmers with holdings of 50 to 200 acres either remained unchanged or declined at each intercensal period. These larger Protestant farmers indeed may have adopted the new techniques, but their static or declining numbers reveal that little consolidation of smaller Protestant holdings took place. The increase in the proportion of all Protestant farmers with 50 acres or more shown in Table 45, therefore, was due entirely to the decline in smaller farmers and not to an increase in the number of larger farmers.

In contrast to the Protestant pattern, the increase in the number of Catholic farmers with 50 to 200 acres between 1946 and 1961 is consistent with changes expected during a period of rapid adoption of agricultural labor-saving devices. The decline among Catholic farmers with from 30 to 50 acres after 1946 runs counter to the steady increase among farms of this size recorded between 1926 and 1946. Such a reversal would be expected if standards of what comprises a farm of "adequate" size rose from the 30 acres of horse-drawn techniques, to the 50 to 100 acres of the modern tractor-powered agriculture. Similarly, the accelerated rate of decline among Catholic farmers with 30 acres or less after 1946 would be related to increased dissatisfaction with the style of life provided by such small holdings. The rural occupations most affected by such a change in technique — agricultural laborers and farmers' assisting sons and daughters — present the largest differences in rates of decline before and after 1946. It would be reasonable to conclude that the increase in Catholic emigration after 1946 was in large part due to the widespread adoption of agricultural labor-saving techniques.

Since the usual interpretation of rural-urban migration leaves much of the Protestant patterns unexplained, we are led to conclude that certain factors made emigration from Ireland attractive for rural Protestants regardless of their relative economic status or their ability to adopt more productive agricultural techniques. And since the rate of population decline was at times greater among urban than rural Protestants, these factors also must have been important to the urban Protestants. In my opinion, the best explanation of the Protestant demographic trends is in the reaction of native-born Irish Protestants to the Anglo-Irish war of 1919–21, to the granting of "dominion status" to the 26 Counties in 1921, and to subsequent political and economic events.

The Protestant Reaction to Irish Nationalism

The emergence of modern Ireland during the early 1920s, and the decline by one-third in the Protestant population of Ireland between 1911 and 1926, were not linked in any way, so far as I know, by direct discriminatory actions against Protestants on the part of the new government. On the contrary, the revolutionary leaders of Irish nationalism went out of their way to care for the Protestant minority. In the constitution of the Irish Free State (1922) the state was specifically prohibited from endowing any one religion, imposing any discrimination or disability because of religious affiliation, or acquiring church property by compulsion (except for certain specified public works and then only with compensation); such provisions were publicly intended to allay Protestant fears of the new government.[5] Protestant schools were permitted to continue without interference and were even given special transportation facilities; in the Judiciary the more than representative proportion of Protestants was maintained; and as a symbolic act, under the 1937 constitution the first president of Ireland was a Protestant, Douglas Hyde.[6]

Many of these provisions flowed from the long tradition of separation of church and state in Irish nationalism (Chapter Two). There was also an immediate political object in guaranteeing the rights of Protestants. Most Irish nationalist leaders hoped eventually to convince Northern Ireland to end the partition and join with Ireland to reestablish once again a united nation for the entire island. And because Northern Ireland was predominantly Protestant, the Irish nationalists felt they had to demonstrate that Northern Irish fears of Catholicism in Irish government were groundless. Hence the sensitivity to specifying the equal rights of non-Catholics, the granting of special facilities to Protestant schools, and the desire to place Protestants in high public positions.

The emigration of native-born Irish Protestants, then, was a voluntary movement and was not caused by any governmental policies directed against them as a religious group. But several political decisions and policies of the new government did indirectly contribute to Protestant emigration. The close association of the Protestant Irish with British interests and ideals meant that conflicts beween Ireland and Britain could have direct personal consequences.

Conflicting loyalties. The events of the early 1920s partitioned Ireland and gave the 26 Counties Commonwealth status, but Ireland remained part of the British Empire. For example, the oath of allegiance was still taken to the Crown. The Anglo-Irish Protestant who remained in Ireland after the turmoil of the early 1920s could think of himself as still living in part of the British Empire. Gradually the political links with Britain were severed, however, and it became increasingly clear that the Irish nationalist leaders wanted their own state, independent of Britain. De Valera replaced Ireland's Commonwealth status with a looser form of association; he removed the oath of allegiance to the Crown in 1933; he abolished the office of Governor General in 1936; and also he removed the Crown from the constitutional machinery of the state.[7]

Maintaining dual loyalties to England and Ireland became even more difficult during the 1936–46 decade because of Ireland's neutrality during World War II. The Irish government strictly observed its neutrality, imprisoning with impartiality both Allied and Axis armed forces (mostly airmen), and refusing to permit the Allies to take control of Irish ports during the battle of the Atlantic. De Valera even expressed his condolences to the German Embassy on the death of Hitler, an act which further provoked resentment among the English,[8] and supposedly, among England's supporters in Ireland. It is not unreasonable to interpret the much larger relative emigration among Protestant than Catholic young men during the war years (Table 38), as due in large part to the more intense loyalties of the Protestant Irish with Britain.

In the spring of 1948 de Valera was defeated after having governed continuously since 1932. But the coalition government which replaced him was no improvement in the view of some

Protestants, and was in some respects even less satisfactory. One of the first acts of the coalition government was to withdraw Ireland from the British Commonwealth and to declare Ireland a republic.

Economic uncertainties. Because of their favored economic position (Table 1), Protestants were particularly concerned with events that might damage the Irish economy. The increasing civil disorders which eventually led to the Anglo-Irish war of 1919–21, and the civil war of 1921–23, convinced many Protestants that the country was sinking into chaos. No doubt some Protestant businessmen closed their Irish offices and transferred their companies to Britain because of their pessimism about Ireland's economic future. Some of their employees, who may have been sympathetic with the Irish nationalists, nevertheless followed their jobs out of Ireland. Similarly, probably several thousand individuals left Ireland after 1921 not for political reasons but simply to maintain their British welfare benefits, or their military and civil service pensions.

The optimism of those Protestant businessmen who remained in Ireland was dampened when de Valera waged an "economic war" against Britain during the 1930s. Ireland had been paying annuities to Great Britain for land which had been transferred to tenant farmers under the various land acts. De Valera did not believe that the Irish should pay the British for Irish land, and when he came to power in 1932 he suspended their payment. In retaliation, Britain placed a tariff on Irish agricultural produce, to which de Valera responded by putting a tariff on British coal and iron. De Valera wished to increase the self-sufficiency of Ireland and to substitute, insofar as possible, trade with other nations for British trade. The "war" was settled by a compromise in 1938 in which the British withdrew their forces from certain Irish ports which they had continued to occupy after the 1921 Treaty.* From the Irish nationalist point of view, de Valera was attempting to become economically as well as politically independent of Britain. From the private businessman's perspective, on the

---

* The full importance of this concession became clear only after Ireland declared its neutrality during World War II. J. C. Beckett, *A Short History of Ireland*, pp. 170–171.

other hand, de Valera was robbing economic Peter to pay political Paul.

"Brain-Drain" emigration. Let us define this concept as the relatively greater emigration of the better educated and the more highly skilled. The economic problems of Ireland after World War I created a situation in which many well educated and highly skilled persons could have earned more, and had more promising careers, if they left Ireland and went to more rapidly developing nations. Relatively more Protestants than Catholics would have been involved since they were disproportionately represented in highly skilled occupations (Table 1), and, as a group, were better educated. In 1926, for example, Protestant males accounted for only 6 per cent of all males aged 15 to 24 years, but represented 23 per cent of all male medical and law students, and 17 per cent of all other students over 18 years of age (excluding theological students).[9]

The generally unpromising economic situation in Ireland may have been overcome for many young Protestants, on the other hand, by the major Protestant influence in several professions and businesses. A young Protestant man interested in a career in banking, to take the most extreme case, might have had more to gain by staying in Ireland where half of all bank officials were Protestant (in 1926), than by trying his luck in a foreign country where the bank officials did not share his same religious background. The Irish Protestant bank officials were in a position of maintaining the status quo, if they chose to do so, by continuing to give preferential treatment to their co-religionists in hiring and promotions.

The importance of Protestant influence in certain occupations in keeping young Protestants from emigrating can be examined with data from the 1926 and 1946 Censuses. Unfortunately the occupational system used in the 1911 and earlier Censuses prevents comparison with the post-1926 data; it is known, however, that Protestant domination of the better urban jobs increases the farther back in time one goes through the nineteenth and eighteenth centuries because of the Penal Laws (Chapter Two). The data from the 1961 Census cannot be used for this analysis because religion was cross-classified only by occupational groups and not by individual occupations. There is no reason to assume, however, that the 1926–46 trends did not continue through 1961.

For my analysis, I selected those occupations in which at least one-third of employed males were Protestant in 1926, and which were also listed in the 1946 Census (Table 47). In each of the 12 occupations, the status quo was not maintained — in every case the Protestant proportion declined. The table has been arranged to account for the logical possibility that the declining proportion of Protestants was due to a greater increase in the number of Catholics, and not necessarily to any decline in the number of Protestants. But again in every occupation the number of Protestants declined regardless of whether the total number of males employed in the occupation increased or decreased. In some occupations the Protestant patterns were extreme. For example, one might expect Protestants to at least maintain the same *number* of lawyers (solicitors and barristers), since 36 per cent were Protestant in 1926, and it was a slowly growing occupation. But instead the number of Protestant lawyers declined by 44 per cent between 1926 and 1946, a rate about double that of the total decline in the male Protestant labor force (−23 per cent). As a result, the Protestant proportion among all lawyers declined from 36 to 19 per cent.

It appears that Protestants on the whole were not attempting to maintain their relative position in occupations in which they had succeeded in the past; they were not interested in keeping the status quo. Judging from the much greater rates of emigration among older Protestants than Catholics between 1936 and 1946 (Table 37), presumably some older Protestant men, already established in their careers, chose to emigrate from Ireland after concluding that their long-term advantage would be better served by absorbing the short-term loss in relocating. Younger Protestant men did not replace their fathers or other Protestants in certain occupations to the degree they might have, perhaps because they shared their fathers' pessimism about Ireland's economic future. Being at the beginnings of their careers, the short-term costs would have been less, and the long-term gains greater for the Protestant sons than their fathers.

Replacement of Protestant elite by Catholics. The voluntary emigration after 1926 of many highly skilled and well edu-

TABLE 47. Number and Percentage Protestant in Certain Occupations, Males, Ireland, 1926 and 1946.

Occupation (a)	Number of males				1926–1946 Percentage Change		Protestant as a percentage of all males	
	All males		Protestant (b)		All	Protestant	1926	1946
	1926	1946	1926	1946				
Growing occupations								
Insurance clerks	518	758	205	154	+46	−25	41	34
Engineers, mgrs., foremen of printers, etc.	291	369	125	112	+27	−10	43	30
Heads of commercial sections of businesses	372	420	154	145	+13	−6	41	34
Solicitors, barristers	1,348	1,410	486	272	+5	−44	36	19
Commercial travelers	3,088	3,215	1,011	690	+4	−32	33	21
Church officials (not clergymen)	593	605	203	170	+2	−16	34	28
Declining occupations								
Bank officials (not clerks)	960	937	495	330	−2	−33	52	35
Employers, mgrs. of metal workers (not shoe-forging)	551	538	182	157	−2	−14	33	29
Bank clerks	2,344	2,198	821	660	−6	−20	35	30
Watch, clock makers, repairers	711	656	244	141	−8	−42	34	21
Auctioneers, valuers	669	551	229	137	−18	−40	34	25
Navigating, engineering officers	744	473	309	156	−36	−49	42	33
Total in all occupations (thousands) (c)	963.8	963.5	67.9	52.1	0	−23	7	5

SOURCES: *Census of Population of Ireland, 1926*, Vol. III, Part I, Table 17, pp. 114–129; *1946*, Vol. II, Table 13B, pp. 198–209.
(a) Occupations in which at least 33 per cent of males were Protestant in 1926, and which were also listed in the 1946 Census.
(b) Protestant Episcopalian, Presbyterian, and Methodist.
(c) 12 years and over in 1926; 14 years and over in 1946.

cated Protestants also could be taken to illustrate the decline of the old Protestant elite. During the last part of the nineteenth century and the first part of the twentieth, many Irish Protestants opposed breaking political ties with Britain not only for fear of being excluded from careers in British public and military service, or of Ireland falling into economic stagnation, but for other reasons: Protestants of all classes still clung, even if only half consciously, to the old notion of Protestant ascendancy, and the establishment of an Irish parliament would bring what remained of that ascendancy to an end and would establish a new Roman Catholic ascendancy in its place.[10]

The possibility of a self-fulfilling prophesy was strong in bringing about such a replacement of elites. The Protestant elite could be eliminated quickly only through mortality or emigration, but before 1921 the presence of the British army in Ireland, the existence of the Royal Irish Constabulary, and the sheer number of Protestants in Ireland (330,000 in 1901), all made the elimination of the Protestant elite through death alone an unlikely prospect. And between 1861 and 1901 there was little difference in the rate of population decline between Protestants and Catholics, indicating that most Protestants still wanted to stay in Ireland. Certain events had weakened the Protestant Establishment well before the turn of the century, however. In 1869 the Church of Ireland was disestablished and some of its land was sold to the tenant farmers who had actually been working it; in 1870 the home-rule movement was founded by Isaac Butt, who wanted to establish an Irish parliament with control over Irish domestic affairs; in 1872 secret voting was introduced and for the first time Catholic tenants could vote without fear of retribution by their Protestant landlords; in 1874 Butt's new party won more than half of all of the Irish seats in Parliament; and during the 1870s the first land acts were passed which began the transfer of land from the Protestant landlord class to the predominantly Catholic tenant farmer class. The "land war" of 1879–82 convinced many British statesmen of both major parties that the landlord system as it existed in Ireland was no longer defensible, and acts passed during the 1880s established the legal precedent of state-aided land purchase for tenant farmers.[11] The establishment of County Councils in 1898 replaced the old system of grand juries (consisting mainly of the Protestant landed gentry), with elected officials who were predominantly Catholic.

The greater decline among Protestants than Catholics, and especially among native-born Protestants between 1901 and 1911 (Table 42) might very well indicate the first major crack in Protestant efforts to maintain the status quo. The triggering event probably was the sudden acceleration in the rate of transfer of land ownership from landlord to tenant farmer after the Birrell Act of 1901 and the Wyndham Act of 1903. These two acts provided the legal machinery and state funds which permitted a total of about 261,000 tenant farmers to buy their own land.[12] Although some landlords may have kept their country homes, and maintained game rights on the land they sold, the general effect of the transfer of land ownership was to end the social institution of a landlord class in Ireland. With the sudden decline of a major rural pillar of the Irish Protestant Establishment, Protestant anxiety about a replacement of elites became greater. And the greater the number of Protestants who emigrated from Ireland, the less secure was the influence of those who remained.

Protestant fear of physical harm to themselves or their property is an unmeasurable factor, but it is still relevant in determining the attractiveness of emigration for some individuals. Terrorism, burning, and threats of violence directed against the landlord class were not unusual during the nineteenth century, and to become relevant to the increased rates of Protestant emigration after 1901 some changes in the situation must have occurred. The most relevant changes would have involved the ability of the established government in Ireland (until 1921 this was, of course, Britain), to maintain law and order. Breaks in British authority in Ireland included the formation of private armies in 1913 and 1914 on the part of both Ulstermen and Irish nationalists; the open gunrunning in 1914; the Easter Rising in Dublin in 1916 and its aftermath; the adoption of a provisional constitution and declaration of independence by Sinn Fein representatives in Dublin in 1919; and the Anglo-Irish war of 1919–21. The replacement of British with Irish law enforcement resulted in the withdrawal of thousands of British troops and the disbanding of the national police (the

Royal Irish Constabulary), and some Protestants may have interpreted this as the termination of the protection they trusted. But probably more Protestants became more fearful about the breakdown of law and order not merely because power had been transferred from Britain, but because of the internal conflicts existing in Ireland itself. The end of the Anglo-Irish war in 1921 was followed in 1922 by a civil war which did not end until 1923. Fear of physical harm to themselves, their families, or their property, I believe, accounts for at least part of the one-third decline in the number of Protestants between 1911 and 1926. And with such a great exodus, the replacement of elites became that much more of a self-fulfilling prophesy.

Church and state. With the achievement of a separate Irish parliament in 1921, the matter of Catholic ideology in governmental matters once again became topical. As pointed out above, if Ireland ever was to incorporate the six counties of the north it was necessary to demonstrate to the predominantly Protestant Northern Irish that the church and state were in fact separate in the 26 Counties. De Valera in particular was consistent in resisting clerical pressure: he did not take the Franco side during the Spanish Civil War; he was prepared to support sanctions against Catholic Italy; his government rejected a plan to convert Ireland into a corporate state, on the Portuguese model (a system in line with Catholic social teaching); and he refused to establish Catholicism as the state religion in his 1937 constitution.[13]

On the other hand, Protestants could point to some changes under the new government and claim that Catholic doctrine was being imposed upon them. For example, laws banning contraceptives were passed in 1929 and 1935;[14] article 41 of the 1937 Constitution stated that "no law shall be enacted providing for the grant of a dissolution of marriage;" no previously divorced person could be married in Ireland; and a government board was established to censor published material. But except for the divorce law, which would apply only to a small part of the population in any case, the ban on contraceptives and the censorship of printed matter were easily circumvented. Copies of banned books could be brought over the border from England or Northern Ireland, and the marital fertility of non-Catholics demonstrates that effective birth control methods were available to those who wished to use them.[15]

It should be remembered that many Irish Protestants were conservative on such issues as divorce and censorship, and did not react in the 1930s as their children and grandchildren might react today to such sumptuary laws. Because these acts had little practical effect on most Protestants, they cannot be taken as major reasons in themselves for Protestant emigration from Ireland. Their importance lies rather in the precedent they set, and in their keeping alive the church-state issue. It could be argued that the institutionalization of Catholic mores in Irish law concerning divorce, censorship, or birth control were harbingers of future legislation with which even conservative Protestants might disagree. The government of de Valera was careful to keep church and state separate, but what of future governments?

Such an incident occurred under the first coalition government of John A. Costello in 1951 over a maternal and child health program. When the government acquiesced to a secret request from the Catholic hierarchy to reject the health plan, the Minister of Health, Dr. Noel Browne, resigned and made the correspondence public.[16] A bitter controversy arose between Catholics concerning the boundary between church and state with the result that the coalition government resigned in that same year. Even though the result of the incident was a reaffirmation of a policy with which Protestants agreed, many Protestants probably interpreted the incident as just one surfacing of many secret requests from the church hierarchy to the Irish government.* At the very least, it could be said that the continuance of the church-state issue in Ireland contributed to the alienation that some Protestants felt from the new Irish nation.

The greater population decline of Protestants than Catholics in Ireland after the turn of the century was due to the economic, social, and political changes accompanying the emergence of the modern nation-state of Ireland. The greater Protestant decline

---

* Another example occurred in April of 1971, when a bill to legalize contraceptives was shelved by the Irish Senate after the Catholic hierarchy, according to newspaper reports, fought to maintain the status quo. From the Associated Press, *Chicago Sun-Times*, April 2, 1971, p. 44.

was not due to differences in natural increase nor to the movement of foreign-born persons from Ireland. In fact, consideration of the foreign-born population shows that the decline among native-born Irish Protestants was greater than indicated by figures for the total Protestant population. Contrary to the normal rural-urban pattern of much of Irish migration, the Protestant urban population has consistently declined since 1911. Furthermore, among rural persons the decline was greater among Protestants than Catholics in spite of the advantaged position of rural Protestants. Because the Irish government was careful to protect the rights of the Protestant minority, it seems reasonable to conclude that the Protestants left voluntarily.

CHAPTER VII

Postponed Marriage and Permanent Celibacy

T HE extreme degree of postponed marriage in Ireland is perhaps that nation's most widely known contemporary demographic characteristic. While the Irish willingness to remain single receives the best publicity, at least in English-speaking countries, Ireland actually is the most extreme example of a general European pattern. For example, in 1945–46 the average age of grooms in Ireland was 33 years; but there were eight other European countries in which the groom's average age was 30 years or over.* Among brides at that time, the average age in Ireland was

---

* Switzerland, Northern Ireland, Netherlands, Sweden, Denmark, Spain, Italy, and England and Wales; Ireland, *Commission on Emigration and other Population Problems, 1948–1954,* "Reports" (Dublin, The Stationery Office), Table 54, p. 69. Because age at marriage was not recorded in Ireland until 1957 (up through 1956 the only indication of age required by law on the marriage registration form was either "full age" or "minor"), estimates of the average age at marriage have had to be made from information collected at the time of the census. But this was not done at every census. The date of marriage or duration of marriage was asked in censuses taken from 1841 through 1871, and then again in 1926, 1946, and 1961. In 1911 the duration of marriage was asked only of women. See, M. D. McCarthy, "The 1961 Census of Population," *Journal of the Statistical and Social Inquiry Society of Ireland,* Vol. XX (1960–61), Table 1A, p. 87. It was not until the 1926 Census that this information was published as the average age at marriage. Among males the average age at marriage was 35

28 years, while in ten other European countries the average age was from 26 to 28 years.[†] Because the average age at marriage does not give any indication of how many people are indefinitely postponing marriage (since, of course, persons who never marry do not influence the average age at marriage), a better measure of postponed marriage is the proportion single among young adults. With this measure Ireland still is the most extreme case among the generally late-marrying European countries, both in recent times and during the 1930s, when the amount of postponed marriage was higher (Table 48).

Europeans not only marry later than persons in many other parts of the world, they also have higher proportions of persons who remain permanently single, and once again, Ireland is the most extreme example of the general European pattern of "permanent celibacy." As we use the term it refers merely to those who remain unmarried beyond the end of the normal childbearing age for women — age 45 or 49. No assumption is made about the sexual behavior of these individuals, and the word "celibacy" is not used in the secondary sense of having taken a vow to remain single. Some of these older persons eventually marry, so the term applies to the group and not to particular individuals. The most direct measures of permanent celibacy are simply the proportions never married among persons 45 years and over, or from 45 to 54 years. Comparing Ireland with other European nations and the United States during the 1930s and more recently, we see that permanent celibacy not only was most prevalent among the Irish, it was much more common among Irish males than females (Table 49).

---

in 1925–26, 33 in 1945–46, 31 in 1961 and 29 in 1967; among females it was 29 in 1925–26, 28 in 1945–46, 27 in 1961 and 26 in 1967. *Census of Population of Ireland, 1946–1951*, "General Report," Table 45, p. 63; Ireland, *Report on Vital Statistics*, 1964, Table 11, p. ix; *1967*, Table 11, p. ix. In the Irish censuses only three categories are used to record marital status: single, married, and widowed. Divorced and separated persons residing in Ireland are enumerated as "married." The error introduced by divorced or separated persons claiming to be single is probably very small.

† Switzerland, Northern Ireland, Netherlands, Sweden, Denmark, Spain, Finland, France, Scotland, and England and Wales. Ireland, *Commission on Emigration*, Table 54, p. 69.

TABLE 48. Postponed Marriage in Selected Countries, 1930s and 1960s.

Country and Exact Years	Percentage Single Among Persons Aged 25–34 Years			
	Females		Males	
	1930s	1960s	1930s	1960s
Ireland (1936, 1966)	55	31	74	50
Northern Ireland (1937, 1966)	47	20	55	29
Finland (1930, 1965)	44	19	50	28
Sweden (1930, 1958)	43	16	54	30
Norway (1930, 1960)	43	15	51	32
Scotland (1931, 1966)	41	13	44	21
Austria (1934, 1967)	41	19	53	30
Iceland (1940, 1966)	40	14	55	26
Switzerland (1930, 1960)	39	23	46	35
Spain (1940, 1960)	35	28	46	39
England, Wales (1931, 1966)	33	12	35	21
Italy (1936, 1966)	32	21	41	38
Netherlands (1930, 1967)	30	12	36	22
Belgium (1930, 1961)	22	12	29	20
U.S.A. (1930, 1967)	18	7	29	14
France (1936, 1967)	15	14	17	27

SOURCES: United Nations, *Demographic Yearbook, 1960*, Table 10, pp. 408, 420–430; *1968*, Table 7, pp. 226, 248–64.

Because Ireland is the most extreme example of the general European pattern, it becomes the best nation to examine in order to better understand why Europeans marry later and accept a higher degree of permanent celibacy than many other peoples of the world. But caution must be used in making generalizations, since the Irish pattern was not exactly like that of the other European countries. Permanent celibacy, for example, was more prevalent among males than females in Ireland, while the reverse was true among all other northwest European countries, both during the 1930s (with the exception of Finland) and more recently. The issue to be taken up in a discussion of Irish marriage patterns, as in the other chapters of this book, is to distinguish those features of Irish life that are shared with other countries from those that are unique to Ireland.

Ireland did not always have unusually high rates of postponed marriage. The proportion single among females around 30 years of age was almost three times higher in 1961 in Ireland than in England (37 compared with 13 per cent, Table 50), but the two

TABLE 49. Permanent Celibacy by Sex in Selected Countries, 1930s and 1960s.

| | Percentage Single Among Persons Aged 45 Years and Over | | | |
| Country and | Females | | Males | |
Exact Years	1930s	1960s	1930s	1960s
Northern Ireland (1937, 1966)	25	21	22	18
Ireland (1936, 1966)	24	23	29	28
Iceland (1940, 1966)	24	20	17	20
Finland (1930, 1965)	21	16	22	9
Sweden (1930, 1965)	21	15	14	14
Scotland (1931, 1966)	21	18	15	12
Norway (1930, 1960)	20	18	12	13
Switzerland (1930, 1960)	18	17	13	12
Austria (1934, 1967)	16	13	11	7
England, Wales (1931, 1966)	16	12	10	8
Belgium (1930, 1961)	14	10	11	8
Netherlands (1930, 1967)	14	11	10	7
Italy (1936, 1966)	12	13	9	8
Spain (1940, 1960)	12	14	8	7
France (1936, 1967)	10	10	8	8
U.S.A. (1930, 1967)	9	6	10	6

SOURCES: United Nations, *Demographic Yearbook, 1960*, Table 10, pp. 408, 420–430; *1968*, Table 7, pp. 227, 249–65.

countries had much more similar rates a century before (39 and 33 per cent in 1851). And the Irish rate in 1851 was considerably higher than it had been just ten years before. Obviously a great change occurred between 1841 and 1851 in the proportion of Irish persons willing to postpone marriage, a change associated with the events surrounding the 1845–48 famine. There is a tendency, however, to compress subsequent changes and to overlook what actually happened after the adjustments to the 1845–48 famine had worked themselves out. The amount of postponed marriage in Ireland did not gradually increase after 1851, as is commonly believed, but instead decreased among both males and females between 1851 and 1871. If the amount of postponed marriage existing in Ireland in 1871 had remained unchanged by the 1930s, then Irish males would have had about the same amount of postponed marriage as the males of six other European countries, and Irish females would have had *less* postponed marriage than females in eight other European countries (Tables 48 and 50).

Ireland also did not always have an unusually high degree of permanent celibacy. In 1851 the proportion single among persons aged 45 to 54 years was the same for Irish and English males, and

TABLE 50. Postponed Marriage in Ireland and England and Wales, 1841–1966.

	Percentage Single Among Persons Aged 25–34 Years			
	Males		Females	
Year	Ireland	England and Wales	Ireland	England and Wales
1841 [a]	43	NA	28	NA
1851	61	37	39	33
1861	57	32	39	30
1871	57	32	38	30
1881	62	32	41	29
1891	67	34	48	33
1901	72	36	53	34
1911	74	38	56	36
1921	NA	34	NA	34
1926	72	NA	53	NA
1931	NA	35	NA	33
1936	74	NA	55	NA
1946	70	NA	48	NA
1951	67	27	46	18
1961	58	23	37	13
1966	50	21	31	12

SOURCES: *Censuses of Population of Ireland, 1946 and 1951,* "General Report," Table 32, p. 51; *1966,* Vol. II, Table VII, p. xii; *Census of England and Wales, 1931,* "General Tables," Table 23D, p. 155; *1961,* "Age, Marital Condition and General Tables," Table 12, pp. 33–34; United Nations, *Demographic Yearbook, 1968,* Table 7, p. 262.

[a] Age-group 26–35 years.

slightly less for Irish than English females (Table 51). The amount of permanent celibacy in Ireland also was not characterized by a steady increase after the Great Famine. Generally the same patterns over time appeared as in the case of postponed marriage, but they appeared a decade or so later as successive cohorts aged from their late twenties and early thirties to their late forties and early fifties. Between 1841 and 1851 the proportion single among older women actually declined slightly from 12 to 11 per cent. After a sudden rise between 1851 and 1861, permanent celibacy among Irish females increased very slowly, by one percentage point each decade between 1861 and 1891. Then between 1891 and 1911 there was another sudden increase amounting to an average of about 3.5 percentage points per decade. Subsequently permanent celibacy among females in Ireland increased by only two percentage points between 1911 and 1951 before beginning its recent decline. The trend in permanent celibacy among Irish males was similar in timing, but began to be much more extreme than the female after the 1880s. Before that time, permanent celibacy was not more than one percentage point higher among males than females, while the greatest discrepancy occurred in 1936 when the male rate was nine percentage points higher than the female (34 compared with 25 per cent).

TABLE 51. Permanent Celibacy in Ireland and England and Wales, 1841–1966.

	Percentage Single Among Persons Aged 45–54 Years			
	Males		Females	
Year	Ireland	England and Wales	Ireland	England and Wales
1841 [a]	10	NA	12	NA
1851	12	12	11	12
1861	14	10	14	12
1871	16	10	15	12
1881	16	10	16	12
1891	20	10	17	12
1901	24	11	20	14
1911	29	12	24	16
1921	NA	12	NA	16
1926	31	NA	24	NA
1931	NA	11	NA	16
1936	34	NA	25	NA
1946	32	NA	26	NA
1951	31	9	26	15
1961	30	9	23	11
1966	29	9	21	9

SOURCES: Censuses of Population of Ireland, 1946 and 1951, "General Report," Table 32, p. 51; 1966, Vol. II, Table VII, p. xii; Census of England and Wales, 1931, "General Tables," Table 23D, p. 155; 1961, "Age, Marital Condition and General Tables," Table 12, pp. 33–34; United Nations, Demographic Yearbook, 1968, Table 7, p. 263.
([a]) Age-Group 46–55 years.

As in the case of postponed marriage, by the 1930s there would have been some European countries with more permanent celibacy among males, and several European countries with more female permanent celibacy, than in Ireland if the Irish rates had remained at the 1871 level. The unusually high degree of permanent celibacy in Ireland during the first half of the present century was not due to the Great Famine of the late 1840s, but rather to increases which took place after the 1870s.

In order to understand the distinctive trend in Irish marriage patterns over the past 125 years or so, a knowledge of Irish emigration patterns is required, for two basic reasons. First, both emigration from Ireland and remaining single in Ireland were considered by many persons as alternative solutions to the underlying problem of obtaining a certain minimum desired standard of living. Second, trends in Irish emigration and the character of this emigration account for some features of Irish marriage patterns, particularly the greater celibacy of Irish males than females. Because of the great amount of speculation about the possible reasons for the high rates of postponed marriage and permanent celibacy in Ireland, I have attempted to verify those various arguments which lent themselves to a statistical treatment. This approach, while necessary, has made this chapter more complex than it otherwise would have been. One such argument, that Irish Catholicism accounts for the Irish marriage patterns, is developed in detail because it seems to be so widely accepted. My own belief is that the special character of present-day Irish Catholicism is the result, and not the cause, of a high proportion of single persons in the Irish population.*

Irish Catholicism and Remaining Single

It has been argued that some unusual features of Irish Catholicism are in some way responsible for the high rates of Irish postponed marriage and permanent celibacy. The Irish are said to have a greater reverence than other Europeans for priests, monks, and nuns, a respect which becomes a veneration of the celibate way of life: "Another factor tending to deepen and extend the wholesale practice of celibacy in Ireland is the enormous reverence for the priesthood and the religious life which obtains among the Irish. It is without parallel anywhere on earth. . . . With veneration for the religious life comes unwittingly but inevitably veneration for the celibate state, with which the religious life in the Catholic West is always associated."[1]

* The way rural Irish values on late marriage permeated the Irish Catholic priesthood is extensively discussed in K. H. Connell, "Catholicism and Marriage in the Century after the Famine," *Irish Peasant Society*, pp. 113–161.

Another point sometimes made is to assume that sex is immoral, and then to claim that a high proportion of Irish never marry because the Irish are more moral than other people: "In their adherence to a high personal code of morality, the Irish, both Catholic and Protestant, reach standards which are almost without compare anywhere in the world. The numbers who enter the religious life, and the numbers of lay people who remain celibate throughout their lives, are remarkably high."[2]

These two arguments, however, are actually rationalizations of the high rate of Irish celibacy put forth by Irish lay Catholics. Neither argument represents official Catholic doctrine in Ireland because there, as in other Catholic countries, the Church encourages marriage among lay persons. The Church does not consider sexual union within marriage sinful, and during the nineteenth century early marriage was encouraged by the Church as a deterrent to immorality.[3] The sexual puritanism for which Irish Catholicism is known today is actually a very strong emphasis on the dangers of sex among unmarried persons. As Sean O'Faolain described his upbringing: "Since my boyhood I have heard my elders fulminating about keeping company, night courting, dancing at the crossroads, V necks, silk stockings, late dances, drinking at dances, mixed bathing, advertisements for feminine underwear, jitterbugging, girls who take part in immodest sports (such as jumping or hurdling), English and American books and magazines, short frocks, Bikinis, cycling shorts, and even waltzing, which I have heard elegantly described as 'belly-to-belly dancing.' "[4]

As increasingly greater proportions of persons ignored church encouragement to marry, priests feared the result would be a relaxation of sexual morality, and "The Church thunder[ed] against the dangers of sex."[5] Single persons accepted the puritanism of their clergy because it helped them to avoid emotional involvements which might lead to marriage: "The temptations that years of celibacy imposed on [the unmarried Irish] could obviously only be resisted with the help of a powerful moral code; priests felt it necessary to push sexual license to the head of the ordinary sins against which they preached; and also to seek in every possible way to remove the occasion of sin, such as mixed gatherings for dancing or other relaxations, which elsewhere would have been thought innocent enough."[6]

In spite of the official encouragement of marriage, some persons believe that other aspects of Catholic practice in Ireland contributed to the high proportions of single persons in the population. Irish persons may have been reluctant to marry because divorce is not possible in Ireland, and, in fact, the Irish Constitution states that no laws making divorce possible shall be passed.[7] Because Catholic teaching as well as the Irish Constitution prefers married women not to work outside their homes,[8] marriages which might otherwise have taken place do not occur for financial reasons (a matter which will be taken up again in the discussion of the standard-of-living explanation of Irish celibacy). Distribution of birth control materials is against the Irish civil law and forbidden by Catholic doctrine, so some Irish Catholics may have accepted late marriage or none at all in order to avoid the burden of raising the large families expected of them if they married. Late marriage as a means of family planning was not entirely moral, however, according to the Catholic Bishop of Cork, the Most Reverend Dr. C. Lucey: "Late marriage, particularly if so late as to entail a small family or none at all, is undesirable and in a very real sense unnatural as a population practice."[9]

Explanations of Irish celibacy which are based on the character of Irish Catholicism do not account for the high proportions of single persons among Irish non-Catholics. For example, it is not possible to explain the high rate of non-Catholic celibacy by referring to a reluctance to use birth control because Irish non-Catholics did use birth control and did have small families.* Yet in spite of this, there were only small differences in marital status by religion in Ireland, especially when the Irish rates are compared to the national rates for persons in other European countries

---

* In 1946 marital fertility among non-Catholics was about 36 per cent lower than for Catholics: per 1,000 married women aged 15–44 years in 1946, there were 801 children aged 0–4 years among non-Catholics and 1,244 among Catholics; Census Population of Ireland, 1946 and 1951, "General Report," p. 169. Between 1926 and 1961 the Protestant child-woman ratio was from 60 to 75 per cent that of the Catholic; Table 6E, Chapter VI, "Protestant Emigration." For other measures of fertility by religion, see Chapter Eight.

TABLE 52. Percentage Single Among Persons Aged 25–29 Years and 45–54 Years by Sex and Religion, Ireland, 1946 and 1961.*

Sex and	Age-Group in Years			
	25–29		45–54	
Religion	1946	1961	1946	1961
Male				
Catholic	80	67	32	30
Non-Catholic	78	67	29	25
Female				
Catholic	59	46	25	23
Non-Catholic	52	39	29	23

sources: Censuses of Population of Ireland, 1946, Vol. III, Part I, Table 11D, p. 37; 1961, Vol. VII, Part I, Tables 9B, 9C, pp. 37, 38.
* Only two censuses published cross-tabulations of religion with marital status: 1946 and 1961. There may have been greater differences between the two religions before 1946, but there is little reason to believe so, judging from the proportion single among persons aged 45–54 years in 1946 by religion.

(Tables 48, 49, and 52). In fact, permanent celibacy was greater among non-Catholic than Catholic females in 1946. If non-Catholic marriage patterns cannot be explained by referring to a reluctance to become responsible for large families, then how important was this factor in explaining the celibacy rates of Catholics in Ireland? If non-Catholics had other reasons for remaining single — reasons which overcame the fact that they could have small families if they wished — then might Catholics also share these reasons?

The impact of Irish Catholicism on postponed marriage and permanent celibacy cannot be measured statistically. But at the very least we can conclude at this point that much is left unexplained by such an argument: the rise in postponed marriage after the Great Famine of the 1840s; the second rise after the 1870s; the increasingly greater discrepancy between the sexes in permanent celibacy after the 1880s; and the recent declines in both postponed marriage and permanent celibacy. Some other forces must have been at work. I believe that such forces involved the material and social ambitions of the Irish in much the same way that such aspirations in other European countries also resulted in postponed marriage.

The Standard-of-Living Thesis

The rise in Irish celibacy after 1871 was but one example of the more general change in northwest European marriage patterns at this time as persons became increasingly aware of the link between marriage and personal living standards. In England the proportion single among men aged 25 to 34 went up from 32 to 38 per cent between 1881 and 1911 before declining, while the proportion single among English women in the same age-group increased from 29 to 36 per cent during the same period (Table 50). While English males did not adopt permanent celibacy to any degree, the proportion single among older English women began to rise in the 1890s and amounted to 16 per cent between 1911 and 1931 (Table 51).

A convincing argument has been made that the change in English marital patterns after the 1870s was due to rising material aspirations among the English.* There were two basic reasons to postpone marriage under the standard-of-living argument: by not taking on the burden of supporting a wife and children a person could use his entire income to provide a higher personal standard of living for himself; and by not marrying until finding a spouse of higher social status one could improve one's status and standard of living. In other words, two common reasons for marriage (gratification of the sex urge and the desire to have children), were subordinated to the desire to maintain or to achieve a certain minimum standard of living and social status. Postponement of marriage and reductions in fertility first appeared among the urban, upper-middle classes in England, then were adopted by the middle classes, and in the first two decades of the present century by the working classes. The crucial element in the standard-of-

* J. A. Banks, *Prosperity and Parenthood*. An extensive discussion of the links between delayed marriage, celibacy, and rising standards of living is found in D. E. C. Eversley, *Social Theories of Fertility and the Malthusian Debate*. While stating that the consensus of modern opinion can be summarized under the standard-of-living theory, and that this theory describes past conditions in Western countries, Eversley cautions against treating it as some sort of "natural law" which will automatically be relevant to other countries or even to European countries in the future (pp. 283–84).

living thesis is the aspirations of a social class: "As its income level goes up, its hope for greater wealth goes up faster. When a middle-class woman says she cannot 'afford' another child while women with much lower incomes can and do, the difference obviously does not lie in the cost of subsistence or even of comforts."[10]

Concerns with material and social aspirations among the Irish are commonly given as explanations of postponed marriage. For rural Ireland, Arensberg and Kimball commented, "instances of families of brothers and sisters who stuck together celibate until old age, are more often examples of the force of failure to find a mate of acceptable status than of any other cause."[11] About Dublin in the early 1950s Humphreys wrote, "considerations of social advancement on the part of both boys and girls effectively and increasingly operate, according to the testimony of the New Dubliners, to delay marriage on all levels except among the poorer laborers."[12] About young Irish persons generally, Sean O'Faolain summed up, "All our young people are developing a proper concept of what constitutes decent living conditions, and until they get them they are on strike against marriage."[13]

Under the standard-of-living argument, an increase in the desired minimum standard of living should lead to an increase in postponed marriage and permanent celibacy. Between 1841 and 1851 the minimum acceptable standard of living rose in rural Ireland (where four out of five Irish persons lived) with the widespread rejection of the way of life available to those trying to support a family on less than five acres of land.[14] Persons who might have married and begun such a life were increasingly unwilling to do so because they had three acceptable alternatives. They could remain in an unmarried status on the farm of a relative whom they assisted; they could work a small holding alone and thus keep all of the holding's income for their own personal use rather than sharing it with a wife and children; or they could emigrate. During and after the 1840s, millions did choose to emigrate. But millions remained and among these, hundreds of thousands decided to postpone marriage in order to maintain what social status they had, or to try to improve their status.[15] Between 1841 and 1851 the proportion single among persons in their late twenties and early thirties rose from 43 to 61 per cent among males, and from 28 to 39 per cent among females (Table 50).

The standard-of-living thesis might explain changing trends in postponed marriage but it leaves some fundamental questions unanswered. Why should persons place economic or social status aspirations above becoming married and having children? Why the willingness to give priority to economic concerns over familial concerns? Why should increased living standards lead to still higher aspirations when a seemingly more reasonable reaction would be to use the new-found wealth to marry earlier and have larger families? The answers to these questions require a knowledge of the links between the family as a social institution and the economy. In most of Western Europe the family was organized to prevent the fragmentation of agricultural holdings from generation to generation. To maintain the size of the holding only one child in each generation was permitted to marry and produce the next generation. This family type is commonly called the "stem family system" and contrasts with the "joint family system" of countries such as China, where members of the family traditionally held property in common.[16]

The Stem Family System

The essential feature of the stem family system, for our concerns, was the practice of allowing only one child in each generation to inherit the family holding, marry, and produce the next generation. In the case of Ireland, "inheritance" of the family holding did not necessarily mean actually owning the land, because this was not possible for most Catholic farmers until after the beginning of the present century. Thus the term means inheriting the right to become the tenant farmer who worked a certain piece of land, either through local custom or by taking over the lease from the landlord (if the landlord were willing). There are many variations of the stem family system based primarily on sibling birth order and sex. Primogeniture is an excellent example of the stem family system where the eldest child, usually the eldest son, becomes heir to the entire wealth of the family. While this probably was the desired pattern for many Irish families, other considerations sometimes favored the youngest son. He would be the last to reach adulthood and, all other things being equal, the most likely to still be on the home farm when the transfer of control passed from the parents either through old age or death. Daughters also were eligible for inheritance, and when no sons had been born in a family or when no sons acceptable to the parents had remained on the home farm, a daughter usually became the heir.

Regardless of the variations of the stem family system, the demographic consequences were essentially the same. The custom of only two children per family being permitted to marry locally under stable agricultural conditions (the one who inherited and the one who married a neighbor's heir) resulted in some siblings who never married and hence never became part of the legitimate child-bearing population. These persons did not marry because they could not support a family *at the same level of living* which they shared as a member of a landholding family. If they left the family farm and married without the means of supporting a family they became landless laborers and were considered downwardly mobile. In more general terms, we can say that the stem family system resulted in a willingness to place economic considerations over desires for universal marriage and childbearing, and in a tolerance of never-married adults in all age-groups with no implication of individual sexual deviance.

As the stem family system worked in pre-industrial European societies, it usually had a third demographic impact — a relatively late age of marriage among those who eventually did marry. The heir generally could not marry until his or her parents gave up control of the family holding, and often this transfer of status did not take place until the death of the father was imminent. By that time the inheriting son or daughter was in his or her late twenties or even early thirties, and the average age-gap between generations was about 30 years rather than the 20 years or so of the joint family system. This third feature of the stem family system would, like the acceptance of permanent celibacy for some individuals, yield a lower crude birth rate than that of another society with the same completed family size but with universal and early marriage.

Under the stem family system an increase in productivity *per acre* can result in lowered ages at marriage and reduced proportions of single persons in the population. With each acre producing more wealth, fewer acres would be needed to provide the level of wealth previously considered acceptable for supporting a family. A holding could be divided in order to permit more siblings to marry. On the other hand, an increase in productivity *per agricultural worker* can result in increased ages at marriage and higher proportions of single persons if such techniques permit a single family to work a larger holding. Pressures would be strong to consolidate smaller farms into larger units on which the new labor-saving techniques could be profitably utilized; and under the stem family system such consolidations usually took place through the marriage contract. Consolidation of family holdings increased the proportion of unmarried adults since only one child per family, rather than two, would be able to marry locally; and it also increased the average age at marriage because of the greater difficulty of finding a marriage partner who controlled (or would soon inherit control of) a farm suitable for consolidation in terms of location, access, terrain, and existing capital improvements.

The Standard-of-Living and Stem-Family Synthesis

By systematically combining the main points of both explanations, an argument can be presented which accounts for the general willingness of persons to place economic over familial concerns (the stem family), and for changes in the intensity of this willingness (changing desired living standards). Such a synthesis is necessary for understanding Irish marriage behavior because the stem family alone cannot account for changes over time, and the standard-of-living thesis does not explain why persons should be willing to forgo marriage and parenthood for material aspirations. The introduction of the potato in Ireland in the eighteenth century greatly increased productivity per acre, and with no change in either material aspirations or in the family system, more and earlier marriages would have been expected. Pre-potato family holdings at first could be divided into smaller, more numerous units without lowering the previously accepted standard of living. The process could not go on forever, however, and was limited by the increased productivity per acre which the new potato cultivation produced. The fact that almost half of the Irish rural population in 1841 had less than the desired size of holding (about ten acres), indicates that the subdivision process had gone too far. Large scale emigration had begun before 1841 and there is some evidence that the age of marriage was beginning to increase.[17]

When the way of life provided by holdings of less than five acres was rejected between 1841 and 1851, and when the previously "middle-class' manual farmers suddenly found themselves the new "lower class," the stage was set for higher rates of postponed marriage. With no additional land available to enlarge holdings, the consolidation of holdings into farms of "adequate" size could take place in only two ways: land vacated through abandonment, death, or eviction could be added to existing holdings; and two small farms could be merged into a more acceptable holding through the arranged marriage of the respective heirs.*

The desire to maintain and, if possible, to enlarge the family holding explains why the unmarried assisting relatives could not marry as long as they remained on the home farm. Assuming that the home farm was just large enough to support one household at a time (including the unmarried assisting relatives) at the expected minimum standard of living, then if one of the unmarried relatives married and set up a second household on the same farm, he would be in effect reducing the standard of living of the other persons dependent on the holding to a level below the acceptable minimum. Except for the heir, if one wished to marry, one was thus required to leave the home farm and establish himself elsewhere, either as a landless farm laborer (an unacceptable reduction in social status to most Irish farmers) or in another country after emigration (an alternative which held out the hope of an increase in living standards and social status). The resurgence of this type of inheritance system (one heir per holding) did not cause the permanent celibacy of the assisting relatives or the emigration of those who were unwilling to remain single; it was merely the way in which the rural Irish attempted to achieve the new minimum standard of living given the scarcity of land: "if there are more

---

* "This unaccustomed scarcity of land [after the 1845–48 famine] is, I think, the most powerful of the forces which tended, in succeeding decades, to disseminate the 'arranged marriage.' " Connell, "Marriage in Ireland after the Famine," p. 89.

heirs than can be accommodated at the expected standard of living with the land available, no inheritance system can itself alter this fact."[18]

We are now in a position to understand why it was so difficult for the inheriting son to find an "acceptable" mate if many of his brothers and sister chose to remain in an unmarried status on the home farm. The farm may have been large enough when they were children to support their parents and themselves. But now that they were grown, more land would be required to support them in addition to the new bride and the expected offspring. A bride would have to bring with her, in fact, enough land to support herself and her expected children, since nothing could be taken from the existing home farm without reducing the standard of living of the unmarried assisting relatives. Although the additional land did not have to be contiguous, it did need to be within a reasonable distance of the home farm. But within this restricted area, there were few farmers who had only one daughter and no sons remaining on the home farm. Furthermore, such a daughter would not be able to inherit her parents' holding until after they both had died; a wait which might bring her near the end of her childbearing years and thus reduce her attractiveness as a mate able to produce the male heir necessary to ensure continued family control of the holding. Small wonder few families in this situation found what they were looking for: a relatively young woman in the immediate neighborhood who was already in sole control of perhaps as much land as the family already held. And even if such a person did exist, it was doubtful whether she would want to marry a person who was burdened by the support of unmarried assisting relatives. To her this would be a reduction in standard of living and social status. The mate she desired was, in all probability, someone like herself, a person in the immediate neighborhood who was already in sole control of his family holding (and preferably a larger holding than her own).

As was pointed out in Chapter Five, the distribution of holdings by size of farm indicates that the consolidation of holdings became a very gradual process between 1851 and 1901 after the sudden changes of the 1841–51 decade (Table 26). Insofar as the consolidation of holdings was relevant to the rate of Irish postponed marriage, we would also expect little change in postponed marriage during this time. Indeed, this is what happened for two decades after 1851. The proportion single among males aged 25–34 years increased from 43 to 61 per cent between 1841 and 1851 but decreased to 57 per cent in 1871; among females in the same age-group, the figure increased from 28 to 39 per cent during the decade of the 1840s, and decreased to 38 per cent in 1871 (Table 50). Because there was only a gradual change in the consolidation of holdings after the 1870s, however, this factor cannot explain the second rise in Irish celibacy which took place between 1871 and 1911.

The rise in celibacy among Irish rural residents during the 1840s fits very well with the increase in desired standards of living brought about by the adoption of agricultural labor-saving techniques. But what of urban residents? When Irish peasants adopted higher expected standards of living, then other classes of persons, whose relative social status was judged in comparison with the way of life of the peasant, would have to have raised their minimum acceptable standards in order to have remained distinct from the peasant class. At first it might have been simply an effort by unskilled urban workers to remain equal with the peasants; then the skilled urban workers would have raised their minimum to keep from being mistaken for persons of lower status; and so on up the class structure. If Ireland had been rapidly industrializing and if both living standards and opportunities for social mobility had been increasing, then such a process would not necessarily have to lead to more postponed marriage and permanent celibacy. But the anomalous decline in the Irish urban population between 1851 and 1891 (Appendix Table 3) meant that there were *fewer* urban jobs each year; it was not only extremely difficult to rise in social status, it was a problem to maintain the same social status as one's father. The religious discrimination of Protestant employers and managers against their Catholic workers also meant that it was especially difficult for Catholics, the great majority of the popultion, to realize their expectations. In such a situation postponing marriage and remaining permanently single were the two easiest ways of maintaining available income for one's own personal consumption. Also, if urban workers were unwilling to marry someone of equal or lower status in hopes of rising socially through marriage, then they, like the rural farmers with unmarried assisting relatives, would want a mate who, in all probability, would not wish to marry them.

The increased willingness of the inheriting son to postpone marriage until his father had either died or relinquished the family holding through old age makes the fathers' expected length of life a matter of importance. As Patrick Noonan commented: "There are certain customs inherent in the Irish way of family life which impede early marriage. Chief among these is the custom by which the parents retain the ownership and administration of their property even into the seventies and eighties. Only the grave will terminate their rule. . . . Normally [the heir] abandons all prospects of marriage until they are laid to rest."[19]

If fathers lived longer after the 1840s than before, then the sons would have a longer wait. In this way an increase in life expectancy would result in an increase in postponed marriage, assuming other factors remain unchanged: "Marriage is unusually late because the son has reached his thirties before his father dies or is willing to pass on his land to him. A century or more ago fathers aged more rapidly: they died, or yielded control of their farms at a sufficiently early age for the sons who succeeded them to marry young."[20]

If we take the expectation of life of men in their forties to represent the situation of the fathers, then the inheriting sons would have had to wait an average of six years longer in 1871 than in 1841, assuming the figures for length of life are comparable.* But even though this factor probably explains part of the rise in the average age of marriage immediately after the 1840s, it is not necessarily relevant to subsequent increases in the rate of postponed marriage. First of all, if marriage is later, then the age-gap between fathers and sons is greater and one factor may cancel the

---

* The expectation of life for rural men aged 40 was 23 years in 1841; for all men aged 45 it was 24 years in 1870–72 (note the five-year difference in the age at which the expectation of life was calculated). The 1841 figure refers to the whole of Ireland (32 Counties), and the 1870–72 figure refers to the 26 Counties of present-day Ireland. *Censuses of Population of Ireland, 1841,* "Report," pp. lxxx-lxxxiii; *1946 and 1951,* "General Report," Table 51, p. 68.

other. Secondly, although the Irish inheritance system after the 1840s was one heir per farm, the heir did not necessarily have to be the first-born son. On some Irish farms the parents chose the youngest son as heir. The most important weakness in this explanation of Irish postponed marriage is that it does not apply to the increase in celibacy at the close of the nineteenth century. While the average number of years of life left to men at age 45 remained unchanged at 24 years between 1871 and 1901,[21] the proportion single among men aged 25–34 went up from 57 to 72 per cent (Table 50).

It might be thought that changes in Irish land laws after the 1870s contributed to the rise in the number of persons willing to remain on the home farm in hope of inheriting. The added security brought by ownership of land also could have meant that there were proportionately more persons willing to remain on the home farm as unmarried assisting relatives. But the marriage pattern began to change about two decades *before* a significant proportion of farmers owned their own farms: by 1895 only 12 per cent of all holdings were being worked by farmers who owned them (this figure rose to 64 per cent by 1921).[22] Changing land laws could not have initiated the second period of change in marital status; at most they contributed to the trend and made the rates higher than they otherwise would have been.

After the formation of present-day Ireland in 1921, much more detailed information about marital status began to be published in the various census volumes. For example, the 1926 Census was the first to cross-classify marital status by age and sex, with occupation. Issues which were previously matters of speculation could now be studied directly. One such possibility was that the high Irish rates of celibacy may have been due to a high proportion of priests, monks, and nuns in the Irish population. This particular point, however, did not account for very many of the *permanently single* in Ireland. In 1926 only 2.0 per cent of all single males aged 45–54 were priests and monks, and 4.9 per cent of all single females in the same age-group were nuns, postulates, and lay sisters.[23] Whether or not the proportions themselves were high compared with other Catholic countries is less important than the fact that the celibacy of about 98 per cent of the single men and about 95 per cent of the single women in this age-group in Ireland in 1926 could not be explained by saying they were religious personnel.

Another matter on which data first became available in the 1926 Census is the proportion of married women who worked outside their homes. As I have already mentioned, Catholic doctrine was strongly opposed to married women working and this could be a factor preventing marriages which might otherwise have taken place except for financial considerations. But when the facts themselves are considered, another perhaps even more important matter becomes apparent. Even though there was a strong social norm against married women working (about one in twenty Irish wives were employed outside their homes between 1926 and 1966), there was no such restriction on single women working (about two-thirds or more of younger and about half or more of older single women were employed, Table 53). If few single women worked outside the homes of their parents, then it would matter less that few married women worked because in this situation marriage would mean independence from parental authority and the attainment of adult status. But in Ireland the majority of single women were employed outside the home and if they were not satisfied with conditions at home they could simply move out and rent a room. It was the combination of a permissive attitude toward single women working and a restrictive attitude toward married women working which increased the reasons for remaining single. For the majority of single persons in Ireland, marriage meant two adults living together on one income where two had been living separately on two incomes; other things being equal this would immediately reduce their standard of living.

Was one considered a good Catholic when one postponed marriage in order to enjoy the independence and higher living standards possible through keeping one's income to oneself? Not according to Bishop Lucey: "In general, it may be said that those who remain single through selfishness, or through over anxiety about the future, or for any other such reason — for instance, the woman who does not want to give up her independence or her job, or the man who does not want the burden of supporting a home — are failing in their duty to God, themselves, and the race."[24]

TABLE 53. Percentage Occupied by Marital Status and Sex Among Persons Aged 25–29 Years and 45–54 Years, Ireland, 1926, 1946, and 1966.*

Marital Status and Year	Age Group in Years			
	25–29		45–54	
	Males	Females	Males	Females
Single				
1926	97	63	91	48
1946	97	69	91	49
1966	95	84	92	60
Married				
1926	98	6	97	6
1946	98	5	98	6
1966	99	6	99	6
Widowed				
1926	97	46	96	55
1946	96	36	95	45
1966	98	46	95	44

SOURCES: *Censuses of Population of Ireland, 1926,* Vol. V, Part II, Tables 1A, 1B, pp. 3, 5; *1946,* Vol. V, Part II, Tables 1A, 1B, pp. 3, 5; *1966,* Vol. V, Tables 1A, 1B, pp. 4, 9.

* Percentage occupied is defined as "All persons described on the Census schedules as following an occupation, whether employed or unemployed at the date of the Census."

In spite of this admonition, single women in Ireland made no secret of why they postponed marriage. About middle-class Dublin women in the early 1950s, an observer (himself a Catholic priest) was able to conclude: "The refusal to start marriage at a lower level than that to which she is accustomed, the refusal to forgo the material advantages and enjoyment her wages and her liberty bring her, the need to save to buy a home — all these are as prevalent among clerical girls as among artisans. So is the desire to improve her social position by marriage."[25]

One reason why many Irish ignored their church's teaching about early marriage, while they accepted their church's norm against married women working, was that there were other social and cultural motives which reinforced the restriction of married women to their homes. Many Irish feel that a working wife is an indication of the failure of the husband to provide a standard of living acceptable to his family. Also the slow economic development of Ireland has resulted in a belief that the limited number of available jobs should go to married men first, then single men, widows, single women, and last of all to married women whose husbands are able to work. Concerning women working while married, especially if the women have children, the Irish attitude was much like that of other European peoples and was not a special feature of Irish Catholicism.

Another matter which the post-1921 data permit us to examine is the change in permanent celibacy by size of farm among male farmers. Under the standard-of-living and stem-family argument, the smaller the holding the higher should be the proportion single among older farmers. In 1926 the proportion single among male farmers aged 45 to 54 years was highest for those with holdings of less than 15 acres, but for farmers with larger holdings there was little difference in degree of permanent celibacy (Table 54). Apparently persons in these cohorts in 1926 considered marriage when they possessed a holding of at least 15 acres — the size generally large enough to support a family using the techniques of manual agriculture. Twenty years later the situation changed and the proportion single increased regularly with each smaller farm size. In 1946 there were three broad groups of farmers: those with 200 acres or more who had an average of 19 per cent permanent celibacy; those with from 30 to 200 acres among whom the proportion single ranged from 24 to 27 per cent; and those with less than 30 acres among whom not quite one-third were single. At this time at least 30 acres generally were needed to use animal-powered machines, and persons in this cohort had been less willing to marry without at least 30 acres, compared with cohorts who were twenty years older. And indication of the increased reluctance of the smaller farmers to marry is the fact that in 1946 their degree of singleness was the same or higher than the average for all occupied men, while in 1926 it had been much lower, even among farmers with less than 15 acres.

By 1966 the trends had become much more extreme, and the importance of farm size on the willingness of the farmer to marry (or his success in attracting a mate), was even more important. Among older farmers with less than 30 acres the degree of bachelorhood about doubled between 1926 and 1966, while only among those with at least 100 acres did the proportion single decline between 1946 and 1966. Among farmers with 50 acres or less, the proportion single was greater than the average for all occupied men in 1966. I believe that the increased reluctance of farmers on the smaller farms to marry reflects the increase in the desired "minimum" farm size to at least 50 acres after the widespread adoption of modern agricultural machinery during the 1950s (Chapter Five).

The change in the proportion single among male farmers aged 25–29 years suggests not only that 100 acres might be con-

TABLE 54. Percentage Single Among Male Farmers Aged 25–29 Years and 45–54 Years by Size of Holding, Ireland, 1926, 1946, and 1966.

| Size of Holding in Acres | Age Group in Years | | | | | |
| | 25–29 | | | 45–54 | | |
	1926	1946	1966	1926	1946	1966
200 and over	65	60	44	20	19	18
100 to 200	65	61	53	19	24	23
50 to 100	65	61	63	18	25	27
30 to 50	63	64	67	18	27	33
15 to 30	66	66	71	20	31	39
1 to 15	64	70	71	23	33	42
All male farmers	65	66	65	20	28	33
All occupied men	80	80	57	30	31	28

SOURCES: *Censuses of Population of Ireland, 1926*, Vol. V, Part II, Tables 3A, 6A, 8, pp. 8, 46, 60–64; *1946*, Vol. V, Part II, Tables 3A, 4A, pp. 8, 10–12; *1966*, Vol. V, Tables 1A, 2A, pp. 5, 10.

sidered the new "minimum" to support a wife and family in the near future, but also that the rates of permanent celibacy among men with less than 30 acres will rise to unusually high levels. (Changes in the proportion single among male farmers aged 25–29 do not necessarily represent changes in postponed marriage, because persons who will become farmers usually do their waiting as farmers' assisting sons.) Between 1926 and 1966, the proportion single among these young men declined for those with at least 100 acres, changed but little for those with 50 to 100 acres, and increased for those with less than 50 acres. The proportion single was less than that of all occupied men only for those young farmers with 100 acres or more.

In order to understand the increasingly higher rates of celibacy among smaller farmers in Ireland the selective effect of migration must be considered. Persons who were most dissatisfied with such a way of life did not wait to inherit the home farm but left Ireland for a new life abroad. Those who remained accepted more than the relatively lower standard of living for themselves; they also accepted the possibility that they would not be able to succeed in attracting a female who was willing to accept the standard of living they were able to provide. The element of selective migration generally, and the fact that emigration was at all times an alternative to remaining single in Ireland, calls for a separate discussion of the links between emigration and marriage in Ireland.

Emigration and Marriage

Several writers have argued that Ireland's historically high rates of emigration contributed to the high Irish rates of postponed marriage and permanent celibacy. Perhaps the first person to specifically state the connection was C. H. Oldham, who wrote in 1913: "the young people in the rural parts are all intending migrants: they never think of marrying so long as they still hope to be able to emigrate."[26] Marriage effectively reduced the opportunity for emigration not only because one's spouse might not want to emigrate, or because the cost of passage was higher for a family, but also because of a feeling that the risk of failure after emigration had best be borne alone. It was in this way that indecision about whether to emigrate reinforced the already existing reasons for remaining single under the standard-of-living and stem-family argument.

It is important to distinguish individual indecision about whether to emigrate or to marry from the aggregate effect of high rates of emigration and postponed marriage at the national level. Because there were proportionately more single than married persons among all emigrants, an increase in the rate of emigration would result in a decrease in the proportion of single persons remaining in the population, all other things being equal. Conversely, if the reasons for remaining single in Ireland remained unchanged, then a reduction in the rate of emigration would result in an increase in the proportion of single persons in the population, again assuming all other things remain equal. This pattern explains, I believe, the generally inverse relationship between national rates of postponed marriage and net emigration between the 1890s and the 1950s (Table 50, Appendix Table 2). As rates of emigration fell from 12 emigrants per 1,000 population per year in the 1890s to about 6 per year between 1926 and 1946, the proportion single in the population increased. Postponed marriage measured in terms of the proportion single among persons aged 25–34 years increased between 1891 and 1936 from 67 to 74 per cent for males, and from 48 to 55 per cent for females. During the same period permanent celibacy, the proportion single among persons aged 45–54 years, increased from 20 to 34 per cent for males, and from 17 to 25 per cent for females.

At the individual level the reasons for the decrease in emigration and the increase in postponed marriage were seen in a specific historic context. On the positive side, the attractiveness of emigration declined after the 1890s with the achievement of land reform around the turn of the century and the coming of Irish independence soon after World War I; on the negative side were the reduction in employment opportunities in the United States and in England during the Great Depression of the 1930s and the uncertainty about the future during World War II. Emigration became a less attractive alternative, but for those who remained in Ireland the reasons for remaining single had not changed. Many persons postponed both emigration and marriage during the 1930s and early 1940s while hoping for things to get better. After World War II, the situation did improve for thousands in rural Ireland with the adoption of modern agricultural techniques, but the new techniques required larger holdings. Given the already extremely high levels of postponed marriage, further postponement of marriage was unlikely. The stage had been set for a return to increased rates of emigration. By the late 1940s the main stream of emigration had shifted from the United States to Britain, and the act of emigration was no longer so permanent nor so painful as it had been before the 1920s. During the 1950s and 1960s Britain also became a more attractive destination because of the reduction in British discrimination against the Irish and a widening of employment opportunities for them there.

The increase in emigration during the 1950s resulted in a decline in the proportion of young single persons in the Irish population. The average annual rate of net emigration was about 14 per 1,000 between 1951 and 1961, compared to about 8 between 1946 and 1951 and about 6 between 1961 and 1966, (Appendix Table 2). It is reasonable to conclude that the great increase in emigration was mainly responsible for the decline in the proportion single among persons aged 25 to 34 years between 1946 and 1961 (from 70 to 58 per cent for males, and from 48 to 37 per cent for females). First, the average age at marriage declined only slightly during the fifteen-year period from 33 to 31 for males, and from 28 to 27 for females.[27] Part of this decline in the average age at marriage was due to a probable increase in the proportion of persons who marry in Ireland but intend to emigrate immediately, and of persons who have already emigrated but who return to Ireland only for the marriage ceremony. In 1961, 15 per cent of all grooms said their future residence would be outside of Ireland, and the average age of these men was 28 years.[28] Second, the decrease in the number of single persons between 1946 and 1961 was much greater than the increase in the number of married persons in the 25–29 year age group (Table 55).

Because high rates of emigration could be expected to reduce the proportion of single persons in a population from what it otherwise would be, the different rates of emigration by religion

TABLE 55. Marital Status Among Males and Females Aged 25–29 Years, Ireland, 1946 to 1961.

Sex and Marital Status	Number		Change	
	1946	1961	Absolute	Percentage
Male				
Single	82,976	48,547	−34,429	−41
Married	20,932	23,700	+2,768	+13
Widowed	231	42	−189	−82
Total	104,139	72,289	−31,850	−31
Female				
Single	59,808	32,968	−26,840	−45
Married	43,675	39,960	−3,715	−8
Widowed	566	160	−406	−72
Total	104,049	73,088	−30,961	−30

SOURCE: Census of Population of Ireland, 1961, Vol. II, Tables 1B, 1C, pp. 2, 3.

in Ireland should help explain part of the differences by religion in the degree of postponed marriage. Our analysis of this matter is limited to the periods just before the 1946 and the 1961 Censuses, since these were the only two censuses to cross-tabulate religion with marital status for the 26 Counties of present-day Ireland. In 1946 the degree of postponed marriage was somewhat greater for Catholics than for non-Catholics (Table 52), which could be expected from the 40 to 90 per cent greater estimated net emigration of non-Catholics than Catholics between 1936 and 1946 among persons aged 10 to 34 years in 1936 (Table 38). Between 1946 and 1961 the estimated emigration of Catholics was greater than that of Protestants (Table 37), which leads us to expect a greater reduction in the degree of postponed marriage among Catholics than non-Catholics by 1961. This did happen for males, among whom the difference by religion in postponed marriage was reduced from 2 to 0 percentage points; but it was not true for females, among whom a difference of 7 percentage points between Catholics and non-Catholics existed both in 1946 and in 1961, (Table 52). The greater impact of the emigration factor on the degree of postponed marriage among males between 1946 and 1961 may have been due to the slightly greater proportion of males among all emigrants during that period: there were 103 males for every 100 females (calculated from Table 23).

The inverse relationship between emigration and postponed marriage holds only under the assumption that all other conditions were equal, that emigration and late marriage were considered alternative solutions to the problem of achieving or maintaining a certain life style. Although exact emigration data are not available for the 1851 to 1871 period, it is reasonable to conclude that the rate of postponed marriage was relatively constant partly because of the decision of so many single persons to emigrate. Between the 1870s and the 1890s the rate of emigration was roughly constant (from about 12 to 16 emigrants per year per 1,000 persons in the population, Appendix Table 2), perhaps because increasing proportions of persons decided to remain in Ireland in an unmarried status (for example, the proportion single among Irish men aged 45–54 years rose from 16 to 24 per cent between 1871 and 1901, Table 51). But when conditions were unusually severe, as during the 1841–51 decade, it was possible for both emigration and postponed marriage to increase. On the other hand, unusually prosperous conditions could result in a reduction in both emigration and postponed marriage. Between 1961 and 1966 the rate of net emigration was much reduced, as was the degree of postponed marriage. Both no doubt were influenced by the substantial increase in industrial productivity of Irish workers between 1961 and 1966 (using 1953 earnings per week as a base of 100, the income of wage earners in industries producing transportable goods increased from 147 to 215 between 1961 and 1966).[29]

Emigration and Marriage Patterns by Sex

Part of the increase in postponed marriage in Ireland after the 1870s can be explained, as already mentioned, by saying it was one example of a general rise in postponed marriage and permanent celibacy taking place in several European countries at that time. But another factor contributed to the rise of male celibacy in Ireland: the increasingly greater emigration of females than males after about 1881 (see Chapter Four). As discussed in earlier chapters, in terms of relative deprivation rural females had more to gain by going to urban areas in the United States and in England than did rural Irish males. But if the greater female out-migration continued long enough, a time would come when there would not be enough females left in rural Ireland to marry all of the single males even if all of the rural females married. Just when this took place is indicated by a comparison of the number of men per 100 women among single persons in the relevant age-groups.

Because Irish husbands are on an average a few years older than their wives,* the number of single men in the 25–29 year age-group is compared with the number of single women in the next youngest age-group, 20–24 years. Since the percentage single

* The average age of husbands was higher than the average for brides by 5.8 years in 1925–26, 5.1 years in 1945–46, 3.7 years in 1961, and 3.3 years in 1966. Ireland, *Commission on Emigration and other Population Problems, 1948–1954*, "Reports" (Dublin, The Stationery Office), Table 53, p. 69; Ireland, *Report on Vital Statistics, 1964*, Table 11, p. ix; *1966*, Table 11, p. ix.

among persons aged 45–54 years is a measure of permanent celibacy rather than delayed marriage, no adjustment is made for the difference in age at marriage between the sexes. Among older persons there were not enough single women to marry all of the single men in Ireland after 1881, and the shortage of older single females reached peak levels between 1926 and 1936, and then again in 1966 (Table 56). There were always enough single girls available among persons in the younger age groups, but there too the sex ratio rose to a high point during the 1930s.

TABLE 56. Males per 100 Females Among Single Persons in Selected Age-groups, Ireland, 1861–1966.

| Year | Age Group in Years | |
	Males 25–29 Females 20–24	Both Sexes 45–54
1861	59	98
1871	68	96
1881	59	100
1891	65	110
1901	NA[a]	108
1911	NA[a]	125
1926	85	142
1936	90	141
1946	89	128
1961	80	137
1966	65	144

SOURCES: Censuses of Population of Ireland, 1926, Vol. V, Part I, Tables 7A, 7B, pp. 22, 24; 1966, Vol. II, Tables 1B, 1C, pp. 2, 3.
([a]) In 1901 and 1911 the age-group 25–29 years was not tabulated.

The national sex ratios among single persons, helpful as they are for indicating long-term trends, do not show the actual availability of single persons to one another because of the opposite preferences of the sexes for rural or urban areas. Between 1926 and 1966 data were published which permit a breakdown of the overall sex ratios into rural-urban sex ratios (Table 19). Single persons in Ireland were concentrating in areas where they would be more likely to find companionship among other single persons of their own sex than to find a partner for marriage. Once again the shortage of single females was more marked among older than younger persons. In 1961, for example, in rural areas there were 244 single men for every 100 single women among persons aged

45 to 54, compared with 125 single men aged 25–29 years for every 100 single women aged 20 to 24. As early as 1926 there were not enough single older women to marry all of the older single men in rural areas (the sex ratio was 176), while among younger rural persons single women were outnumbered by single men sometime between 1926 and 1936. It should be remembered that these sex ratios among single persons were the result not only of greater female out-migration but also probably of greater male re-migration to rural areas.

The impact of the changing sex ratios in rural and urban areas shows up in the contrasting patterns of postponed marriage and permanent celibacy by sex and rural-urban residence (Table 57). The rural-urban contrast in postponed marriage was much greater for males than for females between 1926 and 1966, reflecting the relative scarceness in rural areas or surplus in urban areas of prospective brides on the one hand, and on the other, the greater willingness of Irish women to marry urban men. The preference of some rural women for urban husbands has been commented on by an Irish sociologist: "The modern country girl is turning away

TABLE 57. Percentage Single Among Persons Aged 25–29 Years and 45–54 Years by Sex and Rural-Urban Residence, Ireland, 1926–66.*

| | Age-group in Years | | | | | | | |
| | 25–29 | | | | 45–54 | | | |
Sex and Year	All Areas	Rural Areas (A)	Urban Areas (B)	Rural Excess (A–B)	All Areas	Rural Areas (A)	Urban Areas (B)	Rural Excess (A–B)
Male								
1926	80	86	68	+18	31	34	25	+9
1936	82	89	71	+18	34	37	25	+12
1946	80	86	68	+18	32	37	23	+14
1961	67	80	54	+26	30	36	20	+16
1966	58	73	46	+27	29	36	19	+17
Female								
1926	62	65	58	+7	24	22	27	−5
1936	64	67	61	+6	25	23	28	−5
1946	58	58	57	+1	26	24	29	−5
1961	45	47	44	+3	23	20	26	−6
1966	38	40	37	+3	21	18	24	−6

SOURCES: *Censuses of Population of Ireland, 1926,* Vol. V, Part I, Table 8, pp. 26, 27, 32–35; *1936,* Vol. V., Part I, Tables 7, 8, pp. 23, 25, 32–35; *1946,* Vol. V, Part I, Tables 9, 10, pp. 33, 35, 44–47; *1961,* Vol. II, Tables 6, 7, pp. 8–13; *1966,* Vol. II, Tables 6, 7, pp. 8–13.

(*) Urban areas include places of 1,500 and more inhabitants.

from the land. The wealth of the prospective husband, although still important, is not so decisive as his personal appearance, his manners, and the kind of home he can provide. She objects to the 'muck and dirt' of the farm life and would prefer to marry a professional man or even a white collar worker."[30]

But regardless of the desires of many rural females for an urban husband, the fact remained that so many rural females migrated to urban areas that there were not enough single urban men available to marry them all. The result was the degree of permanent celibacy among females was higher in urban than in rural areas, at least between 1926 and 1966. The fact that spinsterhood was more characteristic of Irish urban than rural residents needs to be emphasized to counter the general impression that permanent celibacy in Ireland was primarily a rural phenomenon.

It has been said that Ireland's high celibacy rates have contributed to the high Irish rates of emigration.* At first this might appear self-evident; but under the standard-of-living and stem-family argument it becomes clear that emigration and celibacy were alternative solutions to the problem of maintaining a certain desired way of life. Furthermore, if the Irish were emigrating to avoid celibacy, why should more females than males have emigrated from Ireland? The higher rates of celibacy among Irish males should have resulted in greater male than female emigration. It is not possible to explain this by claiming that males are somehow psychologically more suited to a celibate life because there was as much or more permanent celibacy during the 1930s and the 1960s among females as among males in each of the other European countries listed in Table 49 — except Finland in 1930. It is more reasonable to conclude that many Irish males were willing to continue living in rural areas even though they knew there were not enough single women in their area for all of them to find wives; and that many Irish females moved to urban areas, both in Ireland and abroad, to escape living, even in a married state, in Irish rural areas.

* "Ireland's low marriage rate over such a long period has had an unfavorable effect on the outlook of young people, and has contributed to discontent, unsettlement, and emigration." Ireland, *Commission on Emigration*, p. 79.

The decision to remain in an unmarried status in Ireland was a compromise. Emigration offered the greatest chance of realizing material aspirations, but it also involved the greatest personal cost in terms of leaving one's family, friends, and native culture. At the other extreme, marriage, even marriage with the use of birth control, meant the immediate loss of the wife's income and two adults living on one income where two had been living separately on two incomes. If few Irish women worked as single persons, this would not have been very important; but the contrary was true and the majority of young single women were employed (at least between 1926 and 1966). The reluctance to become responsible for any size family, large or small, is probably a major reason why the rates of postponed marriage and permanent celibacy were similar for Catholics and non-Catholics even though the non-Catholics did use birth control and did have smaller families. By remaining single a person could continue to live in Ireland and maintain a standard of living which, while less than that available through emigration, was still acceptable.

There were three periods when the minimum standards of living rose markedly in Ireland: between 1841 and 1851, with the rejection of manually working a holding of less than 5 acres; after the 1870s, with changing land laws, rising nationalism, and as part of the general Western European rise in material aspirations; and after 1946, with the transition in Irish agriculture from horse to modern agricultural techniques, the increased productivity of Irish industrial workers, and the increased prosperity of the United States and Britain. The first two rises in material aspirations resulted in increased proportions of Irish persons choosing to postpone marriage and to remain permanently single. The higher level of aspirations after 1936, however, could not be realized simply by remaining in an unmarried state in Ireland. Only through the alternative of emigration could most Irish persons meet their aspirations, and the greater movement of single than married persons from Ireland after 1946 reduced the proportion of single persons remaining in the population.

Emigration from Ireland or remaining single in Ireland were alternative solutions to the same basic problem of obtaining a respectable adult status. This status was more difficult for females than males to achieve in Ireland because of the female's extremely subordinate role in the rural areas. After the 1880s, the proportion of females among all emigrants during normal times began to increase as more females than males chose emigration as their own personal solution. The surplus of single males remaining in rural Ireland contributed to the higher male rate of permanent celibacy after the 1880s. Compared with other northwest European countries during the 1930s and the 1960s, permanent celibacy was not as unusual for Irish females as it was for Irish males (Table 49).

The arguments made under the standard-of-living and stem-family thesis, and the importance of Irish emigration, explain much about the changes in the amount of postponed marriage and permanent celibacy in Ireland over the last 125 years. This does not mean that there were not other contributing factors. But the other explanation most often heard, that certain features of Irish Catholicism encouraged celibacy among lay Catholics, appears to be mistaken. Although it is difficult to put this hypothesis into a form which can be tested, it appears that a willingness to ignore the teachings of the Catholic Church on marriage increased rather than decreased in Ireland between 1871 and 1926. Furthermore, explanations of Irish celibacy based on special features of Irish Catholicism do not explain the high rates of postponed marriage and permanent celibacy among Irish non-Catholics; and these rates might have been higher except for the generally greater Protestant than Catholic emigration from Ireland since the turn of the century. The Irish Catholic emphasis on the sinfulness of pre-marital sex, I believe is a result rather than a cause of the high proportion of single persons in the Irish population.

CHAPTER VIII

High Marital Fertility

THE standard-of-living thesis explains important aspects of Ireland's high rates of emigration, late ages at marriage, and high proportions of persons who choose never to marry. But advocates of the standard-of-living argument usually falter when confronted with what seems to be the most puzzling element of Irish demography—an unusually high legitimate fertility rate (Table 58). It seems paradoxical that Europe's best example of the standard-of-living thesis for some demographic trends should also be its worst example in the case of marital fertility. Ireland's unusual position cannot be explained simply by referring in general terms to Catholic doctrine on the family because there are other European countries with high proportions of Catholics in their populations which have lower rates of marital fertility. The Irish acceptance of Catholic teachings on the family is, in fact, part of the problem to be explained.

The Irish were able to persist in their high rates of marital fertility because they did not have to face the problems of rapid population growth usually associated with such reproductive behavior. Because the average age of marriage was late and because a large proportion of the population never married, a large number of births per 1,000 married women did not result in a large number of births per 1,000 people in the total population. Of those countries listed in Table 58, the crude birth rates of several were as high or higher than Ireland's. A low crude birth rate has existed in Ireland since the second half of the nineteenth century, when it was one of the lowest in Europe. Comparing Ireland with England, for example, the Irish crude birth rate was the lower of the two until the second decade of the twentieth century (Table 59). Because of Ireland's low crude birth rate, the nation has had a relatively low rate of natural increase — about one per cent or less in each decade of the past 95 years (Appendix Table 2). And even this expected population growth did not materialize because the amount of emigration from Ireland has been greater than the surplus of births less deaths in each inter-censal period since 1841 except 1946–51 and 1961–66 (Appendix Table 1).

This chapter focusses on the fertility of married women not only because it is relatively high but also because the more general measure, the crude birth rate, is an insensitive indicator of fertility given the unusually high proportions of single persons in the Irish population. The marital fertility rate, furthermore, accounts for 96 per cent or more of all births occuring in Ireland in each intercensal period since 1871, because of the low level of reported illegitimacy.[1] The basic sources of information about Irish fertility are data from the registration of births since 1864, and replies to questions asked about marital fertility during the 1841, 1911, 1946, and 1961 Censuses. Even though the first two censuses refer to the 32 Counties and the last two to only the 26 Counties, for my purposes the information is sufficiently comparable.* A more serious difficulty is the fact that the first two Censuses tabulated the information only by area, age of the wife and husband at marriage, and duration of marriage. So for some important points, such as fertility by religion or by occupational group, our only sources of information are the data from the 1946

* In 1841, 1946, and 1961 the questions were asked of all married women, (excluding widows in 1946 and 1961) whether or not their husbands were residing with them at the date of the census. In 1911 the questions were asked only of women aged under 50 years at marriage whose husbands also appeared on the same Census schedule. *Censuses of Population of Ireland, 1841,* "Report," pp. xl, xli; *1911,* "General Report," p. lxiii; *1946 and 1951,* "General Report," pp. 209–210; *1961,* Vol. VIII, p. v.

TABLE 58. Marital Fertility Rate, 1960–64, and Crude Birth Rate, 1961, in Selected Countries.*

Country and Exact Year of Marital Fertility Rate	Number of Legitimate Births per 1,000 Married Women Aged 10–49 Years	Total Number of Births per 1,000 Total Population in 1961
Ireland, 1961	195.5	21.2
New Zealand, 1961	154.6	27.1
Canada, 1961	152.9	26.0
Portugal, 1960	148.9	24.5
Spain, 1960	142.1	21.3
Netherlands, 1963	138.4	21.3
United States, 1960	132.7	23.3
Australia, 1961	131.9	22.8
Poland, 1960	130.1	20.9
Scotland, 1964	124.5	19.5
Finland, 1963	119.8	18.4
France, 1963	118.5	18.2
Switzerland, 1960	117.2	18.1
Austria, 1961	116.4	18.6
Norway, 1960	109.8	17.3
England and Wales, 1964	108.3	17.6
Belgium, 1961	106.3	17.3
Denmark, 1963	103.2	16.6
Sweden, 1963	86.9	13.9

SOURCES: United Nations, *Demographic Yearbook, 1964*, Table 16, pp. 530–35; *1965*, Table 25, pp. 569–73; *1969*, Tables 12, 26, pp. 258–65, 446–49.
* The most recent period for which comparable marital fertility rates for all of the countries listed above are available is 1960–64.

and 1961 Censuses. Because the age of the husband at marriage had practically no effect on fertility among husbands married at under 40 years of age, at least according to the 1946 Census results,[†] the husband's age at marriage will be disregarded and the focus of interest will be on fertility differences taking into account the wife's age at marriage and the duration of marriage.

Between 1871 and 1966 the Irish marital fertility rate declined by 38 per cent (Table 59). While the decline was modest compared with the 65 per cent decrease in English marital fertility over the same period, it was significant because it happened at all.

† After standardizing marriages for the age of the wife at marriage, among marriages of 25 to 29 years duration the average number of children born per family was 4.97 for husbands aged 20 to 24 years at marriage and 4.84 for husbands aged 35 to 39 years at marriage. *Censuses of Population of Ireland, 1946 and 1951*, "General Report," Table 197, p. 216.

The issue is not why the Irish rejected control over marital fertility but rather why the Irish acceptance of fertility control was later and less extensive than that of several other European countries. In other countries the spread of family limitation has been explained not only by the standard-of-living thesis but also by "the breakdown of the family as an economic unit, the growth of urban living, the decline in religious belief, the emancipation of women."[2] In attempting to explain the Irish trends in family limitation these variables must also be accounted for, keeping in mind the persistence of subsistence agriculture in Ireland, the low rate of Irish urbanization, the association of Catholicism with Irish nationalism, and the dominance of the male in Irish society. Due to the complexity of the subject, I shall first discuss the fertility levels and trends to show what actually happened, and then interpret the statistical facts under four broad subjects: the possi-

TABLE 59. Crude Birth Rate and Marital Fertility Rate in Ireland, and in England and Wales, 1871–1966.

| Period | *Average Annual Number of Births per 1,000 Total Average Population* | | *Period or Year* | *Average Number of Legitimate Births per 1,000 Married Women Aged 15–44 Years* | |
	Ireland	*England & Wales*[a]		*Ireland*	*England & Wales*[b]
1871–81	26.2	35.4	1870–72	307	295
1881–91	22.8	32.4	1880–82	284	275
1891–1901	22.1	29.9	1890–92	287	250
1901–11	22.4	26.3	1900–02	292	230
1911–26	21.1	20.1	1910–12	305	191
1926–36	19.6	15.0	1925–27	271	140
1936–46	20.3	15.9	1935–37	256	111
1946–51	22.2	18.0	1945–47	270	129
1951–56	21.3	16.3	1950–52	248	105
1956–61	21.2	17.4	1961	190	97
1961–66	21.9	17.7	1966	190	104

SOURCES: *Statistical Abstract of Ireland, 1950*, Table 7, p. 11; *1968*, Table 7, p. 20; *Censuses of Population of Ireland, 1946 and 1951*, "General Report," Table 199, p. 219; Ireland, *Report on Vital Statistics, 1961*, Tables X, XIII, p. xv, xvii; *1966*, Tables X, XIII, pp. xv, xvii; England and Wales, *Registrar General's Statistical Review, 1964*, Part II, Table C, p. 11.

([a]) For England and Wales the periods or years were: 1871–80, 1881–90, 1891–1900, 1906–10, 1916–20, 1931–35, 1941–45, 1946–50, 1956–60, 1961, and 1966.

([b]) For England and Wales the periods or years were: 1871–75, 1881–90, 1891–1900, 1901–5, 1911–15, 1926, 1936, 1946, 1951, 1960, and 1965.

bility of effective fertility control; Catholic encouragement of large families; fertility and the standard-of-living thesis; and fertility and the Irish family system.

Trends in Marital Fertility

As in the case of crude birth rates, Irish marital fertility has not always been unusually high compared with other European countries. Taking the English as the basis for comparison, during the 1870s and 1880s the Irish marital fertility rates were only 3 to 4 per cent higher (Table 59). After the 1890s, the difference between the two countries widened and by 1911 the Irish rate was 60 per cent higher than the English. Not all of the increasing difference was due to the declining English rate, however, for the Irish rate increased between 1881 and 1911 from 284 to 305. In the section below on fertility and the standard-of-living thesis, this increase in Irish marital fertility at the end of the nineteenth century will be discussed using age-standardized marital fertility rates. For now the point is that Irish marital fertility is high only in a relative sense, and is unusual primarily because it did not decline during the first half of the twentieth century as rapidly as did the marital fertility of most other Western European countries.

The decline in Irish fertility which did occur after 1911 can be precisely analyzed in terms of the age of the wife at marriage and the duration of the marriage due to the detailed data available from the fertility censuses of 1911, 1946, and 1961. The decline was not caused by any change in the fertility of newlyweds because the average number of children born to women married four years or less at the time of the census increased between 1911 and 1961, especially among women in their thirties at the time of marriage (Table 60). One reason for the increase in fertility, especially among older brides, was probably a higher level of fecundity in 1961 than in 1911 because of improved nutrition, better prenatal care, the generally improved social status of females (see Chapter Three), and higher living standards for the population as a whole. The interesting point is that apparently no greater effort was made to control fertility by newlyweds in 1961

TABLE 60. Average Number of Children Born per 100 Married Women Classified by Selected Ages at Marriage and Durations of Marriage, Ireland, 1911, 1946, 1961.

Duration of Marriage [a] and Census Year [b]	Age of Wife at Marriage in Years				
	20–24	25–29	30–34	35–39	All Ages (15–44)
0–4 Years					
1911	114	101	90	63	99
1946	116	105	89	62	103
1961	117	112	103	72	107
% Change, 1911–61	+3	+11	+14	+14	+8
5–9 Years					
1911	312	301	258	168	283
1946	291	266	228	135	255
1961	303	281	242	144	263
% Change, 1911–61	−3	−7	−6	−14	−7
10–14 Years					
1911	480	435	352	213	421
1946	422	365	280	149	354
1961	425	373	291	152	350
% Change, 1911–61	−11	−14	−17	−29	−17
15–19 Years					
1911	609	529	395	251	525
1946	513	414	297	172	416
1961	499	410	300	160	403
% Change, 1911–61	−18	−22	−24	−36	−23
20–24 Years					
1911	700	577	438	305	596
1946	562	439	319	183	449
1961	527	412	298	161	416
% Change, 1911–61	−25	−29	−32	−47	−30
25–29 Years					
1911	750	628	484	345	648
1946	587	465	339	218	478
1961	547	419	304	177	438
% Change, 1911–61	−27	−33	−37	−49	−32
30–34 Years					
1911	788	668	545	384	677
1946	608	493	385	242	494
1961	555	434	327	195	457
% Change, 1911–61	−30	−35	−40	−49	−32

SOURCES: *Censuses of Population of Ireland, 1946 and 1951*, "General Report," Table 196, p. 212; *1961*, Vol. VIII, Table 4A, p. 6.

[a] Figures below the horizontal lines represent completed family sizes, that is, children ever born to women aged 50 years or over at the time of the census.

[b] 32 Counties in 1911.

than in 1911 — a matter which will be discussed below under the topic of the possibility of effective fertility control. The limited data available from the 1841 Census about fertility indicates that there has been little change in efforts to control fertility among recently married couples for over a century. Among persons married from five to nine years at the time of the census, marital fertility was less in 1841 than in any of the three twentieth-century fertility censuses (Table 61). Once again fecundity probably was lower in 1841, and the errors of under-reporting or of under-enumeration were probably greater in 1841, but the pattern given by the 1841 data is nevertheless consistent with that of the more recent figures.

TABLE 61. Average Number of Children Ever Born per 100 Married Women for Selected Ages at Marriage Among Marriages of 5 to 9 Years Duration, Ireland, 1841, 1911, 1946, 1961.

| | Age of Wife at Marriage | |
Year	15 to 24 Years	25 to 34 Years
1841 [a][b]	278	248
1911 [a]	314	285
1946	296	252
1961	310	267

SOURCES: *Censuses of Population of Ireland, 1841,* "Report," Table V, pp. 486–87; *1911,* "General Report," Table 165F, pp. 457–59; *1946,* Vol. IX, Table 4, p. 6; *1961,* Vol. VIII, Table 5, p. 6.

([a]) 32 Counties.
([b]) In 1841 the age-groups were 17 to 25 years and 26 to 35 years.

Reductions in marital fertility after 1911 were greatest among those women who married later in life, and among those who had marriages of longer duration at the time of the census. Except for newly married couples, the two factors operated independently with the percentage decline in fertility consistently rising within each age at marriage as the duration of marriage increased, and for each duration of marriage with an increasing age of the wife at marriage (Table 60). When the two factors combined, as for women in their late thirties at marriage and married 25 to 34 years, the reduction in fertility was 49 per cent — the same percentage decline that was recorded for England and Wales between 1911–15 and 1960 (Table 59). These trends show that the greatest reductions in fertility took place among those women who postponed marriage until their thirties, even though for biological reasons alone they would have had smaller families than women marrying earlier. The other major pattern shown is that, regardless of age at marriage, the greatest reductions in fertility took place during the later years of childbearing. This apparently reflects a decision to have no more children as opposed to evenly spacing children throughout the childbearing period, or of postponing childbearing for several years after marriage. In other words, by 1961 Irish women, especially those who postponed marriage until their thirties, were no longer as tolerant as they had been around 1911 of having very large families, or of continuing childbearing into their forties.

Changes in completed family size can be used to illustrate the importance of age at marriage on fertility reductions between 1911 and 1961. In Table 60 a line separates those with completed families — persons who were 50 years or older at the time of the census. I have extended the childbearing period through age 49 because a meaningful proportion of births to women who have large families occur among women who are aged 45 and over. For example, in 1961 births to women 45 and over accounted for only 0.6 per cent of all births, but they accounted for 2.2 per cent of births to women who had had six or more previous live-born children.[3] The influence of age at marriage is shown by the much larger completed family size of younger brides, and their smaller reduction in fertility. Among women married from 30 to 34 years at the time of the census, in 1911 the total number of live births to women married in their early twenties was 7.9, while to women married in their late thirties the number was 3.8. Fifty years later the completed fertility of the younger brides had declined by only 30 per cent to 5.6 children, while that of the older brides had declined by 49 per cent to 2.0 children.

Changes in the composition of the completed family can be studied by examining the percentage distribution of women over 50 years of age, who were in the same age-groups at marriage, and with marriages of the same duration at the census date, by the number of children ever born to them. Taking the age-group at marriage which includes the average age at marriage (age-group 25–29), and that duration of marriage which brings the youngest of these women to at least 50 years of age (from 25 to 29 years), the proportion of women with seven or more children declined from 50 per cent in 1911 to 18 per cent in 1961 (Table 62). This is direct evidence of the increased reluctance on the part of many wives to have very large families. At the other extreme, however, th proportion of childless marriages changed hardly at all over the 50-year period. If the proportion childless in 1911 is assumed to have been due to biologically caused barrenness, then biology would remain today the main cause of childlessness among Irish married couples. This point, coupled with the relatively unchanging rate of marital fertility during the first years of marriage, suggests that almost all Irish couples hope to have children when they marry.

For couples able to have children who nevertheless did not wish to be burdened by the very large families of seven and more children resulting from uncontrolled fertility, the problem was one of matching actual fertility with desired family size. I know of no public opinion surveys inquiring about "ideal family size" in Ireland, but judging from the increase from 12 to 34 per cent in the proportion of couples with from one to three children in Table 62, apparently the small family is becoming increasingly popular. Throughout the rest of this chapter I shall use the term "desired family size" to refer to the size of the completed family and not necessarily to the number of children desired by newly-weds or yet to be married persons. I personally doubt whether many Irish couples rationally calculate an exact number of children that they consider to be ideal and then consistently hold to

TABLE 62. Percentage Distribution of Completed Families by Number of Children Ever Born to Women in Selected Marriage Cohorts, Ireland, 1911, 1946, 1961.

Census Year	*Percentage Distribution of Women Aged 25–29 Years at Marriage and Married from 25 to 29 Years by Number of Children Ever Born*					
	0	*1–3*	*4–6*	*7–9*	*10– Over*	*Total*
1911 [a]	7	12	31	36	14	100
1946	9	27	38	21	5	100
1961	8	34	40	15	3	100

SOURCES: *Censuses of Population of Ireland, 1911*, "General Report," Table 165, p. 471; *1946*, Vol. IX, Tables 7, 7B, pp. 25, 46; *1961*, Vol. VIII, Tables 7, p. 23.
([a]) 32 Counties.

this ideal throughout their entire childbearing years. The more common pattern, I believe, is for virtually everyone who marries to want to have at least one child, and their desire for additional children then changes with each additional birth and with their own personal circumstances as they proceed through life. From this perspective, the desired family size is the number at which they stop having additional children, and assumes that the first- or second-born offspring were more highly desired, perhaps, than the last born. In Ireland as in many other countries, many parents come to "want" the number of children they have, even though most of them may have been unplanned. Nevertheless, persons who stopped at the third child no doubt wanted a smaller completed family than those who stopped at six — all other things, being equal, such as age at marriage, duration of marriage, and ability to effectively control fertility.

Looking again at Table 62, we see that the distribution of completed families in Ireland in 1961 was bimodal, with families of from four to six children being somewhat more common than families with from one to three children. Were there two different desired family sizes or were the families with from four to six children caused by an inability to effectively control marital fertility?

The Possibility of Effective Fertility Control

If the large completed families of the Irish were simply due to a lack of proper contraceptive materials, or of an inability to obtain abortions, then there would be no problem in understanding Irish reproductive behavior. Contraceptives and the advertisement of contraceptives are banned by law in Ireland under the Censorship of Publications Act, 1929, Section 16, and the Criminal Law Amendment Act, 1935, Section 17.[4] Nevertheless, contraceptives are available in Northern Ireland and in other parts of Britain and can be smuggled into Ireland. Because the contraceptive pill can be used for other purposes, it is available by prescription in Ireland. Even though doctors in Ireland should not, by law, prescribe it as a contraceptive, about 25 per cent of the Catholic doctors did in 1966, according to The Irish Times.[5] Until the recent change in English law concerning abortions, abortions were relatively expensive; but for those Irish who could afford it, abortions probably were as accessible to them in Britain as to the British in Britain.

The question to be answered about the large family size of the Irish concerns the *willingness* to use any method, including permanent abstinence, to avoid having additional children. As long as a couple desired a pregnancy they would not be interested in fertility control; on the contrary, they might seek medical help to overcome a barren marriage. Once a couple decided to have no more children, the question then became which spouse should use which method or whether marital sex should be reduced or eliminated. I have been unable to find data on the patterns of use of the various means of birth control in Ireland, but my personal impression is that the most important methods are periodic and permanent abstinence. There is no more effective fertility control than total abstinence; the problem concerns the willingness to practice it.

The willingness to limit fertility existed throughout Irish society by 1946, for by that time all social groups had lower marital fertility than the nation as a whole in 1911 (Table 63)* Among women in their late twenties at marriage, and married from 20 to 24 years at the census date, the proportion with seven or more children was 44 per cent in 1911, 22 per cent in 1946, and 17 per cent in 1961. Semi-skilled manual workers, unskilled manual workers, and farmers and farm managers were the social groups with the highest proportions of seven or more children in 1946 with 28, 27, and 28 per cent respectively; but these figures, while high in absolute terms, were much lower than the average for the nation in 1911. By 1961 the completed fertility of these three social groups had declined further to 17, 21, and 25 per cent respectively. Once again, the point is that a reduction in fertility,

---

* I selected marriages of from 20 to 24 years duration for Table 63 because the 1946 Census did not tabulate fertility by social group, age of wife at marriage, and exact number of children born for marriages of from 25 to 29 years duration. Had the data been published for the longer duration of marriage, the family sizes shown in Table 63 would have been somewhat larger.

however modest in comparison with certain other Western nations, had occurred in Ireland between 1911 and 1961 and took place among persons in all social classes.

Table 63 also shows that the relatively small proportion of childless couples, and the bimodal pattern of completed families also were found in all social groups. The proportion of childless marriages ranged from about 6 to 9 per cent among agricultural occupations and the less skilled urban workers to from 7 to 13 per cent for higher status social groups. The bimodal pattern is especially apparent among the higher status occupations. For example, even though half of the higher professional families had from one to three children in 1961 (indicating effective control over fertility), almost one third had from four to six children. Since most persons in this occupational group were successful in avoiding the very large families of seven or more children (only 9 per cent had seven or more children compared to the 44 per cent expected from the 1911 national fertility levels), it appears that many did not want to stop having children after having had only three — they wanted four, five, or six.

A good illustration of the degree of fertility control possible in Ireland is found in the completed family sizes of Irish non-Catholics (Table 64). By 1946 over half of the non-Catholic completed families (in this selected age at marriage and duration of marriage) had from one to three children, a proportion which increased to almost two-thirds by 1961. The pattern of non-Catholic marital fertility shows that effective birth control techniques, including abstinence, were available to those who wished to use them. The higher marital fertility of Irish Catholics can be traced to a greater reluctance to use, rather than an ignorance of effective birth control methods or an inability to obtain them.*

The fact that completed families among non-Catholics in Ireland were larger than English completed families should not be written off simply as a result of less effective fertility control

* The same pattern was found in Northern Ireland. In 1951 the estimated number of births per 1,000 married women was 289 for Catholics and 155 for non-Catholics. A. T. Park, "An Analysis of Human Fertility in Northern Ireland," *Journal of the Statistical and Social Inquiry Society of Ireland*, Vol. XII, Part I (1962–63), p. 7.

in Ireland. No doubt some couples had more children than they wanted in both countries. The more important point is that more Irish non-Catholic than English couples apparently wished to have at least one child, and more Irish non-Catholic than English

TABLE 63. Percentage Distribution of Completed Families by Social Group and by Number of Children Ever Born to Women in a Selected Age-Group at Marriage, Ireland, 1946, 1961.

Social Group and Year	Percentage Distribution of Women Aged 25–29 Years at Marriage and Married from 20 to 24 Years by Number of Children Ever Born					
	0	1–3	4–6	7–9	10– Over	Total
Salaried Employees						
1946	11	36	37	14	2	100
1961	9	46	37	7	1	100
Higher Professionals						
1946	11	45	34	9	1	100
1961	11	49	31	8	1	100
Employers and Managers						
1946	13	38	35	11	3	100
1961	11	48	34	6	1	100
Skilled Manual Workers						
1946	10	32	39	15	4	100
1961	7	39	39	13	2	100
Lower Professionals						
1946	11	34	38	15	2	100
1961	8	36	43	11	2	100
Semi-Skilled Manual Workers						
1946	6	25	41	21	7	100
1961	7	36	40	14	3	100
Agricultural Workers						
1946	9	32	37	18	4	100
1961	8	33	39	16	3	100·
Unskilled Manual Workers						
1946	8	28	37	20	7	100
1961	6	32	41	17	4	100
Farmers and Farm Managers						
1946	8	23	41	23	5	100
1961	7	25	43	20	5	100
All Groups						
1911 [a]	8	15	33	33	11	100
1946	10	29	39	18	4	100
1961	8	35	40	14	3	100

SOURCES: Censuses of Population of Ireland, 1911, "General Report," Table 165, p. 468; 1946, Vol. IX, Tables 7, 16, 16B, pp. 27, 181, 187; 1961, Vol. VIII, Table 14, p. 164.
([a]) 32 Counties; given as an example of large completed family sizes.

couples wished to have families with from four to six children.* The proportion of childless marriages can be taken as a case in point. If we assume that biologically caused barrenness would result in about 7 or 8 per cent childless couples among all persons in this particular age at marriage and duration of marriage, then a much greater proportion of English than non-Catholic Irish couples married with the desire to have no children at all. These voluntarily childless couples accounted for about 12 per cent of all English couples with this particular age at marriage and duration of marriage (20 per cent total childless less 8 per cent childless for biological reasons), 4 or 5 per cent of all Irish non-Catholic couples, and virtually no Irish Catholic couples. I believe there were few voluntarily childless couples in Ireland, even among the Irish non-Catholics, because the desire to have children was itself an important reason for getting married. If one did not wish to become a father or mother, one did not marry. Because of the high proportions of single persons at all ages in Ireland, remaining single did not normally mean the gradual lessening of social activities and friendships, which in many other countries may have made life increasingly lonely for the permanently single. Marriage with the intent to remain permanently childless, a marriage for companionship, was alien to Irish thinking, especially among the rural Irish.

A strong social norm against married women working probably also reduced the number of voluntarily childless marriages among Irish persons in both major religious groups. To a woman who did not wish to have children, marriage meant not only the loss of her current income and independence, but also the possibility of boredom once the daily round of housework was finished. Activity in an occupation outside the home was not socially accepted, yet virtually all of her neighbors of similar age would have less time than she for socializing because of the attention demanded of them by their children. Reducing the difference in proportion of childlessness between Catholics and non-Catholics

* The legitimate birthrate of the nonCatholic population of Northern Ireland also was higher than that of England: 155 compared with 105 in 1951. *Ibid.*, p. 7.

TABLE 64. Percentage Distribution of Completed Families by Number of Children Ever Born to Women in a Selected Age-Group at Marriage in England and Wales, 1961, Ireland, 1911, and by Religion in Ireland, 1946, 1961.

Country, Religion, and Year	*Percentage Distribution of Women Aged 25–29 Years at Marriage and Married from 25 to 29 Years by Number of Children Ever Born*					
	0	*1–3*	*4–6*	*7–9*	*10– Over*	*Total*
Ireland						
1911 [a]	7	12	31	36	14	100
Catholic						
1946	9	24	39	23	5	100
1961	8	31	42	16	3	100
Non-Catholic						
1946	13	53	27	6	1	100
1961	12	62	22	4	0	100
England and Wales [b]						
1961	20	71	8	1	0	100

SOURCES: *Censuses of Population of Ireland, 1911,* "General Report," Table 165, p. 471; *1946,* Vol. IX, Table 11, p. 130; *1961,* Vol. VIII, Table 11, p. 128; England and Wales, *Census, 1961,* "Fertility Tables," Table 2(i), p. 4.

([a]) 32 Counties.

([b]) Children ever born to women in selected age-group at, and duration of, current marriage.

in Ireland by a few percentage points to account for occupational rather than religious differences,* the two groups would turn out to be remarkably alike; a pattern which coincides with their similar rates of postponed marriage and permanent celibacy (Chapter Seven).

Of course, some social groups did have more knowledge of artificial fertility control methods and easier access to them. This partly explains why in both religious groups the unskilled manual workers had larger completed families than the higher professionals (Table 65).[6] But the larger completed families of Catholics

* A greater proportion of non-Catholics than Catholics were in the relatively low fertility occupations of higher professionals, employers and managers, and salaried employees. In 1946, 33 per cent of non-Catholics and 14 per cent of Catholics were in those occupations, and in 1961 the respective proportions were 34 and 8 per cent, among families with wives aged 25–29 at marriage and married for 20 to 24 years at the time of the census. *Censuses of Population of Ireland, 1946,* Vol. IX, Table 17, p. 197; *1961,* Vol. VIII, Tables 11, 15, pp. 127, 194.

TABLE 65. Average Completed Family Size by Religion and Social Group Among Women in a Selected Age-Group at Marriage, Ireland, 1946, 1961.

Social Group	Average Number of Children Ever Born per 100 Women Aged 25–29 Years at Marriage and Married 20 to 24 Years			
	Catholics		Non-Catholics	
	1946	1961	1946	1961
Salaried employees	413	360	200	219
Higher professionals	389	364	191	218
Employers and managers	410	365	206	202
Skilled manual workers	429	405	314	244
Lower professionsl	424	411	161	237
Semi-skilled manual workers	499	415	477	212
Agricultural workers	443	428	355	288
Unskilled manual workers	478	450	287	350
Farmers and farm managers	490	486	363	329
All groups	452	425	273	247

SOURCES: *Censuses of Population of Ireland, 1946*, Vol. IX, Tables 11A, 17A, pp. 133, 199; *1961*, Vol. VIII, Table 11A, 15A, pp. 136, 203.

than non-Catholics *within* every social group cannot be explained by such differences in access to certain birth control materials. Apparently, many Catholics in every social group wanted larger families than non-Catholics did.

As an example of a large desired family size of one group of Catholics, we can consider Catholic lower professionals. There is no reason to assume that knowledge of or access to effective fertility control methods was less among lower than among higher professionals. Yet completed family size was larger among Catholic lower professionals than among Catholic higher professionals both in 1946 and 1961, and the decline in completed family size between 1946 and 1961 was less among Catholic lower professionals (3 per cent) than among Catholic higher professionals (6 per cent, Table 65). Furthermore, the decline in fertility among lower professionals of all religions between 1946 and 1961 took place entirely among families with seven or more children. For this occupational group between 1946 and 1961 the proportion with three or fewer children, including childless couples, remained about the same at 45 to 44 per cent; the proportion with seven or more children declined from 17 to 13 per cent; and the proportion with four to six children increased from 38 to 43 per cent, (Table

63). In contrast, the fertility decline among higher professionals of all religions occurred among families with four or more children, and the proportion with one to three children increased from 45 to 49 per cent. It seems reasonable to conclude that the desired family size of lower professionals was larger than that of higher professionals, and that many lower professionals wanted families which included four to six children. There is always the possibility, of course, that lower professionals remained at the lower level because they had more children. But I would take this to mean that their willingness to limit fertility in order to further their careers was less than among those who had smaller families and achieved a higher-status occupation.

Under the assumption that the poorer and more isolated farmers would have the least knowledge about effective contraceptive methods and the least access to them, it might be argued that the larger families of Catholic than non-Catholic farmers were caused not by a difference in desired family size but by the fact that most of the poorer and more isolated farmers in Ireland are Catholics. However, a tabulation of completed family size by religion, valuation of holding for taxes, age of wife at marriage, and duration of marriage made in the 1946 Census (Table 66), shows that regardless of valuation of the holding Catholic farmers continued to have larger families than non-Catholic farmers. Furthermore, the assumption that poorer farmers had larger families was not true for Catholics, at least for this age at marriage and duration of marriage in 1946. Although the differences were small, family size increased among Catholic farmers as the value of their farms increased. I interpret this to mean that the better off a Catholic farmer was in Ireland, the better a Catholic he tried to be, at least in terms of having a larger family.

Differences in completed fertility by social group among Catholics, and between Catholics and non-Catholics in the same social group, demonstrate that couples who desired to limit their family size were able to do so. Knowledge about and access to artificial birth control methods explain part of the differences, of course, but traditional methods such as coitus interruptus and either periodic or permanent abstinence were widely known and available to all married couples, given sufficient motivation. The willingness to limit fertility is the heart of the issue, and instead of being a matter of appropriate birth control technology, the explanation of the high rate of Irish fertility involves attitudes about family size, especially the viewpoint of Irish Catholicism.

TABLE 66. Average Completed Family Size by Religion and Rateable Valuation of Agricultural Holding for Women in a Selected Age-Group at Marriage, Ireland, 1946.

Rateable Valuation of Holding in Pounds	Average Number of Children Ever Born to 100 Women Aged 25–29 Years at Marriage and Married from 25–29 Years	
	Catholics	Non-Catholics
Under 4	509	327[a]
4 and under 10	511	356
10 and under 20	528	389
20 and under 50	533	382
50 and over	549	344
All Valuations	523	367

SOURCE: *Census of Population of Ireland, 1946*, Vol. IX, Table 15A, p. 177.
[a] 15 women, 49 children.

A Large Ideal Family Size and Catholic Teachings

The issue here is not what the Catholic Church taught about marital fertility but rather the way in which the Irish people chose to interpret the doctrine of their Church. In some instances involving politics and land, many Irish Catholics openly rebelled against their hierarchy, and occasionally disregarded the Pope (Chapter Two). On the matter of late marriage and permanent celibacy for reasons of personal selfishness, a great many Irish persons chose to ignore Catholic teachings dealing with the encouragement of early and universal marriage among lay persons (Chapter Seven). Having shown themselves independent of Church advice on these matters, why did so many apparently accept Church teaching on a large ideal family size?

It is possible to express simply the Church's teachings about how people are expected to behave without going into the theological reasoning underlying Catholic doctrine about marriage and the family. The virtual absence of voluntarily childless couples among Irish Catholics is consistent with the Catholic perspective of the purpose of marriage: "The primary purpose of marriage, in the natural order of things, is the birth of children. This is not to say that people do not, or may not, marry for other reasons; it is but to say that the most fundamental reason, the one to which all others must yield precedence, is the raising of a family."[7]

But since voluntarily childless couples were also uncommon among Irish non-Catholics, this type of marriage cannot be attributed to Catholic doctrine alone. The greatest area of difference in family size by religion in Ireland is the greater preference of Catholics for four or more children in all social classes, and among farmers of all property categories. Part of the difference between the two religious groups may have been due to differences in knowledge about or access to artificial birth control methods, but there can be no doubt that Catholics were acting in a way consistent with the teachings of their religion:* "The ideal family is the large family. People are not expected, of course, to have as many children as they possibly can. But they are expected to have as many as they can hope to bring up properly. *Per se* there is no inherent reason why people should not 'plan,' 'space,' 'control,' their family, *i.e.*, what number of children they will have, when they will have them, etc. If family-planning, family spacing, family limitation and the like are to be condemned, it is because of the methods by which and the *motives* from which they are practiced."[8]

The key word here is "properly." Apparently more Irish Catholics in 1961 than in 1911 believed that they could "properly" bring up only one to three children: completed families with this number of children among Catholic women aged 25–29 years at marriage increased from at least 12 per cent to 31 per cent during

---

* The relatively high fertility of the Netherlands also is apparently due to the acceptance of a large family ideal on the part of Dutch Catholics. See van Heek, "Roman Catholicism and Fertility in the Netherlands: Demographic Aspects of Minority Status," *Population Studies*, 10:2 (November 1956), pp. 125–138. Just why Dutch Catholics accepted their church's teachings on a large family size, however, is a matter of debate. See Petersen, "Fertility Trends and Population Policy: Some Comments on the Van Heek-Hofstee Debate," *Sociologia Neerlandica*, 3:2 (Summer 1966), pp. 2–17.

the 50-year period (Table 64). The behavior of these women presents no problem because they acted as other Western women acted, and probably for the usual reasons given in the standard-of-living thesis. In the United States, for example, a family size of three or fewer children was thought to be the ideal size by from 30 to 68 per cent of Catholic women, and from 45 to 77 per cent of non-Catholic women between 1943 and 1961 according to national surveys. This meant that the average ideal family size of American Catholics was on an average less than one child greater than that of American non-Catholics.*

The puzzling aspect of Irish Catholic fertility in 1961 is the behavior of the remaining 61 per cent of women in this particular group who had four or more children by the end of their childbearing years. I believe that the best explanation of the persistence of their high fertility norms concerns the selective effects of the extreme marriage and emigration trends in Ireland. Because so many young women emigrated in each cohort, and because so many of those who remained postponed marriage or remained permanently single, the proportion who remained in Ireland and married young has been very small. The proportion of 10- to 14-year-old girls who survived, were still in Ireland, and married by their early twenties amounted to only from 9 to 18 per cent of the original cohorts between 1861 and 1966 (Table 67). Over the same period, among women aged 30 to 34 years the figure was from 23 to 42 per cent of the original cohorts. In other words, the majority of young girls in Ireland chose to emigrate, postpone marriage until their thirties, or to remain permanently single. It was only a minority which chose to remain in Ireland and to marry while in their twenties.

How did the Irish women who remained in Ireland and who married in their twenties differ from the great majority of their cohort? It has been pointed out that those who might have pressed most strongly for change in their home communities in Ireland

---

* The similarity of the two religious groups in the United States led Judith Blake to conclude, "lay Catholics are generally farther from their Church's views concerning family size than they are from sharing those of non-Catholics." Judith Blake, "The Americanization of Catholic Reproductive Ideals," *Population Studies*, Vol. XX, No. 1 (July 1966), pp. 27–43.

TABLE 67. Married Females in Selected Age-Groups as Percentages of All Females in the Same Cohort at the Census Date, Ten or Twenty Years Before, Ireland, 1861–1966.

	Married Females Aged 20–24 Years As a Percentage of		Married Females Aged 30–34 Years As a Percentage of	
Year	All Females Aged 20–24 Years At Census Date	All Females Aged 10–14 Years 10 Years Before	All Females Aged 30–34 Years at Census Date	All Females Aged 10–14 Years 20 Years Before
1861	24	16	67	23
1871	22	18	69	27
1881	17	13	66	35
1891	14	9	61	27
1901 [a]	12	9	NA	NA
1911 [a]	11	9	NA	NA
1926	13	10 [b]	56	32 [c]
1936	14	11	54	32 [c]
1946	17	14	60	42
1951	18	13 [b]	62	42 [c]
1961	22	13	70	41 [c]
1966	25	17 [b]	75	42

SOURCES: *Censuses of Population of Ireland, 1926,* Vol. V, Part I, Tables 1, 7B, pp. 1, 24, 25; *1966,* Vol. II, Table 1C, p. 3.

[a] Data were not published for the 30–34 year age-group.

[b] Percentage of the same cohort 15 rather than 10 years before.

[c] Percentage of the same cohort 25 rather than 20 years before.

were the most likely to emigrate.[9] This is not to say that all emigrants left because they disagreed with the traditions of Catholicism in Ireland, of course. It is rather to say, that the most disaffected Irish Catholics were more likely to be found among the Irish abroad than at home. Those who were most willing to go along with the conventional expectations of their church were also the ones more likely to remain in Ireland, to accept the large family ideal of Catholic teaching, and to marry early enough in life to turn the ideal into actuality.

In the preceding chapter I argued that most persons who postponed marriage to a late age, or who remained permanently single, were less influenced by their church (in this one matter at least), than those who married early. If this were so, then the desired family size of persons marrying late should be smaller than that of persons marrying early, and the permanently celibate population should include persons who would have had no children if they had married. The latter point is a matter of speculation, of course, but my thinking on differences in ideal family size between those who married early or late in life can be tested. Even though older women could be expected to have smaller families because of their lower fecundity and fewer number of childbearing years left to them after marriage, the percentage decline in marital fertility between 1911 and 1961, as described above, was greater the older the wife was at marriage (Table 60). This finding is not something to be routinely expected, at least on the basis of the English experience. Among marriages of 30–34 years duration in England, the greater age of the wife at marriage *did not* result in greater percentage declines in marital fertility between 1911 and 1946: among wives aged 20–24 years at marriage in England, the percentage decline in marital fertility for that 35-year period was 47 per cent; among those aged 25–29 years at marriage, 49 per cent; and among those aged 30–34 years at marriage, 46 per cent.[10]

If the desired family size of Irish women marrying in their late thirties had been about four children, then they could expect to have that number, on the average, if they had exercised no control over their fertility. The reasoning behind this thinking lies in the fact that the average number of live births to Irish women aged 35–39 years at marriage, and married from 30–34 years at the 1911 Census, was 3.8 (these women were married between 1877 and 1881, Table 60). Yet women who married in their late thirties, and were married from 15–19 years at the 1961 Census had only 1.6 live births on an average (these women were married between 1942–46). The reduction from 3.8 to 1.6 live births represents a 58 per cent decline, just under the 64 per cent decline recorded for marital fertility in England as a whole between 1881–90 and 1960 (Table 59). The fact that late-marrying Irish women on an average did not wish to have even four children suggests very strongly that they disagreed with Catholic teachings on a large family ideal; an average completed family size of 1.6 children does not even come into the medium-size range.

The probability that the most conservative (or most passive) Irish Catholics were more often found among the ranks of the early married population in Ireland than among the late married, the permanently celibate, or the emigrant population abroad, I believe, is one of the most important explanations of the Irish acceptance of the large family ideal advised by Roman Catholicism. From this point of view, the persistence of a desired family size of four to six children among Catholics in Ireland was closely related to Ireland's other extreme demographic trends: among the most extreme ages at marriage and proportions permanently single in all Europe, and over a century of high rates of emigration.

A Large Desired Family Size and the Standard-of-Living Thesis

The conservatism of Irish Catholicism about the family, it might be argued by advocates of the standard-of-living thesis, should have been countered by the extreme gap in living standards between those who remained in Ireland and those who emigrated to the United States or to England. Since most Irish non-migrants knew about their relative deprivation through the medium of personal letters, and through the English-speaking mass media, there should have been stronger social forces leading to a more rapid acceptance of family limitation in Ireland than in, say, Portugal or Spain. The fact that this did not happen calls for a separate discussion of the relation between desired family size and personal material standards of living in Ireland.

In other European countries the link between family size and personal living standards rests on two basic assumptions: the raising of children and their establishment in a socially respected position in life is the responsibility of the children's mother and father; and, the desire to have children of one's own is balanced by the desire to achieve or to maintain a certain minimum standard of living for oneself. The more sacrifices required to establish one's offspring in life, and the higher one's own personal minimum standards of living were, the smaller the family size one was supposed to desire. The heavy rates of emigration from Ireland during the last century, however, resulted in an attitude held by some Irish that there was not much that a parent could do to prepare his children for their adult lives. As a small farmer in Kerry remarked :"Ah, the place is so small that only one can have it, and the rest will have to go. And sure, it's little one can do for them, for you don't know what to tell them. You can only teach them to be good men and to be true to their faith, and hope that, if they do that, they will be all right."[11]

The farmer may have been right about his inability to prepare his children in any technical sense for life in the quite different environment of urban America or England, but what is more important is that his attitude lifted from his own shoulders the burden of establishing his offspring in life. If the sacrifices one feels socially bound to make for one's children are reduced to the provision of food, clothing, shelter, and elementary education until they are able to earn their own keep during the interim before emigration, then one of the basic reasons for family limitation in other European countries was of little concern to many Irish families. This point, of course, was more germane to some groups than others, and probably it was most applicable to farmers, other agricultural workers, and unskilled and semi-skilled manual workers, who accounted for about 49 per cent of all married couples living in Ireland in 1961.[12]

The other assumption underlying the usual standard-of-living argument has also been modified in Ireland by the selective processes of Irish emigration and marriage. Every point which was made for the effect of emigration and marriage on the likelihood that the most conservative Catholics would be found among the early married persons in Ireland also applies to those who cared least about their own personal standard of living. But now non-Catholics can be included in the discussion. In previous chapters I have argued that a strong desire to achieve or maintain a certain minimum standard of living was one of the most important factors distinguishing those who emigrated from those who did not; those who married from those who did not; and among the married population, those who married early from those who did not. If the desire to have children was to be balanced against the desire to achieve or maintain a certain minimum standard of living, then this second basic reason for family limitation in other European countries has been greatly reduced for the married population of Ireland.

The relatively large completed fertility of some Irish non-Catholics can be taken as a case in point. The proportion of Irish non-Catholics of the age at, and duration of, marriage given in Table 64, for example, with seven or more live births in 1961 was very small compared with the 50 per cent expected under the 1911 levels of fertility; it appears that the prevention of very large families was almost as complete among Irish non-Catholics as among the English. Yet over one-fifth of the Irish non-Catholic families had from four to six children compared with only one-twelfth of the English families. Catholic doctrine on family size has no relevance here, but Irish demographic trends do. The Irish non-Catholics have had greater rates of emigration than Irish Catholics over the last fifty years or so, and the rates of postponed marriage and permanent celibacy for both religious groups in Ireland were similar. In other words, the selective processes of emigration and marriage were as important to distinguishing what type of Irish non-Catholic remained in Ireland and married early as they were to the Irish Catholics. When the married non-Catholic population of Ireland is compared with the total married population of England, it is actually a comparison of a disproportionate number of persons least concerned with their own personal standard of living in one group with a rather normal population of married persons in the other group.

The selectivity of the processes of emigration and marriage in Ireland helps to understand not only why the reduction in marital fertility has been less extensive in Ireland than in other European countries but also why the decline in marital fertility in Ireland did not begin until several decades after England's (Table 59). In England, and in almost all other northwestern European countries, the major reason for the decline in the crude birth rate was the decline in the marital fertility rate. It is generally known that the Irish crude birth rate declined not because of a decline in the marital fertility rate but because of the increased proportions of single persons in the population after the 1870s. What is generally not realized is that the selectivity of who postponed marriage and who married early in Ireland actually *increased* the marital fertility rate, especially after the rate is standardized for possible differences in age distribution at different times (Table 68).

The Irish women who married late contributed to Ireland's high marital fertility rate, in spite of the fact that they had small completed families. If they had married earlier and still had the same number of children by the end of their childbearing period, then they would have added their numbers to the population of Irish married women in their childbearing years without increasing the number of births. This would have lowered the Irish legitimate birth rate. It was not a coincidence that the marital fertility rate in Ireland rose between the 1870s and 1911 as the degree of postponed marriage increased over the same period. A decline in Irish marital fertility occurred only after the amount of postponed marriage and permanent celibacy among females in Ireland reached near maximum levels in 1911 (Table 68). The greater postponement of marriage after the 1870s of those who cared more about their personal living standards also meant that a higher proportion of the early married population included those individuals who cared less about such matters. Between 1891 and 1911, only 9 per cent of original cohorts of females had remained in Ireland and married in their early twenties (Table 67), yet these early marriers had the largest families (Table 60).

The standard-of-living thesis operated in Ireland as in other European countries, but because of the extreme degree of selectivity through the processes of emigration and postponed marriage, it resulted in an increase in legitimate fertility from what it otherwise might have been. Irish persons who cared most about

TABLE 68. Percentage Single in Selected Age-Groups by Sex, and Age-Standardized Legitimate Birth Rate, Ireland, 1871–1951.

	Percentage Single				Age-Standardized Average Number of Legitimate Births per 1,000 Married Women Aged 15–44 Years in the Three-Year Period Centered on Each Census Date[a]
	Age-Group 25–34 Years		Age-Group 45–54 Years		
Year	Males	Females	Males	Females	
1871	57	38	16	15	278
1881	62	41	16	16	275
1891	67	48	20	17	284
1901	72	53	24	20	286
1911	74	56	29	24	307
1926	72	53	31	24	272
1936	74	55	33	25	258
1946	70	48	32	26	261
1951	67	46	31	26	248

SOURCE: Censuses of Population of Ireland, 1946 and 1951, "General Report," Tables 32, 199, pp. 51, 219.

([a]) The age-standardized rates represent what the rates would have been if the age distribution of married women aged 15–44 years at the earlier censuses had been the same as it was in 1951.

the gap in living standards between Ireland and the United States or England were most likely to leave the country, or if they remained in Ireland to postpone marriage (perhaps indefinitely), and to have a small family once married. By default, the persons who married in their early twenties in Ireland not only had the greatest biological potential for having large families, they were also less likely to care about matters of relative material living conditions. The interpretation applies to the marital fertility of both Catholics and non-Catholics in Ireland. But since the fertility of Catholics was consistently higher than that of non-Catholics, the argument is secondary to the selective effect of emigration and late marriage on what type of Catholic was more often found among the early married Irish.

A Large Desired Family Size and the Irish Family System

The demographic trends discussed up to now help in understanding why the large family ideal persisted for so long in Ireland. But the trends themselves tell nothing about the form in which the large family appeared in Ireland in terms of family structure and roles, and of the place of women in the Irish society. Because comprehensive descriptions of the Irish family, both in rural and in urban areas, are available,[13] I shall mention only those features which seem to be most germane to Ireland's high legitimate birth rate. It is important to realize, however, that many aspects of the Irish family have continued for the same reason that the high rates of Irish legitimate fertility have persisted: those who were most likely to have changed the family system either left Ireland or remained in Ireland and chose not to marry.

The importance of selective emigration in explaining the persistence of the Irish family system can be better understood, perhaps, by considering what might have happened if emigration from Ireland had not been possible and all persons born in Ireland had had to remain in Ireland for better or worse. When large scale emigration from Ireland began during the 1830s, there were already over six million persons living in the 26 Counties, most of whom were existing on a subsistence level. Famine and disease were part of everyday life, and a high death rate kept the average annual rate of population growth probably down to about 1 per cent. If it is assumed that late marriage and permanent celibacy would have been adopted to the same extreme degree that they actually were, then a decline in the birth rate would have permitted some decline in the death rate without increasing the average annual increase in the population. At 1 per cent a year the population of Ireland today would be over twenty million instead of the 2,900,000 recorded in the 1966 Census.[14] Clearly, an Ireland without emigration would be quite different than the Ireland which actually exists. It is debatable, however, whether the standard of living of over twenty million Irishmen (or even of over twelve million at a 0.5 per cent average annual rate of increase), would be as high as that currently enjoyed by less than three million Irishmen.

If the Irish had had to face the problems of a growing population without an easy outlet for the surplus, then I believe they would have met their population-related problems as the peoples of all other northwestern European nations have — through the adoption of the small family ideal (in addition to late marriage and permanent celibacy). I hold this view not only because of the sheer numbers involved, but also because persons who cared most about achieving or maintaining a certain material standard of living would have composed a larger proportion of the married population of Ireland than is presently the case. Because virtually unlimited emigration was possible, however, the Irish family system was allowed to persist and to influence some aspects of Irish demography, especially the heavy emigration of females and the related pattern of opposite sex ratios for the rural and urban areas of Ireland (Chapter Four).

Limited Alternative Roles for Married Women. The relevant feature of Irish family life involved here is the custom by which very few married women worked outside the home. The primary role of a married woman being at home as a wife and mother was compatible with Catholic teachings, but it was not limited to members of that religion alone. The sentiment is expressed in secular terms in the Irish constitution: "In particular, the State recognizes that by her life within the home, woman gives to the State a support without which the common good cannot be achieved. The State shall, therefore, endeavour to ensure that mothers shall not be obliged by economic necessity to engage in labour to the neglect of their duties in the home."[15]

The State was not imposing its will upon a reluctant people, but rather expressing the general opinion of married persons, both Catholic and non-Catholic, in Ireland. It should not be forgotten that the selective effects of emigration and non-marriage also would have meant that the additional income earned by the wife working probably had less appeal to the married Irish in Ireland than to some permanently single persons, or to many Irish abroad. Regardless of the possible reasons why the Irish accepted the limitation of a married woman's life to her home and family, the important result for marital fertility was that she was expected to find her purpose in the rearing of children and the care of her husband and home. All other things being equal, this would lead to a larger rather than a smaller desired family size. This point should not be overstressed, however, because Irish non-Catholics did have much smaller families than Irish Catholics even though their married women probably were no more extensively employed outside the home.[16]

Desired Number of Children among Farmers. The facts that Ireland is still a heavily rural nation, and that most of the farms in Ireland are family farms rather than large-scale commercial enterprises, have important consequences for Irish marital fertility. The farm family was conducive to a larger desired number of children, as illustrated by comparisons with other occupational groups for both Catholics and non-Catholics (Table 65). The desire for several children, however, did not result simply from a need to create an unpaid labor force, as is commonly believed. The great majority of holdings in Ireland were small enough to be worked by a man and his wife without the assistance of their children because of the custom of cooperating with their neighbors in doing the heavier jobs. In fact, several years would pass in this manner before the first-born child would be large enough to help in any essential way. Even if a farm couple had children with the express motive of creating helping hands, the needs of most Irish farms would be met by the survival to adulthood of just one son. Additional children would be a drain on the farm's resources and they would not necessarily increase the farm's productivity if the farm size and the farming techniques remained unchanged. If the need for unpaid labor was the only factor determining family size in rural Ireland, a small rather than a large family would be the ideal.

One possible reason why families were larger in rural areas is an extension of the discussion concerning the limited alternative roles for women. Only now the issue is broader than employment outside the home; it concerns the opportunity for social activities outside the home which were especially limited for rural women before the recent advent of radio and television, and the rural electrification program of the last twenty years. After describing the extensive social life enjoyed by males in rural areas, and the occasional dances for young single girls, John M. Mogey comments about the Northern Irish: "It will be obvious that the women are not well represented in this social life. Family ties and household duties, no doubt, absorb much of their time."* And many Irish farm wives could not depend on their husbands to take them out: "The Irish farmer seems mortally afraid to take his wife to a place of amusement — a trait far more marked on the western seaboard than in the Midlands — for the sole reason that he dreads the censure of his neighbours."[17]

Young children were not only the major source of enjoyment for the rural mother, they were also an important factor in determining her status in her family and community — probably more so than was the case for the urban mother. The rural mother had virtually complete control over young children, and as long as she was caring for them she could look forward to occupying a central place in the family circle. The close association of the mother with her offspring in the Irish family system is well described by Arensberg and Kimball. As they point out, in contrast to the father, the mother is the young child's guide and companion: "Her authority most often makes itself felt through praise,

* Later, in discussing women's organizations in rural Northern Ireland, Mogey concludes, "[for] the great majority of all countrywomen, outlets other than those provided by the home and the church are practically non-existent." John M. Mogey, *Rural Life in Northern Ireland*, pp. 118, 202.

persuasion, and endearment. Only when a grave breach of discipline demands a restraining power greater than hers, or when an appeal to ultimate authority is needed, does the father begin to play his role."[18]

Another major reason for the larger families of farmers involves the lineage needs of farmers under the stem family system. Arensberg and Kimball place considerable emphasis on the needs of lineage as an explanation of both the low rate of childlessness and the large desired family size: "For the small farmers marriages are for the purpose of producing children and assuring continuity of descent and ownership."[19] Ideally the heir to the family holding should be the first-born child who would be: a male; alive when the property changed hands; living on the home farm and willing to take over control; and acceptable in all other respects to his parents to play the role of heir. In actuality many of these conditions were not fulfilled by the birth of the first, or even the second or third, child. A family by chance alone might have two or more daughters before having a son. With the levels of mortality existing in the nineteenth century, there was a meaningful chance that one's only son might not survive to adulthood and the family line would be broken — the family name would cease to be on that particular piece of land. At the end of the nineteenth century and the beginning of the twentieth, mortality conditions improved but the extremely high rates of emigration continued and were as effective in taking sons away from the family holding. Ironically, the greater the proportion of any cohort which left the family farm, the greater would be the desire of parents to have enough sons to ensure that at least one would remain and be willing to take control of the home farm when his time came. As discussed in earlier chapters, the son's willingness to remain depended not only upon satisfying his aspirations for material standards of living (Chapter Five), but also upon his willingness to postpone marriage until his thirties or even forties (Chapter Seven). And finally, it could happen that the one son who was willing to inherit the family holding was not, for some reason, acceptable to his parents as their heir. How often this situation occurred is open to question, but since the consequences to the parents would be serious, it was a possibility to be considered.

The solution to all of these contingencies for the farming parents was simple: have enough children to have at least two surviving sons remaining on the home farm. Since the sexes are roughly equally divided at birth, this would mean having on an average at least four live births. But given the extremely high rates of emigration from rural Ireland, many parents no doubt believed they would need at least three sons to have some assurance that at least one, and preferably two, would remain on the home farm as potential heirs. This would result in a total number of live births of from four to six, depending on the sex of each additional off-spring. For most small farmers, the additional children would be a great burden on their limited resources. Nevertheless, the needs of lineage in the stem family system and the need to retain control of the family holding from generation to generation took prece-dence over considerations of material living standards. It should not be forgotten that the selective effects of migration and non-marriage probably resulted in those who cared most about lineage and the family farm, and least about material living standards, being the most likely in each generation to become the heirs and the parents of the following generation.

Because the family system of the Irish farmer is well known, it is important to point out that an explanation of high fertility based on rural lineage needs is limited and leaves unexplained two major aspects of Irish fertility. First, it omits the higher fertility of Catholics. Presumably the lineage needs of non-Catholic farm-ers were the same as those of Catholic farmers, yet in 1961 the completed fertility of the former was only 3.3 births compared with 4.9 births for the latter (among women aged 25–29 years at marriage and married from 20–24 years in 1961, Table 65). Second, it ignores the relatively high fertility of the urban Irish. For example, among women in their late twenties at marriage, and married from 20–24 years in 1961, 56 per cent of lower profes-sionals had four or more live births compared with 68 per cent for farmers and farm managers (Table 63). The need to retain control over the home farm might explain the difference between the farmers and the lower professionals, but the argument leaves un-explained the major part of the desire for four to six children among lower professionals, and probably among farmers as well.

The persistence of a high rate of marital fertility in Ireland cannot be understood without considering other Irish demographic patterns. Neither can it be understood without reference to Catholic teachings about a large ideal family size. The selectivity of emigration and Irish marriage patterns resulted in the most conservative (or most passive) Catholics being found in greater proportions among the early married persons remaining in Ireland than among the permanently celibate, the late married or the emigrants from Ireland. A secondary result of the selective processes of emigration and marriage in Ireland reinforced the selection on religious grounds: persons least concerned with their own personal standard of living were also the most likely to remain in Ireland and to marry early. Marital fertility has remained high in Ireland because those who agreed most consistently with Catholic teachings on family life, and those who cared less about their own personal standard of living, made up a disproportionately large share of the married population of Ireland.

Although the most important reason for the high rate of marital fertility in Ireland is a large completed family size, two other demographic trends also have contributed to making the legitimate fertility rate higher than it otherwise would have been. First, the very low proportion of childless marriages among both Catholic and non-Catholic Irish persons suggests that almost all persons who married in Ireland wanted to have at least some children (this contrasts with countries such as England, where a large minority of married couples remained voluntarily childless). Second, the extremely late ages at marriage raised the legitimate fertility rate in the sense that these women spent many years of their child-bearing time in an unmarried status and then had a small completed family, while in other countries women marrying earlier but also having a small family, spent more of their child-bearing period in a married status but produced no children.

CHAPTER IX

The Interrelationship of Historical Trends

I N the preceding chapters I assumed that no particular demographic pattern in Ireland today can be understood without considering its past relationship with other demographic trends and with historic social, economic, and political conditions. The chapters themselves, however, explained certain theoretical issues using Ireland as a test case. It is only appropriate that this final chapter cover what happened in Irish emigration, marriage, and fertility during the past century and a quarter from the perspective of descriptive Irish history. While the first chapter is addressed to persons interested in certain social regularities found in many societies, this chapter is written for persons primarily interested in Irish society itself. Because the documenting details have already been presented, the story that follows has been made purposefully concise so that the interrelationship of the major patterns will more clearly stand out.

Underlying the course of Irish population trends were social, economic, and political conditions which can be grouped in three broad categories: the ease of emigration to the United States and to England for English-speaking Irish persons; the contrast in standard of living and way of life between Ireland and the United States and England; and the historical English domination of Ireland and the connection of religion with politics and social class. By 1966 the association of religion and politics had decreased, and the effects of Irish demographic trends on the special character of Irish Catholicism had become apparent.

The rapid rise in emigration and in postponed marriage between 1841 and 1851 was due to an increase in the contrast in way of life between the United States and Ireland combined with a decrease in the hopes of the Catholic majority of bringing about any rapid improvement in their situation in Ireland. The increase in the attractiveness of emigration to the United States resulted not only from "pull" factors such as the exaggerated stories of the 1848 gold discoveries, but also from "push" factors such as the 1845–48 famine, the failure of O'Connell's Repeal movement in 1844, and the death of O'Connell himself in 1847. It is important to remember, however, that the great emigration to the United States of the late 1840s and early 1850s would not have been possible without the pre-paid passages across the Atlantic provided by persons who had already emigrated. Although the statistics are poor, the mass emigration of Catholics from Ireland to the United States was well under way by the 1830s. The population of Ireland declined between 1841 and 1851 not because, as is commonly assumed, mass emigration began at that time, but simply because emigration became greater than natural increase.

Even though unique historical events help us understand why the late 1840s and early 1850s were characterized by suddenly higher emigration rates, I believe that the population of Ireland would have declined within a decade or two in any case if the transition from manual to horse-drawn agricultural techniques was to be accomplished. The new techniques increased productivity per worker many times over the older methods, but a certain minimum size farm was needed before the new techniques began to pay for themselves. With a negligible amount of additional agricultural land available through the reclamation of waste land, the enlargement of most existing holdings could only come about through the consolidation of smaller holdings into farms of adequate size. Although some consolidation was forced through evictions, most was made possible by small farmers or their inheriting sons who voluntarily relinquished their holdings and emi-

grated. A major part of the increased emigration from Ireland between 1946 and 1961 was also a movement of persons out of agriculture accompanying the shift to agricultural labor-saving techniques which required even larger holdings before they became
profitable.

Similarly, I believe that the rise in celibacy between 1841 and
1851 also would have occurred sooner or later as agricultural
labor-saving techniques were adopted and the minimum acceptable standard of living in rural areas rose. With the consolidation
rather than the fragmentation of holdings, the match marriage
system was revived to maintain the size of the family holding and
hopefully to increase its size and capitalization from generation to
generation. The change in agricultural techniques and the necessity for a certain minimum size holding to support the new methods was, in my opinion, as important a determinant of Irish emigration and marriage trends as the change from cultivation to
pasture.

For about two decades after 1851 the situation remained
unchanged, with roughly constant rates of postponed marriage
and permanent celibacy, higher rates of emigration than natural
increase, and a declining population. The rapid adjustments which
had accompanied the rejection of manual agriculture during the
late 1840s had stabilized, the domination of the Protestant minority over the Catholic majority continued unbroken, and hopes
for political change were small. By the 1870s, when the population
trends began to change once again, the compulsory registration
of births, deaths, and marriages had been started and accurate information about fertility, mortality, and emigration became available for the first time.

Some of the more important changes which took place during and after the 1870s were the resurgence of Irish nationalism,
the formation of effective popular political organizations following the introduction of the secret ballot, and the gradual transfer
of land ownership from large Protestant landlords to the predominantly Catholic class of tenant farmers. Although the Irish nationalist movement was widely supported by Irish Catholic lay persons, some members of the Catholic hierarchy of Ireland opposed
many aspects of it. Church pronouncements about politics were

ignored by thousands of Catholic lay persons and even some parish priests. It became clear that the link between Catholicism and Irish nationalism was not one of ideology or of domination of the movement by the hierarchy, but rather was a reaction to historical connection of Protestantism with English rule.

A proper understanding of the relation between Catholicism and Irish nationalism at this time is important because the amount of postponed marriage and permanent celibacy in Ireland also began to rise after the 1870s. As the secular reasons for postponing marriage increased, I believe that there was also an increased willingness to ignore church teachings about early marriage as well as about politics. As the amount of celibacy in Ireland rose, Irish Catholic puritanism probably intensified as priests felt it necessary to prevent possible immorality among the increasing numbers of unmarried persons in Ireland. But the rise in celibacy itself is not explained by changes in the puritanism of the clergy or by changes in any supposed desire of the laity to emulate the celibacy of priests, monks, or nuns. The rise in Irish celibacy after the 1870s is understood by considering certain other demographic trends, and some economic and political factors.

In Ireland after the 1870s, as in several other European countries, there was an increased awareness of the association between marital status and one's own personal standard of living. The motivation to postpone marriage and remain permanently single in Ireland was especially intense, however, because the gap between desired and actual standard of living probably was greater in Ireland than in any other European country. Ireland was and continues to be one of the economically least developed countries in northwestern Europe, yet the aspirations of the Irish were and are strongly focused on standards in England and the United States, two of the most highly industrialized nations in the world. Remaining unmarried in Ireland had long been considered an alternative to emigration, and as the rate of emigration declined after the 1880s, the rate of celibacy rose.

As the number of single persons in the Irish population increased after the 1870s, gradually more females than males began emigrating from Ireland during inter-censal periods unmarked by British wars or rapid change in agricultural techniques. Within

Ireland the greater emigration of females out of rural areas widened the gap between rural and urban sex ratios. Both trends soon meant that there were not enough females in rural areas to marry all of the males even if all of the females had married. The greater female than male migration out of Irish rural areas was due, among other things, to the extremely subordinate status of single females in Irish rural areas; in terms of improving one's personal way of life, females had more to gain from migration than males. The higher mortality rates of females than males in some age-groups, and the extremely low excess of female over male life expectation between 1881 and 1926 are indicators of the lower status of females. After 1926 more detailed information becomes available, and it documents another reason for the high celibacy rates of Ireland: the combination of a permissive attitude toward single women working and a restrictive attitude toward married women working. Since the majority of single Irish women worked outside their homes, marriage meant giving up their jobs and two persons living on one income where two had been living separately on two incomes.

As the Protestant landlord class, which dominated rural Ireland, was gradually replaced by a class of small farmer-owners who were predominantly Catholic, as the movement for Irish Home Rule almost succeeded in Parliament only to be superseded by militant Irish Republican movements in Ireland, and as Ireland won its independence from Great Britain, emigration began to appeal more strongly to native-born Protestants than to Catholics. Between 1926 and 1946, in fact, the population of Ireland would have increased had it not been for the movement of Protestants out of Ireland. This is one of the great ironies of Irish population history because a reversal in the decline of Ireland's population in the second census after political independence and a continuing population increase, however slight, in the next two censuses would have been made much of.

While the high rates of Irish emigration and celibacy can be understood in part by the gap between actual and desired standards of living in Ireland, the high rate of Irish marital fertility seems to defy such an explanation. If some Irish were willing to emigrate and others to postpone marriage indefinitely in order to achieve or to maintain a certain minimum standard of living, why should others have large families after marriage and by so doing reduce their standard of living below what it would have been if they had had small families? I argued that the seeming paradox can only be understood by considering the selective effects of the extreme patterns of Irish emigration and marriage. Even though the completed family size in 1961 of Irish women who had married in their thirties was only from 1.6 to 3.0 children, by their late marriage they made the Irish marital fertility rate higher than that of other countries where couples had the same size completed families but where marriage occurred earlier in life. The Irish women who did have large completed families (from four to six children) generally were those who had married in their twenties. These women were a small portion of their original cohort since most females either emigrated, postponed marriage until their thirties, or remained permanently single. It seems reasonable to conclude that the women who remained in Ireland and who married while in their twenties, compared with all females in their original cohort, were more likely to have been the ones who had most fully accepted Catholic teachings about early marriage and a large ideal family size, and also the ones who cared least about their own personal standard of living.

There is a temptation to believe than an explanation of Irish population trends must be made in terms of events, conditions, or cultural and psychological traits unique to Ireland and the Irish. It is true that some important explanatory factors were particular to Ireland compared with other European countries, factors such as the relatively heavy female mortality rates and the selective effects of emigration and marriage on the persistence of a large family ideal. But it is equally true that other explanatory factors were similar to those found in several European countries, especially the reasons behind much of the out-migration from rural areas and the rise in celibacy after the 1870s. By considering both types of explanatory factors I hope I have contributed to a better understanding of the demographic features Ireland shares, to a greater or lesser degree, with other nations, and perhaps also made less puzzling the more unusual aspects of Irish behavior.

❧ Statistical Appendix

TABLE 1. Population Size and Intercensal Change in Ireland, 1821–1966; Births and Deaths Registered, Natural Increase, and Estimated Net Emigration, 1871–66. All Numbers in Thousands.

Year or Period	Population Size [a]	Births	Deaths	Natural Increase [b]	Population Change	Estimated Net Emigration [c]
1821	5,421 [d]	NA	NA	NA	NR	NA
1821–31	6,193 [d]	NA	NA	NA	+772	NA
1831–41	6,529 [d]	NA	NA	NA	+336	NA
1841–51	5,112 [d]	NA	NA	NA	−1,417	NA
1851–61	4,402	NA	NA	NA	−710	NA
1861–71	4,053	NA	NA	NA	−349	NA
1871–81	3,870	1,037	718	319	−183	502
1881–91	3,469	835	639	196	−401	597
1891–1901	3,222	738	588	150	−247	397
1901–11	3,140	714	534	180	−82	262
1911–26	2,972	968	731	237	−168	405
1926–36	2,968	583	420	163	−4	167
1936–46	2,955	602	428	174	−13	187
1946–51	2,961	322	197	125	+5	120
1951–56	2,898	313	178	135	−62	197
1956–61	2,818	303	171	132	−80	212
1961–66	2,884	313	166	147	+66	81

SOURCES: *Censuses of Population of Ireland, 1946 and 1951,* "General Report," Tables 1 & 2, p. 17; *Statistical Abstract of Ireland, 1950,* Table 6, p. 11; *1968,* Table 6, p. 20.

NA: Not available.
NR: Not relevant.
[a] At the end of each intercensal period.
[b] Births minus deaths.
[c] Natural increase minus population change.
[d] Excluding military and navy.

TABLE 2. Average Annual Rates of Fertility, Mortality, Natural Increase, Population Change, and Estimated Net Emigration, Ireland, 1871–1966.

Intercensal period	Rate per 1,000 of average population				
	Births	Deaths	Natural Increase [a]	Population Change	Estimated Net Emigration [b]
1871–81	26.2	18.1	8.0	−4.6	12.7
1881–91	22.8	17.4	5.3	−10.9	16.3
1891–1901	22.1	17.6	4.5	−7.4	11.9
1901–11	22.4	16.8	5.6	−2.6	8.2
1911–26	21.1	16.0	5.2	−3.7	8.8
1926–36	19.6	14.2	5.5	−0.1	5.6
1936–46	20.3	14.5	5.9	−0.4	6.3
1946–51	22.2	13.6	8.6	+0.4	8.2
1951–56	21.3	12.2	9.2	−4.3	13.4
1956–61	21.2	11.9	9.2	−5.6	14.8
1961–66	21.9	11.7	10.3	+4.6	5.7

SOURCES: *Statistical Abstract of Ireland, 1950*, Table 7, p. 11; *1968*, Table 7, p. 20.
([a]) Births minus deaths.
([b]) Natural increase minus population change.

TABLE 3. Total Population, Urban Population, and Dublin Area Population, Ireland, 1841–1966.

Year	Total Population (thousands)	Urban Population [a] (thousands)	Per Cent Urban	Dublin Population [b] (thousands)	Dublin Population As a Per Cent of Total Population	Dublin Population As a Per Cent of Urban Population
1841	6,529	1,100	17	285	4	26
1851	5,112	1,131	22	321	6	28
1861	4,402	986	22	331	7	34
1871	4,053	934	23	330	8	35
1881	3,870	932	24	343	9	37
1891	3,469	888	26	346	10	39
1901	3,222	911	28	375	12	41
1911	3,140	942	30	398	13	42
1926	2,972	959	32	419	14	44
1936 ([a])	2,968	1,055	36	508	17	48
1936 ([a])	2,968	1,099	37	538	18	49
1946	2,955	1,161	39	583	20	50
1951	2,961	1,227	42	634	21	52
1961	2,818	1,299	46	663	24	51
1966	2,884	1,419	49	735	25	52

SOURCES: *Censuses of Population of Ireland*, 1926, Vol. X, p. 15; *1936*, Vol. IX, Table 10, p. 14; *1946 and 1951*, Tables 4 and 5, pp. 24 and 25; *1961*, Vol. I, Table 13, pp. 140–41; 1966, Vol. I, Tables VI and 7, pp. xvi and 11.

([a]) Two sets of figures are given for 1936 because of changed definitions of town boundaries. For the period 1841 to the first 1936, the town boundaries of towns of 1,500 inhabitants or larger in 1936 were used. From the second 1936 through 1951, the 1951 town boundaries and populations were used. In 1961 and 1966, the town boundaries and populations of 1961 and 1966, respectively, were used.

([b]) Dublin City, Dun Laoghaire, Rathmines, Rathgar, Pembroke, and Blackrock for the period 1841 to 1926; Dublin County Borough and Dun Laoghaire Borough, 1936; Dublin County Borough, Dun Laoghaire Borough and their suburbs, for the period 1936 to 1966.

TABLE 4. Number and Percentage Roman Catholic in the Total Population, Ireland (26 Counties), 1861–1961.

Year	Number in thousands			Percentage		
	Total	Catholic	Non-Catholic [a]	Total	Catholic	Non-Catholic [a]
1861	4,402.1	3,933.6	468.5	100.0	89.4	10.6
1871	4,053,2	3,616.4	436.8	100.0	89.2	10.8
1881	3,870.0	3,465.3	404.7	100.0	89.5	10.5
1891	3,468.7	3,099.0	369.7	100.0	89.3	10.7
1901	3,221.8	2,878.3	343.6	100.0	89.3	10.7
1911	3,139.7	2,812.5	327.2	100.0	89.6	10.4
1926	2,972.0	2,751.3	220.7	100.0	92.6	7.4
1936	2,968.4	2,773.9	194.5	100.0	93.4	6.6
1946	2,955.1	2,786.0	169.1	100.0	94.3	5.7
1961	2,818.3	2,673.5	144.9	100.0	94.9	5.1

SOURCES: *Statistical Abstract of Ireland, 1950*, Table 34, p. 31; *1968*, Table 42, p. 53.
([a]) Including No statement.

TABLE 5. Percentage Single by Sex in Selected Age Groups, Ireland, 1841–1966.

Year	Males				Females			
	20–24 Years	25–34 Years	35–44 Years	45–54 Years	20–24 Years	25–34 Years	35–44 Years	45–54 Years
1841 [a]	NA [b]	43	15	10	NA	28	15	12
1851	NA	61	21	12	NA	39	15	11
1861	92	57	24	14	76	39	18	14
1871	93	57	26	16	78	38	20	15
1881	94	62	27	16	82	41	19	16
1891	96	67	33	20	86	48	23	17
1901	96	72	38	24	88	53	28	20
1911	97	75	44	29	88	55	31	24
1926	96	72	45	31	87	53	30	24
1936	96	74	44	34	86	55	30	25
1946	95	70	43	32	82	48	30	26
1951	95	67	·40	31	82	46	28	26
1961	92	58	36	30	78	37	23	23
1966	90	50	33	29	75	31	20	21

SOURCE: *Census of Population of Ireland, 1966*, Vol. II, Table VII, p. xii.
([a]) Age groupings for 1841 were 26–35, 36–45, and 46–55 years.
([b]) NA: Not available.

❧ Chapter Notes

CHAPTER I

1. Ryan, "Some Irish Population Problems," *Population Studies*, 9:2 (Nov. 1955), p. 185.

2. Including Connell, *The Population of Ireland;* Connell, *Irish Peasant Society;* Drake, "Marriage and Population Growth in Ireland, 1750–1845," *Economic History Review*, 2d. series, 13:2 (Dec. 1963), pp. 301–313; Adams, *Ireland and Irish Emigration;* Lawton, "Irish Immigration to England and Wales in the mid-Nineteenth Century," *Irish Geography*, 4:1 (1959), pp. 35–54; Schrier, *Ireland and the American Emigration;* Cousens, "Emigration and Demographic Change in Ireland, 1851–1861," *Economic History Review*, 2d. series, 14 (1961), pp. 275–288; and Walsh, "Marriage Rates and Population Pressure: Ireland, 1871 and 1911," *Economic History Review*, 2d. series, 23:1 (April 1970), pp. 148–162.

3. For example, Commins, "Recent Population Changes Analyzed by Community Size," *Irish Journal of Agricultural Economics and Rural Sociology*, 1:2 (1968), pp. 195–206; Johnson, "Population Changes in Ireland, 1951–1961," *Geographical Journal*, 129:2 (June 1963), pp. 167–174; Johnson, "Population Change in Ireland, 1961–1966," *Irish Geography*, 5:5 (1968), pp. 470–477; Meenan, "Some Features of Irish Emigration," *International Labour Review*, 69:2 (Feb. 1954), pp. 126–139; Meenan, "Eire" in Thomas (ed.), *Economics of International Migration*, pp. 77–84; Honohan, "The Population of Ireland," *Journal of the Institute of Actuaries*, 86, Part I: 372 (1960), pp. 30–68; Streib, "Old Age in Ireland: Demographic and Sociological Aspects," *Gerontologist*, 8 (Winter 1968), pp. 227–235; Verriere, "L'Évolution Récente de L'Émigration Irlandaise," *Population* (Paris), 20:2 (March–April 1965), pp. 233–252.

4. Woodham-Smith, *The Great Hunger*, p. 200.

5. Ravenstein, "The Laws of Migration," *Journal of the Royal Statistical Society*, Vol. 48, Part 2 (June 1885), pp. 167–277, and Vol. 52 (June 1889), pp. 241–301.

6. Wharton, "The Green Revolution: Cornucopia or Pandora's Box?,"

Foreign Affairs, Vol. 47, No. 3 (April 1969), pp. 467, 468, 474.

7. Geary and McCarthy, "Addendum No. 2," *Commission on Emigration and other Population Problems*, 1948–54, p. 201.

8. See Table 60.

9. See Table 67.

10. See Table 59.

CHAPTER II

1. Beckett, *The Making of Modern Ireland*, p. 159.

2. *Ibid.*, pp. 158–159.

3. *Ibid.*, p. 251.

4. O'Brien, *Economic History of Ireland*, p. 504.

5. Inglis, *The Story of Ireland*, 2d. ed., p. 189.

6. *Ibid.*, p. 177; O'Brien, *Economic History of Ireland*, p. 218; Shearman, *Modern Ireland*, p. 35.

7. O'Brien, *Economic History of Ireland*, p. 242; Adams, *Ireland and Irish Emigration*, p. 392; Schrier, *Ireland and the American Emigration*, p. 105.

8. Adams, *Ireland and Irish Emigration*, p. 105.

9. Schrier, *Ireland and the American Emigration*, p. 111.

10. *Ibid.*, pp. 111, 121.

11. Shearman, *Modern Ireland*, p. 90.

12. L. P. Curtis, *Coercion and Conciliation in Ireland*, p. 417.

13. Inglis, *The Story of Ireland*, p. 181; E. Curtis, *A History of Ireland*, p. 287.

14. Inglis, *The Story of Ireland*, p. 181; E. Curtis, *A History of Ireland*, p. 302.

15. Adams, *Ireland and Irish Emigration*, p. 21.

16. Thompson and Lewis, *Population Problems*, 5th ed., p. 389.

17. Williams, *Nutrition in a Nutshell*, pp. 45–74.

18. Schrier, *Ireland and the American Emigration*, p. 8; O'Brien, *Economic History of Ireland*, p. 210; MacArthur, "Medical History of the Famine," in Edwards and Williams (eds.), *The Great Famine*, p. 264; Woodham-Smith, *The Great Hunger*, pp. 32, 33. On the western seaboard there were "near famines" in 1885 and 1890 following potato failures; Freeman, *Ireland*, p. 126.

19. Carr-Saunders, *World Population*, p. 119.

20. Beckett, *The Making of Modern Ireland*, p. 345.

21. Adams, *Ireland and Irish Emigration*, p. 111; O'Brien, *Economic History of Ireland*, p. 210.

22. Ireland, *Commission on Emigration . . .*, Statistical Appendix, Table 26, p. 314. This figure was calculated from the Reports of the Registrar of Shipping, the Report of the Agent-General for Emigration, the Report of the Irish Census Commissioners, 1841, and from the Reports of the Colonial Land and Emigration Commissioners.

23. The figures for 1845–51 come from the reports of the Colonial Land and Emigration Commissioners; those for 1852–70 from the Returns of the Registrar-General; those for 1871–91 are estimated net emigration. Ireland, *Commission on Emigration . . .*, Statistical Appendix, Tables 26, 28, pp.

314–316, 318, 319; *Statistical Abstract of Ireland, 1950*, Table 6, p. 11; *Census of Population of Ireland, 1966*, "Preliminary Report," Table V, p. 11.

24. *Censuses of Population of Ireland, 1946 and 1951*, "General Report," Table 21, p. 40.

25. Shearman, *Modern Ireland*, p. 99.

26. O'Brien, *Economic History of Ireland*, p. 267.

27. Connell, *The Population of Ireland*, p. 181.

28. Adams, *Ireland and Irish Emigration*, p. 164.

29. O'Brien, *Economic History of Ireland*, p. 59.

30. Chauvire, *A Short History of Ireland*, Earl of Wicklow (tr.), p. 120.

31. Coghlan, *The Land of Ireland*, p. 175.

32. O'Brien, *Economic History of Ireland*, p. 55.

33. Beckett, *A Short History of Ireland*, p. 147.

34. Schrier, *Ireland and the American Emigration*, p. 127.

35. Beckett, *The Making of Modern Ireland*, p. 392.

36. L. P. Curtis, *Coercion and Conciliation in Ireland*, p. 148.

37. Freeman, *Ireland*, p. 178.

38. The proportions refer to the 32 Counties. Schrier, *Ireland and the American Emigration*, p. 118.

39. McNabb, "Social Structure," *The Limerick Rural Survey, 1958–1964*, Newman (ed.), pp. 200–201.

40. Bellerby, *Agriculture and Industry*, p. 164.

41. *Ibid.*, p. 165.

42. Adams, *Ireland and Irish Emigration*, p. 63.

43. Beckett, *The Making of Modern Ireland*, pp. 289–290.

44. O'Brien, *Economic History of Ireland*, p. 516.

45. *Ibid.*, p. 41.

46. *Ibid.*, pp. 414, 415.

47. Shearman, *Modern Ireland*, p. 100.

48. E. Curtis, *A History of Ireland*, p. 370.

49. O'Brien, *Economic History of Ireland*, p. 583.

50. Blanshard, *The Irish and Catholic Power*.

51. Inglis, *The Story of Ireland*, p. 201.

52. E. Curtis, *A History of Ireland*, p. 357.

53. Inglis, *The Story of Ireland*, p. 193.

54. Beckett, *The Making of Modern Ireland*, pp. 332–333.

55. Inglis, *The Story of Ireland*, p. 200.

56. E. Curtis, *A History of Ireland*, p. 373.

57. Moody, "Fenianism, Home Rule, and the Land War," in Moody and Martin (eds)., *The Course of Irish History*, p. 285.

58. Inglis, *The Story of Ireland*, p. 201.

59. E. Curtis, *A History of Ireland*, pp. 380–381.

60. L. P. Curtis, *Coercion and Conciliation in Ireland*, pp. 272, 274.

61. *Ibid.*, p. 236.

62. *Ibid.*, p. 203.

63. *Ibid.*, p. 315.

64. Beckett, *The Making of Modern Ireland*, p. 402.

65. According to the Irish Under Secretary. L. P. Curtis, *Coercion and*

Conciliation in Ireland, p. 324.
  66. Inglis, *The Story of Ireland*, p. 195.
  67. *Ibid.*, p. 194.
  68. Beckett, *The Making of Modern Ireland*, p. 445.
  69. Inglis, *The Story of Ireland*, p. 201.
  70. Beckett, *The Making of Modern Ireland*, p. 445.

CHAPTER III

  1. Woodham-Smith, *The Great Hunger*, p. 200.
  2. Beckett, *A Short History of Ireland*, p. 147.
  3. Figures are from reports made to Dublin Castle by the Royal Irish Constabulary. O'Brien, "The Vanishing Irish," in O'Brien (ed.), *The Vanishing Irish*, Table 3, p. 25.
  4. Adams, *Ireland and Irish Emigration*, p. 392; Schrier, *Ireland and the American Emigration*, p. 105.
  5. Figures are for the 26 Counties. Ireland, *Annual Report of the Registrar General, 1931*, Table 18, p. 28.
  6. Cousens, "Regional Death Rates in Ireland during the Great Famine," *Population Studies*, XIV:1 (July 1960), p. 56; MacArthur, "Medical History of the Famine," in Edwards and Williams (eds.), *The Great Famine*, p. 265.
  7. Williams, *Nutrition in a Nutshell*, Chapter V.
  8. Beckett, *The Making of Modern Ireland*, p. 345. One in nine persons died on board ships which sailed from Cork in 1847.
  9. Ireland, *Commission on Emigration . . .*, Table 81, p. 108.
  10. Carpenter, *Immigrants and Their Children, 1920*, p. 206.
  11. Ussher, "The Boundary Between the Sexes," in O'Brien (ed.), *The Vanishing Irish*, pp. 154–155.
  12. Arensberg and Kimball, *Family and Community in Ireland*, pp. 202–203.
  13. *Ibid.*, pp. 35–57.
  14. O'Casey, *Three Plays*, p. 115.
  15. *Ibid.*, pp. 13, 14.
  16. McNabb, "Social Structure," *The Limerick Rural Survey, 1958–1964*, Newman (ed.), pp. 230–231.
  17. Humphreys, *New Dubliners*, p. 162.
  18. *Ibid.*, p. 163.
  19. Arensberg and Kimball, *Family and Community in Ireland*, pp. 47–48.
  20. *Ibid.*, p. 49.
  21. *Ibid.*, pp. 33–50.
  22. Humphreys, *New Dubliners*, pp. 34, 236.
  23. *Censuses of Population of Ireland, 1926*, Vol. V, Part II, Table 1B, p. 5; *1936*, Vol. V, Part II, Table 1B, p. 5; *1946*, Vol. V, Part II, Table 1B, p. 5; *1961*, Vol. V, Table 1B, p. 5; *1966*, Vol. V, Table 1B, p. 9.
  24. Shapiro, Schlesinger, and Nesbitt, *Infant, Perinatal, Maternal, and Childhood Mortality*, p. 43.
  25. Dublin, Lotka, and Spiegelman, *Length of Life*, p. 129.
  26. Madigan, "Are Sex Mortality Differentials Biologically Caused?"

The Millbank Memorial Fund Quarterly, Vol. XXXV, No. 2 (April 1957), pp. 202–223.

27. Stolnitz, "A Century of International Mortality Trends: II," *Population Studies*, Vol. X (July 1956), pp. 22–25.

28. Preston, "An International Comparison of Excess in the Death Rates of Older Males," *Population Studies*, Vol. XXIV (March 1970), pp. 5–20.

29. El–Badry, "Higher Female than Male Mortality in Some Countries of South Asia: A Digest," *Journal of the American Statistical Association*, Vol. 64 (December 1969), pp. 1234–1244.

30. Arensberg and Kimball, *Family and Community in Ireland*, p. 59.

31. See Chapter Two.

32. Beckett, *The Making of Modern Ireland*, p. 407.

CHAPTER IV

1. Population Reference Bureau, "1970 World Population Data Sheet," Washington, D.C.

2. Meenan, "Minority Report," in Ireland, *Commission on Emigration and other Population Problems, 1948–1954*, "Reports," p. 371.

3. Ireland, *Report on Vital Statistics, 1967*, Table 5, p. 6.

4. Appendix Table 5.

5. *Census of Population of Ireland, 1966*, Vol. II, Table VII, p. xiii.

6. Jackson, *The Irish in Britain*, p. 102.

7. *Ibid.*, p. 104.

8. Several authors have commented on the rural-urban character of Irish emigration, including Adams, *Ireland and Irish Emigration*, p. 49; Ireland, *Agricultural Statistics, 1847–1926*, "Report and Tables," p. lxiv; Schrier, *Ireland and the American Emigration*, p. 7; Meenan, "Some Features of Irish Emigration," *International Labour Review*, LXIX: 2 (February 1954), p. 127; Honohan, "The Population of Ireland," *Journal of the Institute of Actuaries*, Vol. 86, Part I, No. 372 (1960), p. 44; and Davis, "The Theory of Change and Response in Modern Demographic History," *Population Index*, 29:4 (October 1963), p. 361.

9. Although the figures from which this proportion was calculated probably understated the total amount of emigration, I believe the proportion itself is reasonably accurate. For the figures themselves and the various sources for the figures, see Ireland, *Commission on Emigration . . .* , Statistical Appendix, Table 26, pp. 314–316.

10. This is based on data from the Registrar-General and again the proportions probably are reasonably accurate even though the figures themselves may understate the actual amount of emigration. *Ibid.*, Table 94, p. 125.

11. Meenan, "Some Features of Irish Emigration," *International Labour Review*, p. 130.

12. Ireland, *Commission on Emigration . . .* , Table 87, p. 116.

13. *Ibid.*, p. 127.

14. *Ibid.*, p. 127.

15. *Census of Population of Ireland, 1926*, Vol. X, p. 19.

16. Ireland, *Commission on Emigration and other Population Problems*,

1948-1954, "Reports," Table 31, p. 322.

17. Ireland, *Census of Population, 1961*, Vol. III, Table 3, p. 11.

18. Ireland, *Census of Population, 1936*, Vol. II, Table 1A, p. 2.

19. United States Bureau of the Census, *Historical Statistics of the United States, Colonial Times to 1957*, Series D 36–45, p. 72.

CHAPTER V

1. Cottrell, *Energy and Society*, pp. 134–144; Clark and Haswell, *The Economics of Subsistence Agriculture*, p. 56; Habakkuk, *American and British Technology*, p. 50.

2. This was the conclusion reached by the Devon Commission. Freeman, *Pre-Famine Ireland*, p. 58.

3. The exact proportions were 29 per cent in 1851, 18 per cent in 1881, and 13 per cent in 1926. Ireland, *Agricultural Statistics, 1847-1926*, "Report and Tables," p. lx.

4. Green, "Agriculture," in Edwards and Williams (eds.), *The Great Famine*, pp. 102–103.

5. MacDonagh, "Irish Emigration to the United States of America and the British Colonies During the Famine," in Edwards and Williams, *The Great Famine*, pp. 324–325.

6. Ireland, *Commission on Emigration and other Population Problems, 1948-1954*, "Reports," Statistical Appendix, Table 26, p. 314.

7. Jackson, *The Irish in Britain*, pp. 103–104.

8. Attwood, "Trends in Agricultural Development in Europe and Ireland," *Journal of the Statistical and Social Inquiry Society of Ireland*, XXI (1962–63), p. 35.

9. Walsh and Kilroy, "A Half Century of Fertilizer and Lime Use in Ireland," *Journal of the Statistical and Social Inquiry Society of Ireland*, XIX (1956–57), pp. 104–136.

10. Department of Local Government, *Reports, 1945–47*, Appendix XXIV, p. 133; *1961–62*, Appendix 33, p. 112.

11. Ireland, *Statistical Abstract, 1950*, Table 50, p. 46; *1964*, Table 55, p. 76.

12. *Statistical Abstract of Ireland, 1964*, Table 356, p. 338.

13. *Census of Population of Ireland, 1961*, Vol. VI, Tables 22B and 22C, pp. 121–122.

14. Inglis, *The Story of Ireland*, pp. 156, 229.

15. The counties were Roscommon, Mayo, Leitrim, Sligo, Galway, Donegal, Kerry, and Clare; see Attwood, "Agriculture and Economic Growth in Western Ireland," *Journal of the Statistical and Social Inquiry Society of Ireland*, XX (1961–62), Table 5, p. 187.

16. *Statistical Abstract of Ireland, 1968*, Table 64, p. 86.

17. *Censuses of Population of Ireland, 1946*, Vol. V, Part II, Table 4A, p. 12; *1966*, Vol. V, Table 2A, pp. 14–15.

18. Jackson, *The Irish in Britain*, pp. 103–104.

19. Byrne, "Some Provincial Variations in Irish Agriculture," *Journal of the Statistical and Social Inquiry Society of Ireland*, XX (1958–59), p. 67.

20. *Census of Population of Ireland, 1946*, Vol. V, Part II, Table 4A, p. 10.

CHAPTER VI

1. O'Brien, *Economic History of Ireland*, p. 218.
2. *Censuses of Population of Ireland, 1926*, Vol. III, Part II, Table 2A, p. 144; *1946–1951*, "General Report, Table 163, p. 175; *1961*, Vol. VII, Part II, Table 1A, p. 78.
3. There were 1,875 foreign-born (born outside of the 32 Counties), 1,793 non-Catholics, and 1,405 Church of Ireland members, Presbyterians, and Methodists. *Census of Population of Ireland, 1961*, Vol. VII, Part I, Table 7A, p. 12; Part II, Table 2A, p. 81.
4. Protestant includes Protestant Episcopalian, Presbyterian, and Methodist. *Census of Population of Ireland, 1926*, Vol. III, Part I, Table 18B, p. 131.
5. Chubb, *The Constitution of Ireland*, p. 12.
6. Inglis, *The Story of Ireland*, p. 238.
7. Chubb (ed.), *A Source Book of Irish Government*, p. 2.
8. Inglis, *The Story of Ireland*, pp. 216–217.
9. *Census of Population of Ireland, 1926*, Vol. III, Part I, Tables 13A, 17, pp. 99, 124–129. Protestant includes Protestant Episcopalians, Presbyterians, Methodists, and Baptists for the 15–24 year age group; and Protestant Episcopalians, Presbyterians, and Methodists for the student groups.
10. Beckett, *The Making of Modern Ireland*, p. 398.
11. Moody, "Fenianism, Home Rule and the Land War," in Moody and Martin (eds.), *The Course of Irish History*, p. 282.
12. Freeman, *Ireland*, p. 178.
13. Inglis, *The Story of Ireland*, p. 236.
14. Censorship of Publications Act, 1929, Section 16; and Criminal Law Amendment Act, 1935, Section 17.
15. See Chapter Eight.
16. For details of the case see Humphreys, *New Dubliners*, pp. 53–54.

CHAPTER VII

1. O'Brien, "The Road Ahead," in O'Brien (ed.), *The Vanishing Irish*, p. 224.
2. De Freine, *The Great Silence*, p. 216.
3. Adams, *Ireland and Irish Emigration*, p. 32; Connell, *The Population of Ireland*, p. 50.
4. O'Faolain, "Love Among the Irish," in O'Brien, *The Vanishing Irish*, p. 115.
5. *Ibid.*, p. 115.
6. Inglis, *The Story of Ireland*, p. 202.
7. Article 41, Section 3, Constitution of Ireland.
8. Article 41, Section 2, Constitution of Ireland: "The State shall ... endeavour to ensure that mothers shall not be obliged by economic necessity to engage in labour to the neglect of their duties in the home." Under Section 10(1) of the Irish Civil Service Commission Act, 1956, women employed in the Irish civil service (with certain exceptions) are required to retire upon marriage, see Chubb (ed.), *A Source Book of Irish Government*, p. 139.

9. Ireland, *Commission on Emigration*, pp. 356–357.

10. Petersen, *Population*, p. 503.

11. Arensberg and Kimball, *Family and Community in Ireland*, p. 225.

12. Humphreys, *New Dubliners*, p. 243.

13. O'Faolain, "Love Among the Irish," in O'Brien (ed.), *The Vanishing Irish*, p. 112.

14. See Chapter Five.

15. For a historical description of changes in Irish marriage patterns after the 1840s, see a series of articles by Connell, "Marriage in Ireland after the Famine: The Diffusion of the Match," *Journal of the Statistical and Social Inquiry Society of Ireland*, XIX (1955–56), pp. 82–103; "The Land Legislation and Irish Social Life," *Economic History Review*, 2nd. Ser. XI (1958), pp. 1–7; and "Peasant Marriage in Ireland: Its Structure and Development since the Famine," *Economic History Review*, 2nd Ser. XIV (1962), pp. 502–23.

16. Hajnal, "European Marriage Patterns in Perspective," in Glass and Eversley (eds.), *Population and History*, pp. 101–143; and Madan, "The Joint Family: A Terminological Clarification," in Mogey (ed.), *Family and Marriage*, pp. 7–16.

17. Connell, *The Population of Ireland*, pp. 41–46. See also Drake, "Marriage and Population Growth in Ireland, 1750–1845," *Economic History Review*, 2nd. Ser. XVI (1963), pp. 307–313.

18. Davis, "The Theory of Change and Response in Modern Demographic History," *Population Index*, Vol. 29, No. 4 (October 1963), p. 353.

19. Noonan, "Why Few Irish Marry," in O'Brien, *The Vanishing Irish*, p. 31.

20. Connell, *The Population of Ireland*, p. 253.

21. *Censuses of Population of Ireland, 1946 and 1951*, "General Report," Table 51, p. 68.

22. The proportions refer to the 32 Counties. See Schrier, *Ireland and the American Emigration*, p. 118.

23. In 1946 and 1961 the respective proportions were for males 2.2 and 3.5 per cent, and for females 5.1 and 6.5 per cent. In 1966 a slightly different occupational title was used: "Catholic clergymen" accounted for 2.0 per cent of all single men aged 45–54 years; and "Nuns and other religious occupations" composed 7.5 per cent of all single women in the same age group. *Censuses of Population of Ireland, 1926*, Vol. V, Part II, Tables 1A, 1B, 4A, 4B, pp. 3, 5, 10, 26, 36; *1946*, Vol. V, Part II, Tables 1A, 1B, 4A, 4B, pp. 3, 5, 10–12, 25, 26, 32, 33, 37; *1961*, Vol. V, Tables 1A, 1B, 2A, 2B, pp. 3, 5, 6–9, 28, 32, 33, 42; *1966*, Vol. V, Tables 1A, 1B, 2A, 2B, pp. 5, 9, 30, 46.

24. Ireland, *Commission on Emigration*, pp. 356–357.

25. Humphreys, New Dubliners, p. 210.

26. Oldham, *Oxford Survey of the British Empire*, in Herbertson and Haworth (eds.), Vol. I, p. 449, cited in Freeman, "Emigration and Rural Ireland," *Journal of the Statistical and Social Enquiry Society of Ireland*, Vol. XVII (1944–45), p. 418; see also Sheridan, "We're Not Dead Yet," in O'Brien, *The Vanishing Irish*, p. 182; see also the comments of Connell and Geary in Connell, "Marriage in Ireland after the Famine," pp. 91, 97.

27. Ireland, *Report on Vital Statistics, 1961*, Table 48, p. 146.

28. *Ibid.*, Table 49, p. 148. The proportion of such men among all grooms was not recorded in 1946.

29. *Statistical Abstract of Ireland, 1968*, Table 118, p. 132.

30. McNabb, "Social Structure," *The Limerick Rural Survey, 1958–1964*, Newman (ed.), p. 221.

CHAPTER VIII

1. Ireland, *Report on Vital Statistics, 1966*, Table 5, p. 6.

2. Banks, *Prosperity and Parenthood*, p. 207.

3. Calculated from Ireland, *Report on Vital Statistics, 1961*, Table 34, pp. 128–129.

4. Ireland, *Public General Acts . . . 1929*, p. 137; *1935*, p. 141.

5. *The Irish Times*, City Edition, October 14, 1966, p. 1.

6. Again we were forced to use data for marriages of 20 to 24 years duration rather than of 25 to 29 years duration because the 1946 Census did not tabulate this particular combination of factors for the latter duration of marriage.

7. The Most Reverend Dr. Cornelius Lucey, Catholic Bishop of Cork, in his minority report to: Ireland, *Commission on Emigration*, p. 357.

8. Lucey, in Ireland, *Commission on Emigration*, p. 357.

9. Jackson, *The Irish in Britain*, p. 38. This point was also made by Johnston, who suggested that the least dissatisfied persons would remain in Ireland and help "make things continue with less change than might be thought desirable." In the comments to Honohan, "The Population of Ireland," *Journal of the Institute of Actuaries*, Vol. 86, Part I, No. 372 (1960), p. 52.

10. Those aged 35–39 years at marriage were not mentioned in the source. See Glass, "Malthus and the Limitation of Population Growth," in *Introduction to Malthus*, Glass (ed.), p. 36.

11. Cited by Humphreys, *New Dubliners*, p. 237.

12. *Census of Population of Ireland, 1961*, Vol. VIII, Table 14, p. 183.

13. The best known of which are Arensberg and Kimball, *Family and Community in Ireland*, (originally published in 1940); Mogey, *Rural Life in Northern Ireland* (based on field work done in early 1940s and describing many aspects of life also found in the 26 Counties); and Humphreys, *New Dubliners* (based on field work done in Dublin from 1949 to 1951).

14. A greater reduction in the death rate with no corresponding change in the birth rate would result in a greater rate of population growth. At 1 per cent average annual increase Ireland's population would have doubled every 70 years, at 1.5 per cent per year it would have doubled every 47 years. With a higher death rate or a lower birth rate yielding an average annual increase of 0.5 per cent, the population would have doubled every 140 years.

15. Article 41, Section 2. A convenient source of this and other parts of the Irish constitution dealing with the family is Chubb (ed.), *A Source Book of Irish Government*, p. 57.

16. Occupational status by religion, sex, age, and marital status was not published in the Irish censuses.

17. MacMahon, "Getting on the High Road Again," in O'Brien (ed.), *The Vanishing Irish*, p. 208.

18. Arensberg and Kimball, *Family and Community in Ireland*, p. 59.

19. *Ibid.*, p. 207, see also pp. 136–37, 204, and 208.

✥ Bibliography

In addition to the major statistical materials which have formed my primary sources of data (censuses of population, reports on vital statistics, agricultural statistics, statistical abstracts, and the *Reports* of the Irish Commission on Emigration and other Population Problems, 1948–54), several secondary sources were consulted. Of these, I have selected those dealing specifically with Irish population topics and those basic works concerned with matters of direct relevance to an understanding of Irish population (sociological studies of Irish life, standard histories of Ireland, and some American or British studies of fertility, mortality, migration, and agricultural economics). For further guidance to Irish source materials including bibliographies, reference works, parliamentary records, periodicals, and series, see the bibliographies given in J. C. Beckett, *The Making of Modern Ireland: 1603–1923*, pp. 462–479, and in T. W. Moody and F. X. Martin (eds.), *The Course of Irish History*, pp. 349–367.

BOOKS

Adams, William Forbes. *Ireland and Irish Emigration to the New World from 1815 to the Famine.* New Haven: Yale University Press, 1932.

Arensberg, Conrad M. *The Irish Countryman.* Gloucester, Mass.: Peter Smith, 1959. (First published 1937: New York, The Macmillan Co.)

———, and Solon T. Kimball. *Family and Community in Ireland.* 2d. ed., Cambridge, Mass.: Harvard University Press, 1968.

Banks, J. A. *Prosperity and Parenthood.* London: Routledge and Kegan Paul, Ltd., 1954.

Beckett, J.C. *The Making of Modern Ireland: 1603–1923.* London:

Faber and Faber, 1966.

———. *A Short History of Ireland.* 3d. ed. London: Hutchinson University Library, 1966.

Bellerby, J. R. *Agriculture and Industry Relative Income.* London: Macmillan & Co., 1956.

Blanshard, Paul. *The Irish and Catholic Power.* Boston: The Beacon Press, 1953.

Carpenter, Niles. *Immigrants and Their Children, 1920.* Washington, D.C.: U.S. Government Printing Office, Census Monograph VII, 1927.

Carr-Saunders, A.M. *World Population: Past Growth and Present Trends.* Oxford: Clarendon Press, 1936.

Chauvire, Roger. *A Short History of Ireland*, Earl of Wicklow (tr.). New York: Mentor Book, 1965.

Chubb, Basil (ed.). *A Source Book of Irish Government.* Dublin: Institute of Public Administration, 1964.

———. *The Constitution of Ireland.* 2d. ed., Dublin: Institute of Public Administration, 1966.

Clark, Colin, and Margaret Haswell. *The Economics of Subsistence Agriculture.* London: Macmillan & Co., 1964.

Coghlan, Daniel. *The Land of Ireland.* 1st ed. Dublin: Veritas Co., Ltd., 1931.

Connell, K. H. *The Population of Ireland, 1750–1845.* London: Oxford University Press, 1950.

———. *Irish Peasant Society.* Oxford, Clarendon Press, 1968.

Cottrell, Fred. *Energy and Society: The Relation Between Energy, Social Change, and Economic Development.* New York: McGraw-Hill, 1955.

Curtis, Edmund. *A History of Ireland.* 6th ed. London: Methuen & Co., Ltd., 1964.

Curtis, L. P., Jr. *Coercion and Conciliation in Ireland, 1880–1892: A Study in Conservative Unionism.* Princeton: Princeton University Press, 1963.

De Freine, Sean. *The Great Silence.* Dublin: Foilseachain Naisiunta Teoranta, 1965.

Dublin, L.I., A.J. Lotka, and M. Spiegelman. *Length of Life: A Study of the Life Table*, rev. ed. New York: Ronald Press, 1949.

Edwards, R. D., and T. D. Williams (eds.). *The Great Famine: Studies in Irish History, 1845–52.* Dublin: Browne and Nolan, 1956.

Eversley, D. E. C. *Social Theories of Fertility and the Malthusian Debate.* London: Oxford University Press, 1959.

Freeman, T. W. *Ireland: Its Physical, Historical, Social, and Economic Geography*, London: Methuen and Co., 1950.

———. *Pre-Famine Ireland: A Study in Historical Geography.* Manchester: Manchester University Press, 1957.

————. *Ireland: A General and Regional Geography*. 3d. ed. London: Methuen & Co., Ltd., 1965.

Glass, D.V., and D.E.C. Eversley (eds.). *Population and History*. Chicago: Aldine, 1965.

Habakkuk, H. J. *American and British Technology in the Nineteenth Century: The Search for Labour-Saving Inventions*. London: Cambridge University Press, 1962.

Hayden, Mary, and George A. Moonan. *A Short History of the Irish People*. Part II. New Edition. Dublin: Educational Company of Ireland, 1960.

Humphreys, Alexander J. *New Dubliners: Urbanization and the Irish Family*. London: Routledge and Kegan Paul, 1966.

Inglis, Brian. *The Story of Ireland*. 2d. ed. London: Faber and Faber, 1965.

Jackson, John Archer. *The Irish in Britain*. London: Routledge and Kegan Paul, 1963.

Mogey, John M. *Rural Life in Northern Ireland*. London: Oxford University Press, 1947.

Moody, T. W., and F. X. Martin (eds.) *The Course of Irish History*. Cork: The Mercier Press, 1967.

O'Brien, George. *The Economic History of Ireland from the Union to the Famine*. London: Longmans, Green and Co., 1921.

O'Brien, John A. (ed.) *The Vanishing Irish*. London: W. H. Allen, 1954.

O'Casey, Sean. *Three Plays*. London: Macmillan, 1966.

Petersen, William. *Population*, 2d. ed. New York: Macmillan, 1966.

Saville, John. *Rural Depopulation in England and Wales, 1851–1951*. London: Routledge and Kegan Paul, 1957.

Schrier, Arnold. *Ireland and the American Emigration, 1850–1900*. Minneapolis: University of Minnesota Press, 1958.

Shapiro, S., E.R. Schlesinger, and R.E.L. Nesbitt, Jr. *Infant Perinatal, Maternal, and Childhood Mortality in the United States*. Cambridge, Mass.: Harvard University Press, 1968.

Shearman, Hugh. *Modern Ireland*. London: George G. Harrap & Co., Ltd., 1952.

Shryock, Henry S., Jr., *Population Mobility Within the United States*. Chicago: Community and Family Study Center, University of Chicago, 1964.

Thomas, Brinley. *Migration and Economic Growth: A Study of Great Britain and the Atlantic Economy*. Cambridge: The University Press, 1954.

Thompson, Warren S., and David T. Lewis. *Population Problems*, 5th ed. New York: McGraw-Hill, 1965.

Williams, Roger J. *Nutrition in a Nutshell*. Garden City, N.Y.: Dolphin Books, 1962.

Woodham-Smith, Cecil. *The Great Hunger*. London: Four Square Edition, 1965.

ARTICLES

Aalen, F. H. A. "A Review of Recent Irish Population Trends," *Population Studies*, XVII:1 (July 1963), 73–78.

Attwood, E. A. "Agriculture and Economic Growth in Western Ireland," *Journal of the Statistical and Social Inquiry Society of Ireland*, XX:V (1961–62), 172–95.

———. "Trends in Agricultural Development in Europe and Ireland," *Journal of the Statistical and Social Inquiry Society of Ireland*, XXI:I (1962–63), 31–49.

Blake, Judith. "The Americanization of Catholic Reproductive Ideals," *Population Studies*, XX:1 (July 1966), 27–43.

Byrne, James J. "Some Provincial Variations in Irish Agriculture," *Journal of the Statistical and Social Inquiry Society of Ireland*, XX:II (1958–59), 60–78.

Carter, C. F., and Mary Robson. "A Comparison of the National Incomes and Social Accounts of Northern Ireland, the Republic of Ireland and the United Kingdom," *Journal of the Statistical and Social Inquiry Society of Ireland* (1954–55), 62–87.

Commins, P. "Recent Population Changes Analyzed by Community Size," *Irish Journal of Agricultural Economics and Rural Sociology*, 1:2 (1968), 195–206.

Connell, K. H. "Marriage in Ireland after the Famine: The Diffusion of the Match," *Journal of the Statistical and Social Inquiry Society of Ireland*, XIX (1955–56), 82–103.

———. "The Land Legislation and Irish Social Life," *Economic History Review*, Second Series, XI (1958), 1–7.

———. "Peasant Marriage in Ireland, Its Structure and Development Since the Famine," *Economic History Review*, Second Series, 14:3 (April 1962), 520–23.

Cousens, S. H. "The Regional Pattern of Emigration During the Great Irish Famine, 1846–1851," *Transactions and Papers of the Institute of British Geographers*, No. 28 (1960).

———. "Regional Death Rates in Ireland during the Great Famine," *Population Studies*, XIV:1 (July, 1960).

———."Emigration and Demographic Change in Ireland, 1851–1861," *Economic History Review*, Second Seried, XIV:2 (1961), 275–88.

———. "The Regional Variations in Population Changes in Ireland, 1861–1881," *Economic History Review*, 17 (December 1964), 301–21.

Davies, Gordon L. "Population Changes in the Republic of Ireland, 1951–56," *Geography*, 41 (1956), 263–65.

Davis, Kingsley. "The Theory of Change and Response in Modern Demographic History," *Population Index*, 29:4 (October 1963), 345–66.

Drake, Michael. "Marriage and Population Growth in Ireland, 1750–1845," *Economic History Review*, Second Series, XVI:2 (December 1963), 301–13.

El-Badry, M.A. "Higher Female than Male Mortality in Some Countries of South Asia: A Digest," *Journal of the American Statistical Association*, 64 (December 1969), 1234–1244.

Freeman, T. W. "Emigration and Rural Ireland," *Journal of the Statistical and Social Inquiry Society of Ireland*, XVII (1944–45), 404–19.

Glass, D. V. "Malthus and the Limitation of Population Growth," in *Introduction to Malthus*, D. V. Glass (ed.), London: Watts & Co., 1953, 25–54.

―――. "Some Indicators of Differences Between Urban and Rural Mortality in England and Wales and Scotland," *Population Studies*, XVII:3 (March 1964), 263–67.

Herdan, G. "Causes of Excess Male Mortality in Man," *Acta Genetica et Statistica Medica*, 3 (1952), 351–375.

Honohan, W. A. "The Population of Ireland," *Journal of the Institute of Actuaries*, Vol. 86, Part I, No. 372 (1960), 30–68.

Hutchinson, Bertram, "Observations on Age at Marriage in Dublin, Related to Social Status and Social Mobility," *Economic and Social Review*, 2:2 (January 1971), 209–21.

Johnson, James H. "Population Changes in Ireland, 1951–1961," *Geographical Journal*, 129:2 (June 1963), 167–74.

―――. "Population Change in Ireland, 1961–1966," *Irish Geography*, 5:5 (1968), 470–77.

Lawton, Richard. "Irish Immigration to England and Wales in the Mid-Nineteenth Century," *Irish Geography*, IV:1 (1959), 35–54.

Madigan, Francis C. "Are Sex Mortality Differentials Biologically Caused?" *The Milbank Memorial Fund Quarterly*, XXXV:2 (April 1957), 202–223.

McNabb, Patrick. "Social Structure," *The Limerick Rural Survey, 1958–1964*, Rev. Jeremiah Newman (ed.), Tipperary: Muintir Na Tire Rural Publications, 1964, pp. 193–247.

―――. "Demography," *The Limerick Rural Survey, 1958–1964*, Rev. Jeremiah Newman (ed.), Tipperary: Muintir Na Tire Rural Publications, 1964, 158–92.

Meenan, James. "Some Features of Irish Emigration," *International Labour Review*, LXIX:2 (February 1954), 126–39.

Meenan, J. F. "Eire," *Economics of International Migration*, Brinley Thomas (ed.), London: Macmillan & Co., Ltd., 1958, 77–84.

Park, A. T. "An Analysis of Human Fertility in Northern Ireland," *Journal of the Statistical and Social Inquiry Society of Ireland*, XXI:1 (1962–63), 1–13.

Petersen, William. "Fertility Trends and Population Policy: Some Comments on the Van Heek-Hofstee Debate," *Sociologia Neerlandica*, 3:2 (Summer, 1966), 2–17.

Preston, S.H. "An International Comparison of Excess in the Death Rates of Older Males," *Population Studies*, XXIV (March 1970), 5–20.

Ravenstein, E.G. "The Laws of Migration," *Journal of the Royal Statistical Society*, 48, Part 2 (June 1885), 167–277, and 52 (June 1889), 241–301.

Rose, Arthur J. "Irish Migration to Australia in the Twentieth Century," *Irish Geography*, IV:1 (1959), 79–84.

Ryan, W. J. L. "Some Irish Population Problems," *Population Studies*, IX:2 (November 1955), 185–88.

Stolnitz, G.J. "A Century of International Mortality Trends: II," *Population Studies*, X (July 1956), 22–25.

Streib, Gordon F. "Old Age in Ireland: Demographic and Sociological Aspects," *Gerontologist*, 8 (Winter 1968), 227–35.

van Heek, F. "Roman Catholicism and Fertility in the Netherlands: Demographic Aspects of Minority Status," *Population Studies*, 10:2 (November 1956), 125–138.

Vaughan, T. D. "Population Changes in Northern Ireland," *Geography*, 45 (1960), 214–17.

Verrière, Jacques. "L'Évolution Récente de L'Émigration Irlandaise," *Population* (Paris), 20:2 (March–April 1965), 233–52.

Walsh, Brendan M., "A Perspective on Irish Population Patterns," *Eire-Ireland*, (Autumn 1966), 3–21.

———. "Some Irish Population Problems Reconsidered," Paper No. 42 (November 1968), The Economic and Social Research Institute, Dublin, 41 pp.

———. "An Empirical Study of the Age Structure of the Irish Population," *Economic and Social Review*, 1:2 (January 1970), 259–79.

———. "Marriage Rates and Population Pressure: Ireland, 1871 and 1911," *Economic History Review*, 2d. Series, 23:1 (April 1970), 148–62.

———. "A Study of Irish County Marriage Rates, 1961–1966," *Population Studies*, 24:2 (July 1970), 205–16.

Walsh, T., and J. Kilroy. "A Half Century of Fertilizer and Lime Use in Ireland," *Journal of the Statistical and Social Inquiry Society of Ireland*, XIX (1956–57), 104–36.

Wharton, Clifton R., Jr. "The Green Revolution: Cornucopia or Pandora's Box?" *Foreign Affairs*, 47:3 (April 1969).

❧ Index